How to Raise a Chatterbox

How to Raise a Chatterbox

A Parents' Guide to Speech and Language Development

Sandy Chappell

Speech and Language Therapist

Matador
9 Priory Business Park,
Wistow Road, Kibworth Beauchamp,
Leicestershire. LE8 0RX
Tel: 0116 279 2299
Email: books@troubador.co.uk
Web: www.troubador.co.uk/matador
Twitter: @matadorbooks

Paperback ISBN 978 1800464 162
Hardback ISBN 978 1800464 179

British Library Cataloguing in Publication Data.
A catalogue record for this book is available from the British Library.

Printed and bound by CPI Group (UK) Ltd, Croydon, CR0 4YY
Typeset in 12pt Minion Pro by Troubador Publishing Ltd, Leicester, UK

Matador is an imprint of Troubador Publishing Ltd

This book is dedicated to my husband, Si, whose skills as a chatterbox won my heart! And to my four wonderful children: Tom, Ben, Peter and Eve. Helping them develop a love of language in all its forms – talking, reading, singing and sharing jokes – has been the biggest joy of my life.

Contents

Foreword

Hello!

My name is Sandy Chappell, and I am a speech and language therapist – a job that is second only to that of being a mum! I specialise in working with preschool and primary school children, and one of the best aspects of my job is that every child I see is different from any other. My caseload includes babies who don't babble much; toddlers who prefer to point at what they want, rather than ask for it; four-year-olds who are difficult to understand; seven-year-olds who have difficulty sequencing their thoughts and ideas; and children of all ages who stammer.

Every day, my work brings magical moments: showing parents how using a simple strategy can prompt a seemingly reluctant baby or toddler to use a sound or word that they have been desperate to hear; recognising a familiar pattern in a child's mixed-up sound system, so that I am able to understand them, bringing huge relief to the child and their parents; and advising teaching staff on ways of supporting children in their class who have word finding difficulties or who stammer, so that they develop enough confidence to put their hand up and answer a question. A couple of my proudest moments have included a seven-year-old child who never spoke in class, but after a few months of therapy, he chose to tell jokes on stage in a school concert, and an eleven-year-old child who stammered but developed enough confidence to audition for a part in the school play – and got it!

I have over 30 years' experience as a speech and language therapist, working both for the National Health Service (NHS) and in independent practice. My roles have included head of a paediatric speech and language therapy service and a county-wide advisor in child language. In *How to Raise a Chatterbox*, I share many of the ideas and strategies that have worked for me over the years, both as a therapist and as a mum of four.

Often, success lies in making everyday activities fun, and it takes very little effort. By changing how we interact with our children, we can tempt them into talking and show them how powerful language is. Words make things happen: people give us attention when we say their name; we get things we want by asking for them; we can begin a friendship simply by saying, 'Hello'; words tell others what we think and how we feel; we can make people laugh or cry with just a few words; and much of what we learn is by asking questions. I hope that this book will help parents to teach their children the power of words, from that huge reaction that a first word brings (especially if it happens to be 'mama' or 'dada'!) to a child delighting their teacher by expressing their imagination in a made-up story.

For me, being a chatterbox means having the ability to use the power of language every day, in everything you do. My love of language has helped me to achieve the most important things in my life: friendships, a career helping others to improve their communication skills and, most importantly, raising four chatterboxes of my own!

As a mum, I have found that giving children the opportunity to learn any skill at an early age can bring them joy for years to come...

But for me, the most important skill we can help our children to develop is language.

Sandy

Introduction

We typically think of a chatterbox as someone who talks a lot, but I prefer the Oxford Languages definition of 'a person who likes to chatter'. Isn't that what we all want for our children? A love of language and talking? The Cambridge Dictionary uses the phrases 'having the gift of the gab' or 'the ability to speak easily and confidently in a way that makes people want to listen to you and believe you', which I love even more! Every parent I have worked with over the past 30 years whose child has struggled to communicate in some way would have dearly loved to give their child such a gift. Whenever they have said to me, 'I just want to have a little chatterbox,' that is what I think they mean, rather than a child who just never stops talking.

I hope that the information, strategies, tips and activities you will find in this book will enable you to help your child to learn to talk more easily and more confidently. To that end, I explain how speech and language develop, and how you can maximise the time you already spend with your child to best encourage their communication skills to progress. This will mostly involve adapting normal daily activities, such as getting dressed, eating meals, going shopping and travelling in the car, but I have also included lots of games and activities that you can do with your child to give them an extra boost, if you have the time. These will be listed at the end of each chapter in the section *Chatterbox time*.

Your child's speech and language skills may be developing as you would expect, but you might simply want them to be the best they can be before they start school; you may feel they are a bit behind in certain areas, and you would like specific guidance, strategies and games to help them to catch up; or you may have serious concerns about your child's communication skills and want to know if you should consider a referral to a speech and language therapist. Unfortunately, I cannot promise that these pages hold a magic wand for those with children whose skills are not developing as well as their parents would hope, despite their best efforts, and this book should in no way be used to replace speech and language therapy. In each chapter, there is a list of skills you can expect at that age, plus those 'red flags' to watch out for; if any of these apply to your child, I would advise you seek a referral to your local speech and language therapy department at the earliest opportunity. Most NHS departments accept referrals from parents; if yours doesn't, ask your health visitor, general practitioner (GP) or school to make the referral on your behalf. While waiting for your appointment, it will, of course, benefit your child to carry on with activities such as those I have suggested; indeed, they can continue to be used to supplement the specific advice that your speech and language therapist will give you.

Usually, all we want for our children is for them to develop along normal lines, so that they babble when we expect them to, say their first words at around the right time, and start producing sentences using slightly immature but recognisable words and grammar. This book is for all parents, grandparents and carers of preschool children who want to make the most of those precious preschool years, which fly by and which we now know give us the best opportunity to *raise a chatterbox*.

Why Do You Need To Do Anything?

Even if your child seems to be developing as you would expect, why is it important that you do everything you can to ensure that their speech and language skills are the best they can be before they start school?

There are huge benefits that come with a child having a good understanding of language, and the ability to express themselves using gestures, sounds, words and sentences. These begin at birth and include the following:

- Your baby will cry less.

  If you respond to non-verbal signals (body language) and the sounds that your baby makes, and give them what they need, they will use these more and resort to crying less often. Crying is distressing for babies as well as parents, and a baby will only resort to crying when all else fails. [1]

- You can avoid some of the terrible twos.

  Tantrums at this age are often either the result of a child not understanding what is happening or not having the language skills to express how they are feeling, which leads to a build-up of frustration. A child who understands what is said to them and can tell people how they are feeling will be less frustrated and less prone to tantrums. Discipline at all ages is easier if your child has good language skills. I can honestly say that none of my four children ever had what could be described as a tantrum. We had a few little strops or sulks, lots of 'discussions', and made many 'deals', but there was never a full-blown tantrum!

- You can avoid extreme shyness, fears, phobias and nightmares.

  If your child has good language skills, they are likely to be more confident in social situations. They can tell you when they are afraid, and it is easier to help them to understand if there is nothing to be afraid of. It is also easier to reassure them after a bad dream if they can tell you what it was about, and you can explain that it's not a real event.

- You can catch illness early.

  If, instead of just crying, your child has the vocabulary to tell you when they have a sore head, tummy or ears, or if they feel sick or very hot, you can spot and treat illness early.

- It is easier to teach safety issues.

  Concepts such as road safety and stranger danger require a good level of verbal comprehension. The earlier you can help your child achieve this, the safer they will be.

- Your child may be less of a fussy eater.

  If a child refuses to eat certain food, it may not be because of the taste. It may be that they don't like the texture, the food may be too hot or cold, or they may simply be full. If they can tell you why they don't want it, instead of simply refusing it, you can try the same food on another occasion and you may find that they will happily eat it.

- Daily activities that your child may dislike – such as nappy changes, getting their hair washed or brushing their teeth – can be made easier if you can distract them verbally with a favourite song, rhyme or story. You may find that, long after you have finished what you need to do, your child will still be listening intently and will want the interaction to continue.

- Your child will be happier if they can predict what is going to happen next throughout their day. This is easier if they can understand what you are saying to them. If they are taken by surprise or unsure what is going to happen next, it can be unsettling. Using verbal routines – even for small things such as picking your baby up, as well as activities such as bath time or going shopping – will make each day less confusing and more predictable for your child and will help to boost their level of understanding.

- You can give your child a head start at school.

Studies have shown that language development at age two is a strong predictor of children's 'school readiness' at age four, as measured by their scores on baseline assessments of language, reading and maths. [2]

Children's communication environment influences their early language development. The number of books available, the frequency of visits to the library, their parents using a range of activities and the number of toys available are all important predictors of the child's expressive vocabulary at age two. [2]

The following 'communication tree' shows how communication skills develop and how a child's environment influences this development.

The skills that form the roots of the tree are influenced by a child's opportunities to interact and play with those around them. Once the roots are strong enough, the trunk will start to develop, and the child will begin to understand the language they hear. With a strong trunk, the branches and leaves (sounds, words and sentences) can grow. All of these skills will continue to evolve, so the roots and trunk will still grow as more branches and leaves emerge.

The rate of growth of all of these things is influenced further still by the child's environment. The sun represents a language-rich environment with lots of praise, and the rain clouds are the opportunities that a child is given to practise what they are learning. By using the top tips and strategies that you will find in this book, you can give an additional boost to the growth of the whole tree.

The Communication Tree

Long-term Benefits of Having Good Speech and Language Skills

Children with good language skills form better relationships with their teachers. [3]

Vocabulary at age five is a very strong predictor of the qualifications achieved at school-leaving age and even of salary at age 30. [4]

It is much easier to find a job if you have good speech and language skills. Employers now rate communication skills as their highest priority, even above qualifications. [4]

A child's popularity with peers can be predicted by the level of their understanding of spoken language. [5]

Language development at age two is a strong predictor of children's school readiness at age four, as measured by their scores on baseline assessments. [2]

Good speech, language and communication skills can help to reduce the risk factors for mental health problems later in life. [6]

Long-Term Risks for Children with Poor Speech and Language Skills

Children with SLCNs* are at greater risk of being bullied than their peers. [7] [8]

One in three children with untreated speech and language difficulties will go on to develop mental health problems. [12]

At age six, there is a gap of a few months between the reading age of children with good oral language skills and those with poor ones. By age 14, this gap has widened to five years. [9]

Up to 66% of secondary pupils who are at risk of permanent exclusion have language difficulties. [10] [11]

Around 88% of unemployed young men have SLCNs. [15]

Only 20% of children with SLCNs achieve five GCSEs A*-C compared with 70% of children overall. [17]

Children with low language abilities experience a reduced health-related quality of life, and this continues to decline in over half of them. [18]

Communication disability has been identified as the number one public health concern for the 21st century and is the greatest barrier to social mobility. [16]

60-100% of people in young offenders' institutions have SLCNs, of whom only 5% already have this identified. With speech-and-language-therapy support, they are 50% less likely to reoffend. [13] [14]

*Speech, language and communication needs.

How Can This Happen?

0–2 Years
Daniel was late saying his first words and tends to point rather than ask for what he wants. He is a happy, sociable little boy.

3–5 Years
Daniel uses sentences, but his speech is immature. At nursery, he is not very good at sharing toys, and he lashes out at other children. His mum reports that he is well behaved at home.

5–7 Years
Daniel's teacher feels he doesn't listen to class instructions. He struggles with his work, particularly phonics and maths. He gets left out of games on the playground as children find him too rough. His language is delayed, especially his vocabulary. He often tells his mum that he feels too poorly to go to school.

7–11 Years
Daniel is known as a bully. He messes about in most lessons and gets into trouble almost every day. He is very behind with his reading, and his written work is poor. He likes maths, but struggles with some of the concepts. He never puts his hand up in class. Daniel's mum struggles to get him to go to school.

Leaving School
Daniel would like to be a mechanic, but he can't get an apprenticeship. He sometimes doesn't come home at night, and his mum is always worried. He has been cautioned by the police, but he didn't really understand why.

13–16 Years
Daniel spends his evenings and weekends with a group of older boys who are known to the local police. He has no real friends at school. He would like to go to college, but isn't expected to do well enough in his GCSEs. His mum feels he doesn't listen to her any more and worries for his future.

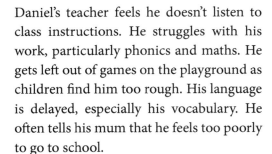

11–13 Years
Daniel has played truant since he started high school. He can't concentrate in class without one-to-one support, and he spends increasing amounts of time in isolation, but doesn't understand why. He has a reputation as a troublemaker and a bully.

Statistics

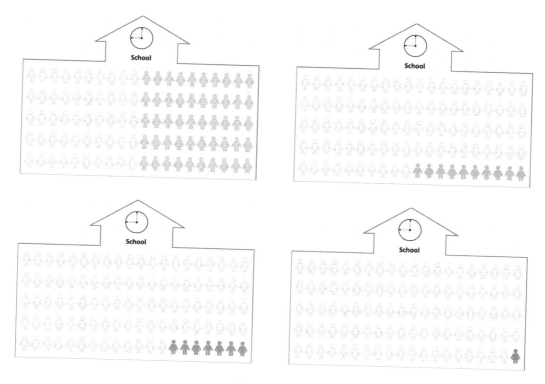

More than 1.4 million children and young people in the UK have speech, language and communication needs (SLCN). [19]

In some parts of the UK, particularly in areas of social disadvantage, at least 50% of children are starting school with SLCNs that can have a significant impact on their educational opportunities. These children may improve, given the right support, but there is clear evidence that their difficulties can persist throughout their school career if they do not receive such support. [20] [21]

More than 10% of all children and young people have long-term or persistent SLCNs, which create barriers to communication or learning. [19]

The 10% of children with long-term needs includes around 7.6% (two in a class) who have an SLCN as their main difficulty, for which there is no known cause; i.e. they are developing typically in other ways with no additional learning, physical or sensory difficulties. This is known as Developmental

Language Disorder (DLD), and it requires specific support; without this, it can have a significant impact on learning. These children may have a rich communication experience, with lots of support from parents, but despite this, will be disadvantaged from the start. [22]

The remaining 2.4% have SLCNs linked with another diagnosis, such as hearing impairment, autistic spectrum disorder and specific learning difficulties. [23]

An estimated 1% of children have the most severe and complex SLCNs, which prevent them from expressing their basic needs. [24]

My Aims for This Book

1. To help you learn more about how your child communicates from birth to five years, so that you are in the best position to help their communication skills develop. I have listed the speech and language skills that you can typically expect at each age. The developmental stages are based on averages, so don't be too concerned if your child doesn't seem to be doing everything at the right time. Sometimes, progress in one area of development can mean a slight delay in another. Focus on the areas where you feel your child needs more support.

2. To help you to maximise the time you already spend with your child, so that, whatever you are doing with them throughout the day, you are using that time to boost their speech and language skills. This will mostly involve adapting normal daily activities – such as getting dressed, eating meals, going shopping and travelling in the car – but I have also included lots of games and activities that you can do with your child to give them an extra boost, if you have the time. These will be listed at the end of each chapter as *Chatterbox time*.

3. To help you make an informed decision about which advice you choose to follow. As well as suggesting what you should do, I have tried to make it clear why those things are important. We are all aware that we should read to our children, for example, and that too much time in front of the TV is not a good idea, but do we know why? I have discussed the reasons behind the advice and the research studies that support it.

4. To make you aware of the red flags at each stage, so that you can seek advice in good time if any apply to your child.

How To Use This Book

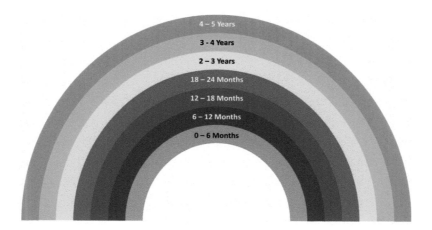

4 – 5 Years

3 - 4 Years

2 – 3 Years

18 – 24 Months

12 – 18 Months

6 – 12 Months

0 – 6 Months

1. Establish at what age level your child is functioning; i.e. where are they on the rainbow diagram? Their chronological age is a good place to start, but for premature babies, use their corrected age, i.e. when they were due to be born rather than their actual date of birth.

2. Read the list of skills that your child should have at their age, and if there are any gaps, go back and fill these in before you move on, e.g. there is no point expecting your 18-month-old child to start using two-word sentences until they have a vocabulary of at least 40 single words. They may be using a few two-word phrases that have been learned as a single unit (e.g. 'All gone!' or 'What's that?') or they may simply be imitating something they have heard you say and are not yet using it meaningfully. It is better to spend some time helping them to develop a larger vocabulary than trying to encourage sentences before they are ready. The obvious comparison is that you would never expect a child to run before they could walk, but, of course, every parent is desperate to know that their child is going to be a little chatterbox.

3. At each stage, keep the 'communication pyramid' in mind (see page xxxi) and make sure you work from the bottom to the top, as each level acts as a foundation for the development of the skills that are higher up. Children will not understand and use language until they have developed skills such as social interaction, attention, listening and turn-taking. If a child presents with delayed speech or language, the root of the problem is often much lower down the pyramid.

4. Choose activities from those listed under the sections *All the time* and *Chatterbox time* that best fit in with your daily routines, the toys and objects you have available, and the activities you know that you and your child will enjoy.

When To Start

It is never too early to start. Children are born to become chatterboxes. With the right support from day one, we can help that happen.

We know that the first three years of a child's life are the most critical time for language development. The brain develops faster between birth and the age of three than at any other time. Around 80–85% of brain development happens in the first three years, with the child's brain developing a million new neural connections every second. [24] As children get older, the neural connections in the parts of the brain that have not been used will start to be lost. [25] [26] Because of this, it is important to stimulate language and literacy during the early stages of life, otherwise a huge opportunity will have been missed. Children thrive when they are immersed in rich language – both oral and written – morning, noon and night. Reading to children regularly, singing and engaging them in conversation, all prepares them to be incredibly successful. [27]

The good news is that you are the person who is the best equipped to help your child to develop their language skills. They don't need apps, flashcards, expensive toys, beautifully illustrated books or even a place in a nursery rated as 'outstanding' by Ofsted. The main tool your child needs to acquire language is *you*.

If your child could choose between a top-of-the-range toy garage with flashing lights and cars that went 'brrm, brrm' or 'beep, beep', and the cheapest toy garage that came equipped with you, making the noises, praising them for copying you, laughing when your cars bumped together and singing a song about cars, they would always choose the latter. And they would be right, because they will learn so much more with you in terms of language and social interaction than playing alone with the best toy money can buy.

Language is developed, not taught. You and your child have an equal role to play. You don't need qualifications to help your child develop language, but it is useful to have as much knowledge as possible about how speech and language develop, so that you can make the most of every interaction with them, whether that is at breakfast time, at bath time, driving to the shops or during that extra-special bedtime story. Parents with this knowledge have higher-quality interactions with their children, regardless of their finances or educational background. Parents who provide good-quality learning support at home for their young child lay the foundation for success for the rest of their child's life.

The amount and the way parents speak to their children has a direct impact on their children's language development and intelligence quotient (IQ). Children's later academic success is directly related to the amount they are spoken to from birth to age three. [2] One study shows that children from professional families hear 30 million more words by the time they are four than children from low-income families. Also, the children in the low-income families 'heard more than double the negative remarks per hour' compared with the children of professionals, who were much more likely to be praised and encouraged with 'Well done' or 'You're right!' 'Even without science, we know intuitively that saying "shut up" 30 million times is not going to help a child develop into an intelligent, productive, stable adult.' [28] However, *the key factor is not the income or education of the parents, but how much they talk to their children and the amount of positive, encouraging language they use.* [28]

What You Need To Do

The good news is that you don't need to make any more time in your day to devote specifically to speech and language development. Obviously, the more time you can spend interacting with your child, the better, but what matters most is that you optimise any time that you do spend so that every minute counts.

And you don't need to buy any special toys or materials. The simplest objects and household items can be used to make great speech and language activities. As babies, my children all used to spend a lot of time playing with items from kitchen cupboards, banging on pans with a wooden spoon or pretending to cook with dried pasta! And they all had simple items that were favourites for a long time, ranging from a potato to a snake knitted by their nana! We used to take these wherever we went and then make up stories about their adventures at the end of the day.

What You Can Do

In each chapter, I have divided this section into two parts:

1. **All the time**

   This will include suggestions of how to make the most of the time that you are already spending with your child throughout the day, so that every minute counts towards boosting their speech and language skills. You may find that you are already doing a lot of the things I suggest, but you may not always realise how very important they are.

2. **Chatterbox time**

   This will include ideas on the best ways to spend any extra spare time you may have that you can devote specifically to one-to-one activities with your child. This may be short periods of time throughout the day or one set time that is a little longer. It can be useful to have one specific period set aside at around the same time each day, so that your child will know they have your undivided attention during this time. It doesn't have to be long – it could even be as short as 10 minutes – but it will be time that they look forward to (especially as they get older) and get huge benefit from.

- You can give this time a name so that your child knows it is a special time.
- Use a time that suits you both so that you are not busy and trying to rush, and they are not tired.
- Try to go somewhere quiet and free from distractions. If at all possible, leave your phone in another room!
- If your child is old enough, let them choose the activity. It should be anything apart from TV or just reading stories, as the aim is to interact with each other.
- Let them be in charge of the play, which means you should avoid giving instructions or asking questions. Simply comment on what you are both doing.
- Try to make sure they are going to do something fun at the end of this special time, such as having a bath, so that they are not too disappointed the time is over.

I have used six categories for these times:

1. Looking/attention skills
2. Listening
3. Sounds and talking
4. Music, songs and rhymes
5. Books and stories
6. Games and activities

Looking/attention skills

These include things that your baby will naturally enjoy looking at, such as your face, and things that you can encourage them to look at to learn about their environment and develop their attention skills.

Listening

This section will include the opportunities you have to help your children focus on the sounds in their environment. A baby will learn to understand the meaning of sounds made by everyday things around them – such as a car, a phone or a dog – before they can understand words.

It is important to keep background noise to a minimum (e.g. TV and radio), as babies and toddlers cannot filter these out to focus on the important sounds. You need to do the filtering for them at first and help them learn which sounds are more important.

Sounds and talking

Speech-sound development takes place over several years, from birth to sometimes as late as seven to eight years old. There are two main things that children have to learn in this time:

1. They need to develop the muscle control to produce each sound accurately. This is called 'articulation'.
2. They need to learn the rules about using sounds in words. This is called 'phonology'.

You need to listen carefully and respond to your children's attempts to communicate, so that they feel they have been successful, and they will then keep trying to use different sounds or words to communicate with us more and more.

If you repeat the sounds a baby makes, it shows them you are interested. It also gives an early opportunity for little turn-taking 'conversations'. Later, you can repeat words and phrases they say and extend them slightly to model what they should be aiming for at the next stage.

Music, songs and rhymes

Songs and rhymes are important for the development of many skills that children need both for good speech and language and for reading. This is why so many have been passed from one generation to the next. I have included separate sections on *Music* (see page 193) and on *Nursery rhymes* (see page 23) to explain why they are so important.

In a nutshell, songs and rhymes do the following:

- Hold children's attention for longer than just speech.
- Help them to learn to listen for patterns in words, such as how many syllables they have and those that rhyme. Awareness of these features is a reliable predictor of later reading ability. [29]
- Help to build awareness of the rhythms in words and sentences.
- Have more stressed words than in speech, and these are the words that attract children's attention and that they learn first.
- Include multiple repetitions of words, which is important for learning vocabulary.
- Help a child's memory skills through learning songs and rhymes.

In each chapter, I have suggested age-appropriate songs and rhymes to share with your child.

Books and stories

Babies love books, so start reading stories from birth.

You don't have to read the text, just talk about the pictures to begin with. As babies grow, keep some books where they can reach them, and you might be surprised how often they bring one to you to share. And remember, read *with* your baby, not *to* them. It is an experience to be shared, with your baby taking an active role. They will show you the pictures that they like by kicking their legs or squealing, and you should respond to this by spending extra time on those pages. When reading board books, encourage them to turn the page. Once they are talking, leave lots of pauses in familiar stories for them to fill in missing words.

For each age group, I have suggested a selection of books to try.

For more information about the importance of reading with your child, see the *Reading* section on page 202.

Games and activities

Children learn through play. It is important for every aspect of a child's development. Toys don't need to be expensive; variety is key. The most important thing is that children engage in play with other people.

Remember that *you* are your child's best toy in their preschool years. Given a choice, they will always choose you. Why?

1. You are multifunctional! You talk, sing, dance, make lots of different noises; you can be jumped on, play indoors and out, and help them learn the true meaning of cause and effect.

2. You can do things that no toy can do: you listen and respond; you take turns; you

know what your child likes best; you can deliberately make them laugh; you know when they've had enough; you encourage your child; you change with their age, ability and interests; you smile; and you make them feel loved and special.

3. You are free and don't require batteries!

Communication Pyramid

Successful communication requires the development of many different skills, all of which are used to different degrees, depending on the age of the child and the situation. Some of these skills are more fundamental than others and form a strong foundation from which other skills can then develop. The following communication pyramid shows the main skills needed and the order in which they need to develop for a child to become a successful communicator. As each new level is added, those beneath continue to develop and become stronger, e.g. a child of five not only uses more sounds and words than a one-year-old but also has much more well-developed attention, listening and play skills.

It is important that we think about each of these areas when we are trying to help our children develop their communication skills and that we don't expect them to develop those near the top of the pyramid before they have a solid foundation in those areas at the bottom. There is no point expecting a child to start using lots of clear words if they are not yet interacting with other people or paying attention to the language around them.

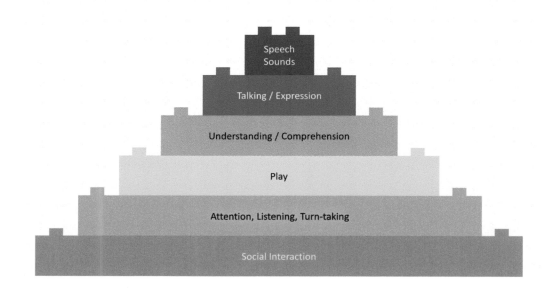

Social Interaction

Language forms the basis of social communication. We need language to communicate with others and understand them.

The main functions of language are all connected to our relationships with other people. We use language to share information, to express our feelings, to influence the behaviour of other people, and to simply interact and maintain social relationships, such as using small talk just to be sociable.

Children are born programmed to respond to people. They prefer to look at faces and listen to voices than anything else; they prefer to be with people than be alone; and as they get older, they prefer to have the company of lots of different people rather than just their parents. These preferences give them the best opportunities for learning language.

For a child to be able to acquire language, there needs to be social interaction between the child and adults in a language-rich environment. This gives the child the opportunity, reason and motivation to communicate.

Attention, Listening and Turn-Taking

In order to develop good communication skills, a child needs to have an awareness of others, and to learn to pay attention to what they hear (including voices) and what they see (including facial expressions and gestures).

Attention is the process of concentrating on one object, sound or event while ignoring others. It involves the ability to focus for increasing periods of time. Children need to be able to pay attention, focus and concentrate in order to learn.

Listening and hearing are not the same. Hearing is a sense; listening is a skill. Hearing is an involuntary process and is simply our ears picking up sounds. Listening is an active process in which you choose to focus on a sound and try to process it to understand what it means. We hear lots of different noises all around us, but we don't listen to them all. We can filter out the sounds that we don't want to listen to, and this is one of the most important skills that a baby needs to learn. Children need to have lots of quiet, distraction-free time throughout the day to be able to learn how to pay attention and listen.

Turn-taking is one of the most important skills that a baby needs to learn to become a good communicator. Studies have used magnetic resonance imaging (MRI) scans to show that being involved in turn-taking activities is a critical step in building speech and language skills. [30]

Taking turns is not the same as sharing. The former is an essential skill for language development, and it involves short, back-and-forth exchanges; the latter is more about forming friendships and being kind. Sharing can involve waiting for longer periods or giving something away to another child, such as sharing a snack.

Communication is very much a two-way process, and for it to be successful, we each need to be aware of our roles as both a listener and a speaker. The back-and-forth interaction forms a key part of our social and communication skills including exchanging facial expressions, looking at what someone is pointing at, imitating each other's sounds and words, sharing simple two-way activities and having a conversation. Even young babies respond to opportunities for turn-taking; they will try to copy your expressions and sounds, and they will love it when you do the same.

Play

Play has been called 'the work of children' because it is through play that children learn how to interact in their environment, discover their interests, and acquire cognitive, motor, speech, language, social and emotional skills. [31] Through various types of play, children learn to discover, create and problem-solve in a safe, caring environment. When you play with your child, they will watch you, listen to you and imitate you, which are all important precursors to language. Once your child is using sounds, words and sentences, they will use these to narrate their own play and direct play with others.

Understanding

This is the ability to understand language, including individual words, phrases and sentences. Children also learn to use other information as extra clues to help their understanding, such as tone of voice, which words are stressed and facial expressions. Some of these skills develop early, so even a very young baby can distinguish a happy voice from an angry one, [32] [33] whereas only a much older child will be able to understand subtle features such as sarcasm.

Expressive Language

This is the ability to convey a message to another person through sounds, words or signs. When we combine words into phrases and sentences, it needs to be done in a way that is as grammatically accurate as possible and makes sense.

Speech Sounds

This refers to the sounds that we produce and the rules by which we combine them to form meaningful words.

I hope I can help to guide you through the early years of your child's speech and language development. If you are lucky enough to have a little chatterbox running out of the school gates to tell you all about their first day, then you will know that all the baby talk, the nursery rhymes, reading the same books, singing the same songs or playing the same games hundreds of times over the years will all have been worth it.

Top Tips

Respond to your child's attempts to communicate

Get down to your child's level, face to face

Imitate your child

Rotate toys regularly

Pause

Narrate the action

Let your child take the lead and play their way

Try not to correct your child's 'mistakes'

Share books, songs and rhymes

Use communicative temptations

Just one more

Chatterbox time

Use more comments and fewer questions

Have plenty of quiet time

Be silly and use surprises

Use gestures

Give your child choices

Consider using a parent-facing buggy

Wait

Monitor TV time

Use repetition

At any age, the following tips will benefit your child's speech and language development:

1. **Respond to and interpret your child's attempts to communicate**

Responding straight away with enthusiasm lets your child know that you are interested in what they are trying to say. Interpreting their attempts lets them know that you are trying to understand. Whether it is your baby babbling, your toddler pointing, or your three-year-old asking a question with immature sounds or grammar, respond as though you understand exactly what they are trying to say, and it will encourage them to keep trying.

Newborn babies cry to let you know what they want, but they very quickly start to use other sounds. At first, it's very much trial and error as they work out which sounds get the desired response, and if you respond as though you understand, it lets them know that they are on the right track, e.g. if your baby shouts to get attention and you respond by picking them up and saying, 'Would you like to play?' they are more likely to try shouting to you again.

You can even interpret what your baby might be thinking. If they look at a bowl of fruit and start kicking their legs, you could interpret this and say, 'That banana looks tasty. Shall we have some banana?'

If your toddler says, 'Up,' and puts their arms up, you know that they want you to pick them up, so interpret this for them and reply, 'Do you want me to pick you up? Up you come.'

If your child says, 'No dot dink,' at lunch time, interpret back what you know they mean; i.e. 'No, you haven't got a drink. Mummy forgot. Here's your drink,' and they will know that you have understood and keep trying.

Another important way of responding to your child's attempts to communicate is to let them have what they have asked for when possible, so that they learn that words are powerful and make things happen. Getting what they want – whether it's food, a toy or some attention – will prompt your child to keep trying. At times when they can't have what they have asked for, such as a treat just before lunch, let them know that you have understood what they said and explain why they can't have it.

2. **Imitate your child**

One of the best ways to encourage your child to communicate more is by copying them. This doesn't have to be speech; you can copy your baby's facial expressions, their actions, as well as any sounds that they make. Get down to their level and copy what they do: if they clap, you clap; if they bang on their highchair tray, you bang on it; and if they shout '*Ah!*' you do the same. Babies love this and will probably want to carry on much longer than you do!

With babies, or toddlers who may be reluctant to talk, imitate any sounds that they make. Try to match the sound as closely as you can, then wait to see if they try again. From a very young age, babies love this vocal turn-taking. It shows them that you are listening to what they have said, that you are interested and that you have responded. It is their introduction to having a conversation, even before they are able to use words.

It doesn't even have to be a speech sound. Try copying your child when they cough or sneeze, and you might find that they keep trying to force another one to make the game go on! You could also try animal noises that you know they can make, a car or train sound, or even blowing a raspberry!

The more you respond in this way, the more likely your child is to try starting another little 'chat'.

3. **Get down to your child's level, face to face if possible**

Babies and young children will communicate more easily when they can see your face. You can hold a young baby to face you on your lap, sit facing an older baby in a highchair, or sit/lie on the floor to play with a toddler or older child.

Any activity can be done face to face: reading a book, singing a song or rhyme, playing peekaboo, rolling a ball to each other, building a tower together, doing a puzzle, etc.

The benefits are as follows:

- You can see the world from their point of view and can watch what they are doing.
- Being face to face allows for good eye contact, which shows your child that you are listening and interested in what they are doing and saying.
- Your child is more likely to keep looking at you and initiate communication or include you in their play if you are looking at each other.
- When children are learning language, they get clues about the meaning of words from watching your facial expressions. They are more likely to be aware of these if they are facing you.
- You will be aware when your child is about to try to communicate, and you can respond in an encouraging way. They are then more likely to keep trying.
- You can easily see when they seem confused or don't understand, and you can quickly try to help them. They will then be less likely to give up or get bored.

4. **Let your child take the lead and play their way**

When you play with your child, let them lead the way, join in with what they are doing and simply comment on what you are both doing. This shows them that you are interested in what they are doing and want to join in. Even if they don't try to communicate with you, just join in and play the way they are playing. To begin with, simply get another toy that is similar to theirs and copy what they are doing. Try not to have a goal in mind, just have fun!

As parents, we often feel that we should be setting up new play activities that teach particular skills, or we may feel that our child isn't playing with a toy in the 'right' way and we step in to show them how to do it. If things don't go to plan or if your child just isn't interested in your idea, it can end up being a waste of time and frustrating for both of you!

If you would prefer them to use a toy in a different way, just get another of the same toy and play with it alongside them, e.g. if all your child does with a car is bang it on the floor, you can get another car and roll it along, say what you are doing and using 'brrm, brrm' and 'beep, beep' sounds to get them interested. Roll the car to them a few times, and you will probably find that they stop banging their car and start joining in with you!

Similarly, if you want to extend your child's play, simply show them the next step and describe what you are doing in an interesting way, e.g. if all your child does with bricks is to build a tower and knock it down, you could sort your bricks into colours and build a tower of each colour, or you could build towers of different sizes and use words such as 'big', 'bigger' and 'biggest'.

There are many benefits of following your child's lead and playing their way:

- **Attention**
  They are much more likely to pay attention to what you are doing if you simply play alongside them rather than try to take over.

- **Listening**
  Don't we all like it when someone takes an interest in what we are doing? Your child is far more likely to listen to you when you are commenting on what they are already doing than when you are trying to get them interested in your play idea.

- **Turn-taking**
  Copying what your child is doing is a good way to start a turn-taking activity, e.g. you may start by playing with a car alongside your child before progressing to rolling the car to each other.

- **Understanding**
  Describing what your child is doing is one of the simplest ways to help them learn new words, e.g. when they roll a car along you could say, 'Push. You push the car. Mummy push the car.' Or for colours, you could tell them, 'Your car is red. Mummy's car is blue.'

- **Speech sounds**
  When children are interested in what you are saying, they will listen more closely to how you are saying it. This is one of the most important ways that children learn how different sounds are used in words.

5. **Pause**

Babies and young children need a little longer to process what we say to them and to plan what they are going to say in response, simply because they are still learning. One of the best things we can do for them is to give them this extra time by pausing. This is important at every age.

Pausing when you are copying the early sounds that your baby makes introduces them to the idea of taking turns and is one of the first little 'conversations' that you will have with them. Pausing lets them know when it is their turn.

Pausing during a familiar activity encourages your child to let you know they want you to carry on. Use activities that can be repeated, e.g. with a baby, you can tickle them, throw them gently up in the air, bounce them on your knee once, or start 'This Little Piggy' or 'Round and Round the Garden', then pause. When your baby is very young, they may simply kick their legs or make a little noise to let you know that they want you to carry on, and that is enough.

With a toddler, you can use activities such as pushing a car or rolling a ball between you, pushing them on a swing, or singing a favourite song or rhyme. As they get older, you will expect them to do more as a prompt for you to carry on, such as take your hands, make a sound or say a word such as 'again'.

Encouraging your toddler to use more words can often be achieved by starting to talk, pausing and waiting expectantly, e.g. saying, 'Ready, steady…' or pausing at a key point in a familiar rhyme such as 'Row, Row, Row Your Boat': 'If you see a crocodile, don't forget to…'

For older children who are trying to use longer sentences, pausing after asking them a question gives them time to find the words they want to use and to link their thoughts together in a sentence. If they don't respond straight away to a 'why' question, for example, don't assume that they don't understand the question or can't answer it. They just need more time to respond than an adult would.

By pausing, we encourage our children to keep trying because when we pause, we listen, and that is all children want when they talk to us.

6. **Use more comments and fewer questions**

We are all proud of what our children achieve and love them to show us, but asking lots of questions such as, 'What's this?' or 'Can you say "dog"?' means that we can miss opportunities for teaching.

Asking lots of questions doesn't help our children to learn words. It helps them learn how to ask questions, but not how to answer them! Questions often limit a child's options for responding, e.g. a 'why' question needs a 'because' answer, and questions will very often only result in a one-word or yes/no answer.

Reducing the number of questions you ask and increasing the number of comments is a really powerful strategy to support language development in young children, which is supported by lots of research.

For example, asking, 'What's that?' doesn't help your child to learn the word 'dog'. Saying, 'Can you say "dog"?' doesn't teach them the meaning of the word. It is much better to use comments such as, 'Look, it's a dog. Hello dog. Listen, the dog's barking. The dog says "woof, woof". Bye-bye dog,' which gives your child several opportunities to hear the word in context and to start to understand its meaning. They are also more likely to try to copy what you say if it is in the form of a comment.

Comments teach, but questions test, so it is important to get the balance right. I advise parents to try to use at least five comments for every question and to sometimes challenge themselves to play for 10 minutes without asking a single question! It isn't as easy as it might sound!

It is sometimes useful to ask your child questions. Make sure they understand the question and give them time to respond. Useful questions include these:

- Questions that give your child a choice, such as 'Would you like a story or a puzzle?'
- Open questions that your child can answer according to their language level, e.g. 'What shall we do?' can be answered with a point, a gesture, a single word, or a long and complex sentence.
- Questions that show your child that you understand and are interested in what they are saying, e.g. 'Did you hear the doorbell?'

7. **Narrate the action**

This simply means describe what is happening during daily routines, using language that is appropriate to your child's age. You can talk about what you are doing or thinking, or what you can see, hear, feel, taste or touch, e.g. 'My hands are dirty. I'm going to wash them. Where's the soap? Oo, the water is cold. Now my hands are clean. I need to dry them.'

It is also useful to narrate what your child is doing, during their daily routines and when they are playing, e.g. 'You're building a tower. It's very tall. One more brick on top. It looks wobbly. Crash! It fell down. Let's build another tower.'

The more language children hear, the better. Narrating the action is one of the simplest ways to model sounds, words and sentences, and it can become such a habit that you may find that you end up narrating what you are doing even when your child isn't there!

8. **Chatterbox time**

Try to have some time each day that you can totally focus on your child without any distractions. Obviously, the more time you can give, the better, but giving your child your full attention for five minutes is better than half an hour where you are checking your phone, tidying up around them or keeping one eye on the TV. If your child is old enough, let them choose the activity, but remember that the aim is to interact with each other, so try to avoid just watching TV.

9. **Just one more/stay one step ahead**

This applies to different areas of speech and language development:

Attention skills
Extending a child's attention span can be achieved gradually every time you play by asking them to put one more brick on a tower, complete one more piece of a puzzle or look at one more page of a book.

Following instructions
Adding just one more word to an instruction helps to develop auditory memory and verbal comprehension skills. Give little tasks throughout the day as part of your routine, adding one more word each time, such as the following:

- 'Go and find your shoes.' →
  'Go and find your socks and shoes.' →
  'Go and find your socks, shoes and coat.'

- 'Can you get a cup?' →
  'Can you put the cup on the table?' →
  'Can you put a red cup on the table?'

Expanding your child's expressive language level

This means modelling the next stage of language to show your child what they are aiming for. You add just one more thing to the sentences they are already using. Think about adding one more piece of information rather just one word:

- If they are not saying words yet, but are pointing or using some gestures, use lots of single words to interpret for them what they are trying to say. Label all the things that they point at. If they give you a cup when they want a drink, say, 'Drink,' or, 'More.' If they wave, say, 'Hello,' or, 'Bye-bye.' If they shake their head at the end of a meal, say, 'No,' or, 'Finished.'
- If they are saying single words or more, think about adding one more piece of information rather just one word; for example, as follows:
  o 'Daddy.' → '*There*'s Daddy.'
  o 'Daddy car.' → 'Daddy's *washing* the car.'
  o 'Daddy wash car.' → 'Daddy's going to wash the *dirty* car.'
- If they are saying short sentences, add another piece of information; for example, as follows:
  o 'More juice.' → 'More juice in the cup,' 'More juice now,' or, 'More juice for Mummy.'
  o 'Daddy do it.' → 'Daddy will read the book,' 'Daddy will kick the ball,' or 'Daddy will fix the car.'

By staying one step ahead, you are showing your child what they are aiming for next, whatever stage of language they are currently at. If you are always several steps ahead, it can be too difficult for your child to learn from what you say to them, e.g. if your child says, 'Car,' and you reply, 'Yes, in a minute we're going to go in the car with Daddy and drive to Nana's house for tea,' this will be too complicated for them to process and won't help them move on to using two-word sentences.

Also, by including what they have said in your response, you are reinforcing the fact that you have heard them, and they have got it right, which will motivate them to keep trying.

Try to include different word types when you expand your child's language, e.g. if they say, 'Dog,' you could respond, 'There's the dog,' 'The dog's barking,' 'It's a big dog,' etc. The more types of words your child has, the easier they will find it to start using sentences.

10. **Try not to correct your child's 'mistakes'**

Learning to say words correctly takes a long time, and part of the learning process is making mistakes. Sometimes, parents put this down to laziness, but children are never lazy with their speech or language. There is simply no point. You may notice that your child can sometimes say a sound, but at other times they get it wrong. This is a perfectly normal part of development. Children often learn to use a sound at the beginning of words, but not at the end (or vice versa); or they may say a word correctly on its own but make a mistake when it's in a sentence. Reacting in a positive way to their attempts will encourage them to keep trying.

When learning language, the mistakes children make often show us that they have learned a rule but are overusing it. English is full of irregular plurals, tenses, etc. and it is our job to provide our children with the opportunity to hear the correct version as often as possible, so that they can gradually learn all the exceptions to the rules.

Correcting children simply lets them know that whatever they have tried to say, they have got it wrong. We would never try to correct the way our children learn to walk! We accept that they are going to be a bit wobbly at first, and we understand that it's because they haven't quite developed the necessary muscle control. It is the same with speech. Also, correcting them doesn't teach them any more than simply providing the correct model of a word.

If your child says, 'It's a dut, Mummy,' then you can respond by saying one of these:

1. 'No, it's not a 'dut', it's a duck. Say 'duck.'
2. 'Is it a dut? Or is it a duck?'
3. 'Yes, it is a duck. The duck's eating the bread. Listen. The duck says "quack, quack".'

The first response lets your child know they have made a mistake, and that you are more concerned about how they have said something rather than what they have said. They may have another go at saying the word but are likely to get it wrong again because they have already tried their best. They will have learned nothing new.

The second response tells them that they have made a mistake and asks a question that they can't get right because they are still likely to say 'dut' again. They try to say 'duck' every time and think they are saying it right. They are more likely to keep trying if you encourage them rather than correct them.

The third response lets your child know that you have understood what they have said, and you are interested enough to carry on the conversation. You are giving them three good examples of how to say the word and you are teaching them some more information about ducks (that they eat bread, and they say 'quack, quack'). They are likely to happily try to say 'duck' again to continue the conversation, and if you are lucky, they might say something you have never heard before such as, 'Quack, quack,' 'Duck quack,' 'Duck bread,' or 'More bread.' This response gives them a lot more options for learning.

If possible, try to give more models of the word throughout the day when the opportunity arises. You can prompt this by leaving a toy, object or picture where they will see it (e.g. a toy duck). Wait until your child mentions it again, and then use the opportunity to model the word several more times while they are interested.

11. Use communicative temptations

These are strategies to encourage or 'tempt' your child into communicating (see *Communicative temptations* section, page 71). They are sometimes referred to as communication temptations.

12. **Give choices**

Giving choices is one of the most powerful tools we have to prompt our children to communicate. All too often, we might ask, 'What would you like?' or 'Would you like an apple?' but the better question to ask is something such as, 'Would you like an apple or a banana?'

Having a choice lets your child know that, by communicating their preference, they will get what they want.

Choices can be used throughout the day as part of your verbal routines, such as at mealtimes, getting dressed, playtime or at the shops:

- 'Would you like toast or cereal?'
- 'Will you wear blue socks or red socks?'
- 'Shall we read a book or do a puzzle?'
- 'Do you want to go on the slide or the swing?'
- 'Shall we buy broccoli or carrots?'

Giving choices helps language development in these ways:

1. Having a choice motivates a child to let you know what they want. Seeing the choice in front of them will prompt them to reach, point or say the word.

2. Choices help your child to learn what words mean by helping them to match the word to the object.

3. Choices provide a model of the words that you want your child to use, whereas asking, 'What would you like?' doesn't.

4. It lets your child know that you expect a specific response. Asking, 'What would you like?' or 'Would you like an apple?' might just prompt a shrug or a nod of the head, even if they are able to use words. You are more likely to get a response that reflects your child's language ability when you give them a choice.

5. Often young children don't know what they want! Giving your child a choice makes the decision easier for them. This is especially true when children are tired or upset.

6. Giving a choice enables your child to respond whatever their language level:
   o For a child who isn't using any words yet, you can show them an apple and a banana, and ask, 'Apple or banana?' and they can simply point or just look at the thing that they want, without even having to understand the words. But if you ask, 'What would you like to eat?' they may not understand the question or have the words to answer.
   o For a child who can use single words, but often doesn't, giving them a choice is often enough to prompt them to talk.
   o For a child with lots of single words, you can give them a choice of two phrases, e.g. saying, 'Would you like a big apple or a big banana?' or, 'Would you like to walk to the park or drive to the river?'

7. It encourages a child to have a go at the next level of language by imitating what you have said. Your child is more likely to try more advanced language when they can copy you.

8. Choices make your child feel that you are taking their wishes into account, even if you are only offering two things that you are happy with! It also removes the problem of asking your child what they want, them telling you, and you having to say no!

Remember to give choices for things other than just names. If your child is labelling lots of objects, and you are trying to encourage more action words, you could play a game where you ask, 'Shall we jump or hop?' or 'Shall we kick a ball or read a book?'

Don't always insist on a spoken word before you let your child have what they want, especially if they are not using many words yet. To encourage your child to use language, it needs to be fun. Accept a look, sign or point, and keep modelling the word.

If they can't choose between two things that they like, make the choice between something you know they would like and something they wouldn't, e.g. an apple or some broccoli. This adds an extra level of motivation so that they end up with something they want!

13. Have plenty of quiet time

Children learn best when there are as few distractions as possible. Young children are unable to filter out background noise, such as the TV or radio, so we need to do this for them. If you are talking to your child or playing with them, the best way to make the most of this time is to remove as much background noise as possible.

Bear in mind that other things can also distract your child, such as having too many toys out at once, being tired or hungry, so you will also need to make allowances for these things. Imagine if you were trying to learn another language when you were tired and hungry, the TV was on, and you could see lots of other things around that you wanted to do. Our children have to try to learn language under circumstances such as these, so as often as possible, we need to try to make the environment the best it can be.

14. Monitor TV time

As busy parents, we all look to CBeebies to help us out sometimes and shouldn't feel guilty about it. We simply need to weigh up the benefits and risks of screen time, according to our child's age, then decide what we allow them to watch, when and how much (see the separate *TV* section on page 197).

15. Share lots of books, songs and rhymes

In each chapter, I explain the importance of these things for helping speech and language development, but at any age, if you are unsure what to do next with your child, doing one of these things will always be beneficial.

Books

Sharing books with children has been shown to have enormous benefits, from helping them to develop early vocabulary and language skills to giving them a head start on their journey as readers (see the section on *Reading*, page 202).

Songs and music

Music has a beneficial effect on language development but also influences the development of other skills such as listening, memory, reading and maths (see the section on *Music*, page 193).

Rhymes

Parents have shared nursery rhymes with their children for hundreds of years and they are still popular today as a means of encouraging early language development (see the section on *Nursery rhymes*, page 23).

16. **Rotate toys regularly**

Some parents think that the best way to help children's play skills to develop is to have as many toys available as possible. However, having too many toys may mean that children only ever play at a very superficial level and never have the opportunity to develop deeper, more meaningful play skills.

Children only ever play with a small number of their available toys in any one day, and the rest are simply a distraction and contribute to a messy environment, which makes it difficult for them to concentrate.

Children will tend to flit from one thing to another if there is too much choice, and they will not spend enough time on one activity to be able to improve their attention skills. If all their toys are visible, they will all be familiar and therefore less interesting, so it is helpful to keep a large number of their toys out of sight and out of reach. Your child will have renewed interest and enthusiasm for toys that they haven't seen for a while.

17. **Consider a parent-facing pushchair or buggy**

This is worth considering, at least while your baby is very young. A study carried out by the National Literacy Trust between 2008 and 2010 shows that parents talk to their babies more than twice as much if they are facing them, [34] they use more varied and interesting speech, and they laugh three times as much. There doesn't seem to be much difference in the amount that the babies talk whichever way they face, but if they can see their parent, they laugh almost 10 times more and they sleep more than twice as much. [35]

Buggies that only face forwards tend to be cheaper, lighter and easier to fold, which are all important considerations and are the features that tend to be highlighted by manufacturers. Naturally, manufacturers will avoid stressing the advantages of parent-facing buggies when most or all of their range will only face forwards.

18. **Be silly and use surprises**

If you introduce little surprises and are silly from time to time, you may find that it encourages your child to respond with more spontaneous language. Even little things can prompt your child into a verbal reaction:

- Talking in a silly voice or doing a funny walk.
- Walking into the room with a hat on.
- Making deliberate mistakes, e.g. saying, 'The dog says "moo"'; handing them a puzzle piece from the wrong puzzle; or giving them a spoon when they want to colour a picture.
- Putting a toy on your head. This can be particularly effective at bath time when you can pretend to sneeze and make the toy fall in the water!

- Pushing a train along a track then deliberately pushing it off.
- Putting an item of clothing on the wrong part of your body or theirs, such as putting a shoe on your hand.

- Burying toys outside in the garden or sandpit for your child to dig for.
- Putting things in a bag. Letting your child pull toys or objects out of a bag is likely to result in them saying something, because they will be surprised by what they find. This is a more natural way to encourage naming rather than simply asking them to tell you.
- Hiding toys up your sleeve and letting them drop out when your child is looking at you.

19. Use gestures

Gestures such as waving, pointing, and clapping appear spontaneously before speech in a child's attempts to communicate and so are a natural precursor to spoken words. Using gestures or signs can benefit a child's understanding of language and help them to express their needs (see the section on *Gestures and Signs*, page 38).

20. Repetition

Repetition is key. It is estimated that a young child learning their first words needs to hear a word around 500 times before they can understand and use it! (see the section on *Repetition*, page 36). [36]

21. **Wait**

Waiting is one of the best strategies to encourage your child to initiate communication with you. This isn't the same as pausing, which is to encourage a response to something you have said. Waiting means not saying anything at all to allow your child to start the conversation.

Don't use this strategy all the time or for too long each time. Communication should always be a positive experience for children, so you don't want them to get upset or frustrated.

Examples of situations when it can be useful to wait include these:

- Choose a book that your child enjoys, sit down with them and wait for them to let you know they want to start the story.
- Keep a favourite toy or object slightly out of reach. Make sure your child can see it and wait for them to let you know in some way that they want it.
- Choose an activity that your child needs help with, such as blowing bubbles or wind-up toys. Wait for them to ask for help in some way, help again a couple more times and then pause again.
- At mealtimes, give your child an empty cup or plate and wait. Then give them a small amount of food or drink and wait again for them to show or tell you that they want more.
- When you are about to leave the house, walk to the door, stop and wait.
- If you know your child wants a snack from the fridge, stand in front of it and wait.
- If you normally open treats such as raisins, crisps or chocolate buttons before you give them to your child, try giving them unopened and waiting.
- At night, walk into a room with your child and wait a minute before you turn the light on.
- When something goes wrong – such as when your child drops, spills or breaks something – wait a few seconds to give your child the opportunity to tell you what's happened. This is often enough to prompt a child to communicate, so try not to step in straight away to fix things.
- Do something silly and wait for your child to react, e.g. put a glove on your head or put their sock on their hand. The surprise may be enough to prompt a reaction.

Chapter 1

0-6 months

Newborn babies have been described as 'A loud noise at one end, and no sense of responsibility at the other.' [37] Many parents will identify with this description and wish that, when handed their baby, they were also presented with some sort of manual! However overwhelmed you might feel in your early days as a parent, you will quickly begin to recognise and make sense of the signals that your baby is giving you. Babies are born with all the communication skills they need to survive, some of them quite subtle, and you will find that you are responding to many of these without even realising it.

At birth, your baby's brain is focused on controlling the bodily functions that they need to survive, so they can breathe, feed, sleep, wee and poo! From birth onwards, cognitive development begins, which is the process by which a baby's brain learns the skills necessary for perception, thought, memory, physical coordination and language. These skills enable a baby to explore and make sense of the world around them.

A newborn baby's brain is about a quarter of the size of an adult brain, and it doubles in size in the first year! [38] From birth, the connections between brain cells are formed through a child's everyday experiences. The amount and quality of the care, stimulation and interaction they receive determines which connections develop and last a lifetime. Children who grow up in a safe, stable and nurturing environment, with lots of positive interaction with familiar adults, will go on to be more successful in later life. [39]

Your baby is a born communicator and, from birth, is already working their way up the communication pyramid.

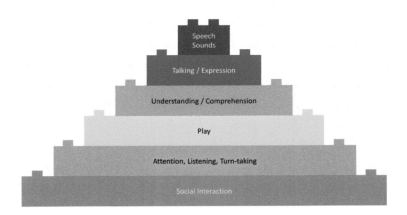

Social Interaction

Although a newborn baby is helpless in many ways, they are already a very social creature and well-equipped to interact with those around them. They show an emotional inclination towards people and naturally engage them in communication.

Soon after birth, a baby will quieten when they are spoken to, given eye contact or picked up. Their eyes focus best at the distance between their face and their mother's face when feeding or the face-to-face distance when anyone is holding them in their arms (20–30cm). By 36 hours old, they prefer their mother's face to a stranger's, and they will actively seek eye contact, but only maintain it for a short time. [40] [41] When someone maintains eye contact with us, it encourages us to keep talking to them, so it is an important skill for a new baby to have. Through eye contact, they will begin to learn about facial expressions and the social aspect of communication.

Your baby is learning about you from the moment they are born. They are watching your movements, gestures and facial expressions, and picking up on the tone of voice you use. Soon after birth, babies have been observed to imitate facial expressions (such as sticking their tongue out or opening their mouth wide) and arm waving. This is one of the ways that they show their preference for familiar people over any other interesting objects. [42] In the early days, you are also trying to make sense of the body language and sounds they are using to communicate with you, so it is very much a two-way learning process.

Attention, Listening and Turn Taking

Even before a baby is born, the process of learning language has already begun. In the third trimester of pregnancy, when a baby's ears have developed sufficiently, the intonation patterns of their mother's speech are transmitted through the fluids in the womb. This is thought to be like listening to someone talking in a swimming pool: it is difficult to make out the individual sounds, but the rhythm and intonation can be heard. By the time a baby is born, they already prefer their mother's language to other languages and can recognise it by the intonation patterns. [43]

At birth, a baby's brain has the ability to tell the difference between the 800 or so sounds that make up all the languages of the world. This means that, from birth, babies can learn any language they are exposed to, but they are born with a preference for around 40 sounds that make up their native language. By the time they are a year old, they will have lost the ability to hear the difference between sounds other than those of their native language. [44]

As soon as babies are born, they start to listen and pay attention to the world around them. Voices and faces will draw a baby's attention. A very young baby has only a fleeting attention span, and they are very easily distracted. Even their favourite things, such as their parents' faces and voices, will only hold their attention for a very short time.

A newborn baby will turn their head towards familiar voices or unusual sounds, showing that they are listening. They can tell the difference between a human voice and other sounds, and from around two weeks, a baby prefers listening to human voices to any other sounds. [45] A baby can recognise their mother's voice at only a few hours old. [46] By six months, they will show excitement when they hear familiar voices and when they hear sounds associated with favourite routines, such as feeding or bath time.

Once your baby is making noises, you will have lots more opportunities for turn-taking with them. When they pause, you can respond by repeating the sounds they have made and then leaving a long pause to encourage them to try again. Babies love this form of interaction. As early as six months old, babies are skilled at taking turns during interaction, responding when there is an opportunity and pausing to allow the other person to respond. [47]

Play

In the early days, you are your baby's favourite toy! They like to look at your face, listen to your voice and grab any part of you within reach! Anything in their hand will end up in their mouth, as this is the best means that they have to explore objects. It is also a useful way to slowly prepare them for weaning, to practise chewing, and to help reduce their strong gag reflex and tongue thrust for when they need to move solid food around in their mouth without spitting it out.

By three months, they like to have other things to look at, hold and explore in a more controlled way, such as shaking and banging, so anything that makes a noise is a bonus. All objects are explored in a similar way, whether it is your hand, a rattle, a ball or your baby's own toes! They will begin to enjoy simple, repetitive games, and will soon start to show excitement and anticipation, waiting for the peekaboo or tickle that comes with a familiar activity.

Understanding

From birth, your baby starts to make sense of their world and understand the many different sounds and words that they hear, as well as the messages conveyed to them through touch, body language, facial expressions, tone of voice, etc. [32]

Your baby will show an increasing interest in sounds of all kinds, but will prefer to listen to speech, especially familiar voices. They will know the difference between a happy and an angry voice, and may be upset by shouting, even though it is not directed at them.

Between three and six months, they will begin to recognise a few familiar words and simple phrases that they hear throughout the day. This will include their own name, the names of family members and phrases associated with favourite routines, e.g. they may get very excited when they hear, 'Splish, splash. Bath time!' or, 'Yum, yum. Dinner time!' Remember to use baby talk and verbal routines as often as you can (see the following sections).

Baby Talk

Traditionally called baby talk, but also known as motherese, parentese and infant-/child-directed speech, this is a pattern of speech that is used instinctively by adults when talking to young children (and often animals!). Young children themselves use this when talking to children who are younger than they are. [48]

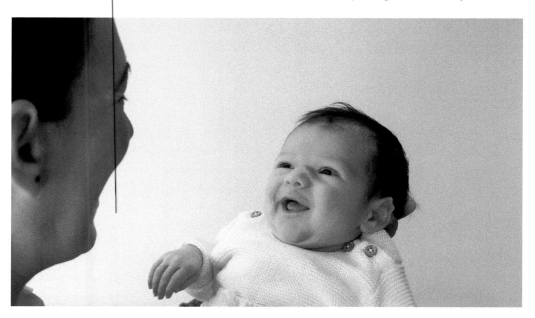

Baby talk is a feature of almost all languages and cultures around the world. [49] [50]

Typical features of baby talk include the following:

- A slightly higher pitch than normal
- A wider pitch range
- A slower rate of speech
- Lots of pauses
- Short, simple sentences
- Lots of repetitions
- Exaggerated intonation (sing-song)
- Clearer articulation
- Exaggerated mouth movements
- Proper names rather than pronouns
- Changes in volume/loudness
- Lots of questions to encourage a response
- Lots of facial expressions and head movements
- Use of special 'baby' words, e.g. 'doggy' or 'yucky'.

Why baby talk is good for babies

1. Babies have been shown to prefer baby talk to normal adult speech and will listen to an adult using baby talk for longer than one using normal adult speech. [51] [52]
2. Babies first start learning language by listening not to individual words but to the rhythm and intonation patterns of the speech they hear around them. These features are exaggerated in baby talk, which is one of the reasons babies prefer it. [52]
3. We all want our children to feel loved and happy; baby talk is perceived by all ages as 'happy talk', and it reinforces the emotional bond between a baby and its carers. [53] [54]
4. Baby talk tends to be spoken at a slower rate. [55] Young children have been found to recognise words more easily when they are produced more slowly than in typical adult speech. [56] When speech is slower, individual sounds and words are produced more clearly and it is easier for babies to pick them out. In addition, babies process language much more slowly than adults, and slower speech gives babies more time to process what they hear. [57]

5. In baby talk, key words often appear at the end of a phrase. For example, the sentence 'Can you see the dog?' is better than 'The dog is eating a bone,' as babies learn words more easily when they appear at the end of a phrase. Words at the ends of phrases are also more likely to be emphasised. [58] [59]

6. Words produced on their own or separated from the rest of a phrase by pauses are also easier for babies to learn, as it is obvious where the word begins and ends. [60] Research has revealed that the first words that babies produce are often those that are heard most frequently on their own, such as 'bye-bye' and 'no'. Baby talk contains lots of single words and lots of pauses between words. [61] [62]

7. Word repetition is beneficial in babies' early word learning. [63] Babies' first words tend to be those that are produced most frequently, such as 'Mummy', 'Daddy', 'bottle' and 'more'. The more often a baby hears a word, the easier it is for them to pick it out from a stream of speech. [64]

8. Reduplicated words (i.e. words that contain repetition, such as 'bye-bye', 'mama' or 'dada') are typical of baby talk and are known to help early word learning. Even newborn babies show stronger brain activity when they hear words that contain reduplication, and older babies find it easier to learn reduplicated words. [65]

9. In baby talk, adults seem to use extended pauses at the end of sentences, helping babies to start to learn how words are grouped together. [66]

Baby talk seems to provide the easiest model for babies to begin to learn language. Adults naturally reduce the amount of baby talk they use as children get older, so that the language they are exposed to is always age-appropriate.

Verbal Routines: Teaching First Words Through Daily Activities

Parents learn quickly that a structured daily routine makes for a happy baby; from feeding to bedtime, it helps to gain a sense of predictability about their day. But what about verbal routines?

A verbal routine is a set of words or phrases that is used in the same way during the same activity, so that it becomes familiar and predictable. Establishing verbal routines is a great way to get preverbal children talking. Familiar, repeated language helps children to recognise the words that they hear and to anticipate which words will come next. By using the same words each time, you help your child to link word meanings with specific objects and events. The predictability of verbal routines means that your child will eventually learn the order of the words, so that if you pause at a key point, they will be able to fill in the gap, and you will have created lots of opportunities for turn-taking.

Opportunities for verbal routines:

- Verbal routines can be as simple as saying, 'One, two, three,' or 'Ready, steady, go.'
- Simple social games are ready-made verbal routines, e.g. 'peekaboo', 'so big', 'Round and Round the Garden' and 'Pat-a-cake, Pat-a-cake'.
- Many children's books are based on verbal routines, e.g. *Brown Bear, Brown Bear, What Do You See?* by Eric Carle.
- Nursery rhymes are based on verbal routines as are many children's songs, e.g. 'Old MacDonald Had a Farm' and 'The Wheels on the Bus'.
- Make up your own verbal routines for mealtimes, bath time, bedtime, getting dressed and undressed, brushing teeth, nappy-changing time, putting shoes and coat on to go outside, shopping, travelling in the car, etc.

During verbal routines:

1. Use vocabulary and phrases that are simple enough to hold your child's attention. Try to stay one step ahead of where your child is: if they don't have many words, use lots of single words and a few simple phrases; and if they are using lots of single words, you should use lots of two-word phrases and some that are a little longer, and so on.
2. Use a sing-song voice with lots of repetition and emphasis on key words (see section on *Baby Talk*, page 5).
3. Have your key words and phrases in mind. You don't need to use all of them every time or say them in exactly the same order, but the more you can do this, the more familiar and predictable the language will become to your child.
4. Watch your child's responses: are they looking at you, smiling, or showing interest and excitement?
5. Leave plenty of pauses for your child to respond, no matter what their language level is, e.g. a baby may kick their legs in anticipation, a 15-month-old may fill in the word that comes next and a three-year-old may say the whole routine with you.
6. Once the routine is familiar, give your child the opportunity to initiate it with a movement, action, sound or word.
7. Initially, your child will imitate their favourite parts of the routine, which may be the actions, certain sounds or particular words. Don't worry if they don't join in with you, they will still be learning by just listening.
8. Try to use as many everyday activities as possible as opportunities for verbal routines. Think of it as making everything your child does a fun game with a simple commentary provided by you. Not only will your child learn language more quickly but you may find that some tasks that were once a battleground become much easier because your child is distracted by the verbal routine.
9. Once your child is familiar with the routine and joining in, you can occasionally make small changes to see if it prompts them to correct you.

Examples of daily verbal routines:

- **Morning**

    'Wakey, wakey!'
    'Rise and shine!'
    'Let's get up. Up, up, up.'

'Nappy time.'
'Let's go downstairs. Down, down, down.'
'Breakfast time. Yum, yum, yum.'

- **Getting dressed/nappy-changing time**

'Arms up. Top off. Over your head. Peekaboo!'
'Trousers off. Where are your toes? I see your toes.'
'Arms in. Where are your hands? I see your hands. Clap hands.'
'Socks on. Bye-bye, toes.'

- **Playtime**

'Let's play. It's playtime!'
'Let's find dolly. Let's find teddy.'
'My turn. Your turn.'
'Tidy-up time! Toys away.'
'Bye-bye, teddy. Bye-bye, dolly.'
'Clean up song…'

- **Mealtimes**

  'Wash our hands. Lunchtime!'
  'Yum, yum, yum.'
  'Tasty sandwich. Mmm.'
  'Let's drink juice.'
  'More apple? Tasty apple.'
  'All finished?'
  'Let's get down.'

- **Bath time**

  'Splish, splash! It's bath time.'
  'In the water. Toes in.'
  'Wash your hands. Wash your tummy. Wash your hair.'
  'All clean!'
  'Lots of bubbles. Pop, pop, pop!'
  'Time to get out. Up you come.'
  'Dry your hands. Dry your tummy. Dry your hair.'
  'All dry. Pyjamas on.'

- **Bedtime**

  'It's bedtime. In you get.'
  'Let's have a drink.'
  'Story time…'
  'Night, night. Sleep tight.'

Expressive Language

Babies cry from the moment of birth. It is the most effective way that they can make their needs known and get their parents to respond. Babies don't have a specific purpose to their cries; they are simply reacting to how they feel and what is happening to them. They quickly develop different cries to express what they need and how urgently they need it; one of the first challenges a new parent faces is to interpret this new 'foreign language' correctly. Babies also communicate through facial expressions and body movements, and these can give you early clues about what they need.

Babies generally cry to express the following:

- **Pain**
  This is generally where a baby gives a sharp scream then pauses, without seeming to breathe, then gives another sharp scream.

- **Hunger**
  This is a low-pitched cry that has a rising and falling rhythm. It gets progressively louder and nothing other than milk will soothe the baby. They may also root for food and suck their fist by mistake, which only makes them more frustrated, and then they will cry more.

- **Tiredness**
  A soft, moaning cry as your baby tries to fall asleep. They may also rub their eyes or pull their ears.

- **Discomfort**
  This can be the most frustrating cry as it is not always obvious what the source of the discomfort is. The baby will give a whining cry, may show increasingly jerky body movements and will not be soothed until you work out what is wrong. It can be anything from a wet nappy to mild colic. Often, trial and error is the only solution.

In the early days, it can be difficult to distinguish some of these cries. A baby that wakes in extreme hunger may sound more like they are in pain, and it may simply be the time since their last feed that suggests to a parent that they are hungry. One of my children spent his first few weeks either full and content or starving, and I quickly learned to try feeding him before anything else!

Crying begins as a reflex. Newborn babies have not had the opportunity to try out other sounds or body language to let their parents know that they need something. If your baby is near you when they begin to get hungry, then you will be able to observe their body language and hear the quiet sounds that are their first attempts at letting you know what they want. However, if your baby is usually in another room and you are relying on a monitor, you may not recognise that anything is wrong until they start crying. It may be worth keeping your baby close in the early days until their routines are more predictable.

Mothers have been shown to distinguish their own baby's cry from other babies within hours of birth. [67] [68] [69] The same is true of fathers, if they spend an equal amount of time with their baby. [70] Mother nature has equipped adults to respond to very young babies in the most appropriate way. We know that this is a natural instinct because it is one of the few things that is seen across almost all cultures. [71] The most difficult part is trusting our instinct and having the confidence to do what we feel is best. Whatever you do, if you are happy and your baby is happy, then you are doing it right!

Before the days of Google and parenting apps, new parents had to rely on their instincts and the advice of a limited number of close friends or family members. Now there is a huge amount of conflicting information available, and parents have the task of choosing what advice to ignore and what to follow. Parents do quickly learn to recognise their baby's attempts at both verbal and non-verbal communication, and once a predictable routine has been established, they will be able to anticipate what their baby needs and not have to wait for them to 'ask' for it.

As soon as a baby learns that their parents will respond to their cries straight away, they have less need to cry as loudly or for as long. By recognising non-verbal cues such as body language, it will help you to predict what your baby wants, so that they resort to crying less and less. [1]

Speech Sounds

Apart from crying, a new baby's other sound-making is related to bodily functions, e.g. coughing, burping and hiccups. If parents respond to these sounds and interpret them as though the baby were making them deliberately to communicate, they will learn that when they make different sounds, they get a different response. As early as possible, you want to teach your baby that their behaviour has a direct effect on what happens to them.

Crying noises are basically long vowel sounds that are 'designed' to be unpleasant to parents so that they act quickly! Towards the end of the first month, other vowel sounds that are shorter may appear; at first, this is just to signal that your baby is content, but they very quickly become used to get your attention. Again, responding quickly to these will encourage your baby to use specific sounds to communicate their needs rather than resorting to crying.

At around two months, your baby will start making some sounds with their tongue at the back of their mouth, partly due to the fact that they will be spending a lot of time lying on their back, and this will be their tongue's natural, relaxed position. They will start cooing or gurgling, making a musical comfort noise, often in response to being spoken to.

From two to three months onwards, your baby will go through a 'primitive articulation' stage where they will be moving their mouth, lips and tongue, just as they move other parts of their body. If they then use their voice to make a sound, they will produce consonant-like sounds; this will be accidental at first, but as they develop greater control of their speech muscles, it will become more deliberate.

At this stage, you may also notice your baby moving their lips and tongue as though they are trying to make a sound, but without any noise. Parents often naturally respond by saying, 'What are you trying to tell me? Have a go; I'm listening,' which is exactly what your baby needs to encourage them to keep trying. It is uncertain why babies do this, but they may be simply watching your mouth while you are talking and are trying to copy you.

By four to five months, your baby will be making a variety of consonant and vowel sounds, and many others that don't appear in the language they will eventually use, e.g. blowing raspberries! Your baby's communication changes gradually from pre-intentional, where they do not expect any particular outcome from their vocalisations, to intentional, where they predict how adults might respond to their sounds, based on the fact that they have responded consistently before. With a sound such as a raspberry, they are likely to get a reaction from people around them and so will use that sound more and more. Similarly, if they shout to get your attention, and you respond, they will use this sound again to communicate their need for attention. Even sounds such as raspberries have an important part to play in giving your baby the practice they need to develop speech. Have a little raspberry-blowing conversation with them! They will love it, and this stage will only last for a short time, so you won't have the opportunity to do it with them in a couple of months.

By four months, you will probably have heard your baby's first proper laugh in response to something you have done. You will happily become their personal comedy show for as long as they find you funny!

By five months, your baby can make deliberate changes to their sounds, in terms of changing the volume, pitch and intonation. Simply playing with sounds in this way gives them a lot of pleasure, and they will become more accurate at copying the sounds that you make. [72]

Dummies

There is always a debate among parents about the pros and cons of using a dummy. All babies are different, and some may be content enough of the time that their parents never need to consider a dummy. Others may go through periods where they are so unsettled that a dummy can be a lifesaver! I want to lay out for you the current research for and against the use of dummies to help you make the decision whether you use one at all, and if you do, how often and for how long.

These are the advantages of using a dummy:

1. Dummies soothe babies and help them to settle and fall asleep.
2. There is some evidence to suggest that using a dummy when sleeping can reduce the incidence of sudden infant death syndrome (SIDS). [73]
3. It tends to be easier to wean a child off a dummy than to stop them sucking their thumb.

However, most speech and language therapists agree that prolonged or frequent use of a dummy is not a good idea. These are the disadvantages:

1. It increases the risk of middle ear infections. [74] [75] [76]
2. When a child has a dummy in their mouth, they are less likely to babble and play with sounds, which is important for speech development. [77]
3. It can affect the growth and position of a child's teeth, causing gaps between the upper and lower teeth, which can then result in speech problems such as lisps. [78] [79]

4. It can cause increased dribbling in children, due to the dummy preventing lip closure, and causing poor lip tone, unfavourable tongue positions and problems with the position of the teeth. [75] [80]

5. Tongue thrust is a normal pattern of swallowing in early childhood, where the tongue either pushes against or through the front teeth. It's function in young babies is to prevent them taking anything other than milk to the back of their mouth and potentially choking on it. Tongue thrust naturally disappears, allowing babies to be weaned on to more solid food. The prolonged use of a dummy can cause tongue thrust to persist, meaning the teeth are pushed too far forwards, which causes difficulty with the articulation of certain sounds such as 't', 'd', 'n', 'l', 's' and 'z'. [80] [81] [82]

6. It restricts the movements of the lips and tongue, and it can cause difficulty in articulating sounds. If a child tries to make a sound that needs their tongue to be at the front of their mouth (e.g. 't' or 'd'), a dummy will prevent their tongue from doing this and they will end up using the back of their mouth, so that 't' becomes 'k' and 'd' becomes 'g'. The more they try to say these sounds with a dummy in their mouth, the more the wrong tongue position will be reinforced. In the end, they will produce the sounds as though they have a dummy in their mouth even when they haven't.

7. There is conflicting evidence about whether dummies are preferable to thumb sucking. Some studies suggest that the effect of thumb sucking can be worse on a child's teeth. [81] Other studies have found that dummies cause more problems. [78]

Occasional use of a dummy to soothe a tired baby will not cause problems, but because of the possible impact on speech development, I would suggest that the use of a dummy is limited to times when your baby cannot settle without it rather than it being used habitually. It is also a good idea to get rid of the dummy as early as you can, preferably by the time your baby is a year old. Speech problems caused by the overuse of dummies can be difficult to correct, even long after a child has stopped using one.

Tongue Tie

The tongue is attached to the floor of the mouth by a flap of skin called the frenulum, which runs from the middle of the tongue. In cases of tongue tie, the frenulum extends right to the tip of the tongue, restricting the amount that it can move in any direction, particularly up towards the nose.

True tongue tie is quite rare, but many children have it to some degree, with no significant effect on their speech or the functioning of their tongue. Some health professionals will attribute feeding problems, such as issues with latching, to a tongue tie, but there are many reasons that a baby may have trouble feeding. It may be suggested to parents that they have the tongue tie snipped to avoid later problems with speech, but again, there are many reasons that children have difficulty with sounds.

I would suggest that, before you decide to have your baby's tongue tie snipped, that you take advice from a feeding expert and/or a speech and language therapist. Leaving the frenulum intact can make it easier for a child to learn to control the movements of their tongue that are necessary for speech, as it keeps the tongue in a more central position in the mouth. If the tongue is not anchored at all to the floor of the mouth, it can be more difficult to develop the finer control needed to produce certain sounds.

Summary

The skills expected by six months of age are summarised as follows.

Understanding

- Your baby turns towards sounds.
- They are startled by loud noises.
- They quieten when spoken to.
- They watch your face when you talk to them.
- They recognise your voice and other familiar voices.
- When upset, they are calmed by your voice.
- They get excited when they hear you approaching.

Expressive language

- Your baby uses different cries to express different needs.
- They show excitement by waving their arms and legs.
- They respond with a smile or laugh to other people smiling and laughing.
- They coo or squeal to get your attention.
- They make noises when spoken to.

Speech sounds

- They play with sounds, making lots of different consonants and vowels, with no real meaning attached, which is known as 'cooing' or 'gurgling'.

Red flags

If any of the following are true for your child at six months old, you should consider seeking the advice of your health visitor, GP, or local speech and language therapist:

- They have some difficulty with eating or drinking.
- They are not startled by loud sounds.
- They do not look at your face when you speak.
- They are not responding to speech (especially familiar voices) or other sounds by turning or quietening.
- They are not interacting socially with eye contact and smiles.
- They are not starting to make a variety of different sounds.

Chatterbox Ideas

Special one-to-one time is important from day one, and at this age, it is easily achieved by simply spending a little more time on daily routines such as feeding, nappy changing and bath time.

All the time

Looking/attention skills

- Watch what your baby is looking at and talk about it. Sharing a baby's focus shows them that you are interested, reinforces their attention and encourages them to focus for longer. A baby's attention is fleeting, so you will find that you have to change what you are talking about every couple of minutes, but that is exactly what your baby needs.
- When your baby looks at an object, bring it closer to them, and if appropriate, let them touch it while you talk about it.

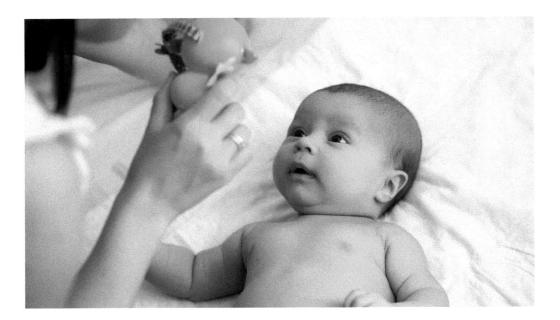

- Watch and copy your baby's facial expressions. This will encourage them to do the same.

Listening

- Keep the environment as quiet and free from distractions as possible, such as TV or music. Babies cannot easily tune out background noise, so we need to control it for them.
- Talk to your baby as you move around the room to encourage them to follow your voice.
- Talk to your baby frequently from the moment of birth. At this stage, it really doesn't matter what you say. Have your baby close to you and facing you, if possible.
- Say your baby's name to attract their attention and establish eye contact when you speak to them. This also prevents them from being startled, which can be upsetting for them. When picking up a young baby try saying their name and telling them what you are going to do, e.g. saying, 'Come to Mummy,' or, 'Come for a cuddle.'
- Name toys and objects around you, showing them to your baby as you say the name.
- Use simple verbal routines (see section on *Verbal Routines*, page 7).

- It is sometimes useful to give a running commentary about what you are doing or thinking or about something that is happening. Your baby won't understand what you are saying, but it will give them the opportunity to hear the overall rhythm and tune of language. It also gives you the chance to get on with things you need to do and teach your baby at the same time!

- When you talk to your baby, speak slowly in short, simple, tuneful sentences with lots of pauses and lots of repetition (see section on *Baby Talk*, page 5).

- It is natural to ask a young baby lots of rhetorical questions, such as 'Who's gorgeous?' It is a natural part of turn-taking, and it exposes the baby to different intonation patterns from an early age.

Sounds and talking

- Listen to your baby's sounds, interpret them, repeat them back and add a few more.

- Reward your baby's attempts at making sounds with lots of smiles, kisses and play.

- Interpret and respond to all the sounds your baby makes, including reflex sounds, e.g. when your baby coughs, you may say, 'Oh dear,' and give them a gentle pat on the back; or when they start to let you know that they are hungry with sounds or body language, say, 'You sound like you're hungry. Let's have some milk.'

- Mirror the sounds that your baby makes back to them. This will show them that you are interested in what they are trying to say. Try extending your baby's vocalisations a little each time, e.g. if they say, 'Ah,' you could reply, 'Ah… boo.' This one-step-ahead approach is important throughout your child's language-learning journey.
- Start taking turns in 'conversations' as early as you can, pausing to allow your baby to 'speak', and speaking to them when they pause. Introduce turn-taking as soon as your baby is making sounds. Wait for them to pause, then repeat their sound back to them or give a short comment such as, 'Oh really?' or, 'I see,' then wait for them to respond with another sound. Maintain eye contact while you are doing this, use lots of facial expression and exaggerated intonation, and your baby will very quickly learn to love this game.

Chatterbox time

Music, songs and rhymes

- **Sing**
  Sing songs and nursery rhymes (see section on *Nursery rhymes*, page 23):
    o 'Head, Shoulders, Knees and Toes'
    o 'Ten Fat Sausages'
    o 'Miss Polly Had a Dolly'
    o 'The Wheels on the Bus'
    o 'Teddy Bear, Teddy Bear'
    o 'See-saw Margery Daw'
    o 'If You're Happy and You Know It'
    o 'This Little Piggy'
    o 'Round and Round the Garden'
  Whenever possible, do the actions with your baby. It will hold their attention for much longer, and they will love the song even more.
  Songs and rhymes are also great for car journeys.

- **Musical instruments**
  Give your baby simple musical instruments such as rattles, bells and rainmakers.

- **Dance**

  Dance with your baby. Not only will they find it enjoyable (it can be either fun or soothing depending on your choice of music), but it will help your baby learn about rhythm as you move in time to the music.

- **Arms and legs**

  Lie your baby on the floor and move their arms and legs in time to some music. You can clap their hands or feet together to the beat.

- **Nursery rhymes**

  Children love nursery rhymes! Some were recorded as early as the 1600s, but they will have been passed down through generations before that. Why have nursery rhymes stood the test of time and why are they still important for children today?

  - They are the perfect first stories. Many are published as board books, which are perfect for babies. This is a great start in developing a love of reading.
  - The bouncy rhythm catches a baby's attention, and they are usually quite short, so you can get to the end before you lose their attention.

- One of the key predictors for early success in reading is how well children know nursery rhymes. [83] Learning about rhyme is an important part of developing phonological awareness which is a key skill in learning to read. [84]
- In normal speech, there are stressed and unstressed syllables. Babies tend to focus on the stressed syllables and ignore the unstressed ones. [58] [85] This is clear in the way that they miss unstressed syllables off longer words, e.g. 'banana' becomes 'nana'. In nursery rhymes, many of the syllables are stressed so they are a perfect tool for teaching sounds and words.
- Some rhymes don't make any sense and just sound silly, which appeals to a child's sense of humour.
- The actions that go along with many nursery rhymes are good for developing coordination and fine motor skills.
- Repetition is key to language acquisition. [63] [86] Words tend to be repeated in nursery rhymes, and children usually like to hear the same rhyme several times.
- Knowing and reciting nursey rhymes helps to build social skills. Children find nursery rhymes easy to learn, and once they know them, your child will want to say them with you. In playgroups, nurseries and schools, children will naturally join in saying rhymes all together, and it becomes a social activity.
- Nursery rhymes connect generations. There is a lot of fun to be had in teaching your child something that you enjoyed when you were a child. Also, grandparents may not be familiar with current TV characters or smartphone apps, but they can always share nursery rhymes with their young grandchildren.

Here are some nursery rhymes to try with your child:
o 'Baa, Baa, Black Sheep'
o 'Twinkle, Twinkle, Little Star'
o 'Humpty Dumpty'
o 'Ring a Ring a Roses'
o 'Hey Diddle Diddle'
o 'Little Bo Peep'
o 'Jack and Jill'
o 'Row, Row, Row, Your Boat'
o 'Hickory Dickory Dock'

- o 'Mary Had a Little Lamb'
- o 'Little Miss Muffet'
- o 'Old Mother Hubbard'
- o 'Mary, Mary, Quite Contrary'
- o 'Old King Cole'
- o 'Little Jack Horner'
- o 'Pat-a-cake, Pat-a-cake'
- o 'Cobbler, Cobbler'
- o 'The Old Woman Who Lived in a Shoe'
- o 'It's Raining, It's Pouring'
- o 'One, Two, Buckle My Shoe'
- o 'Polly Put the Kettle on'
- o 'Pop Goes the Weasel'
- o 'Sing a Song of Sixpence'
- o 'Round and Round The Garden'
- o 'The Grand Old Duke Of York'
- o 'There Was a Crooked Man'
- o 'Three Blind Mice'
- o 'This Old Man'
- o 'This Little Piggy'
- o 'Two Little Dickie Birds'
- o 'Wind the Bobbin up'

Books and stories

It's never too early to start reading to your baby. Babies love the sound of their parents' voices, whether they are using baby talk to speak to them directly, reading a simple rhyming story or reading articles from the morning paper! Sit close to your baby and use baby talk and lots of facial expressions to engage them, and they will happily listen to the news headlines or even the football results!

Books for babies often have simple, rhyming text that even the youngest of babies will enjoy listening to. It has been demonstrated that babies show increased interest in stories that were read to them before they were born, [87] [88] so it really is never too early to start!

Read simple books. Board books are best, so that you can encourage your child to touch them as well as look at the pictures. These are some suggestions:

- Board books with nursery rhymes or any simple, rhyming text.
- Books with different textures for your baby to explore.
- Books where you can make a noise on every page, e.g. animals, vehicles, or common household objects such as a clock, doorbell or kettle. Some books make the appropriate noise when you press a spot on the page, but your baby will enjoy it more, and learn more, if you make the noise.
- Books with a single photo on each page, of objects, people or animals.
- Babies love other babies, so books full of baby photos are always popular.
- Make a simple photo album of familiar people, pets, places, toys, food, etc. This is bound to be a favourite, and it can be updated as your baby grows.

Here are some examples of books that are appropriate at this age:

- *Eyes, Nose, Toes, Peekaboo!* by DK

- *Baby Touch and Feel First Words* by DK
- *Baby Touch and Feel Mealtime* by DK
- *Baby Touch and Feel Farm* by DK
- *My First Words* by DK
- *Baby Faces Peekaboo* by DK
- *Baby Sparkle Funny Faces* by DK
- *Baby Sparkle* series by DK
- *What's That Noise? Guess the…* series by Child's Play and Cocoretto
- *What's That Noise, Spot?* by Eric Hill

Games and activities

- Play social games, such as these:
    - o Peekaboo – Sit facing your baby, then cover your face with a cloth, pull it off and say, 'Peekaboo!' When your baby is a little older, put the cloth over their head, and ask, 'Where've they gone?' As they pull the cloth off, say, 'There they are!' At first, your baby will think that you have gone because they can't see you, but by about five months, they will have 'object permanence' and know that you are still there under the cloth.

o So big – Take your baby's hands and ask, 'How big are you?' Then lift their arms above their head, and say, '*So* big!' As soon as babies develop control of their arms, they love to initiate or join in with this one anywhere and everywhere!

- Make funny faces. Even a newborn baby is fascinated by faces, especially their parents' because they recognise their voices. Pull a series of different faces and watch your baby's reaction; stick out your tongue, then give a huge grin, then open your eyes and mouth wide as if surprised, and so on. It is an important skill for babies to learn to maintain eye contact and to understand different expressions, so it is good to introduce this early. While you are making faces, you can make lots of different sounds.

- Have a bag of common objects that are safe for your baby to explore, e.g. a baby's hairbrush, a plastic ball, a bath toy, and a plastic or cloth book. Give them one object at a time and just let them explore. Each one will end up in their mouth, so they may need a watchful eye.

- Dangle toys or things that move in front of your baby's line of vision. Move them slowly from side to side and let them grasp them if they reach out. Use brightly coloured toys, ones with faces, and ones with different textures that crinkle when you touch them.

- Blow bubbles around your baby, taking care not to let them go too near their face as they can sting a baby's eyes. Babies are fascinated by the shape of the bubbles and the way they reflect the light. Your child will love them even more once they are old enough to try to pop them!
- Blow coloured feathers near your baby. Bring one near their face for them to look at, then stroke the feather around their face for them to feel how soft it is.
- Show your baby two coloured plastic spoons. Bang them together. Give one to them to hold and explore.
- Place a mirror near your baby so that they can look at their reflection as they move and babble.
- Bring a favourite cuddly toy close for your baby to look at, then hide it behind your back and ask, 'Where's Teddy gone?' As you bring it back to the front, say, 'Here he is!' or 'Peekaboo!'

Chapter 2

6–12 months

This is when the fun really begins! Hopefully, your baby will be sleeping through the night, so the worst of the tiredness will be over for you, and their daily routine will be more established, so that your family life should be more predictable and relaxed. They will be sitting up and watching everything that is going on around them, desperately wanting to join in. Their personality will be shining through, and they will spend most of their wakeful hours smiling, laughing, shouting and, generally, willing you to entertain them. That is much easier now, as they will find everything you say or do interesting, and they will be amused for long periods of time by the most basic of household objects!

Between the ages of 6 and 12 months, your baby's gross and fine motor skills develop rapidly. The honeymoon period – when you could leave the room for a few minutes, knowing that when you came back, they would be exactly where you left them – is gone for ever! Remember that they will put everything in their mouth at this stage, so be aware of what is within their reach.

The parts of the brain that play a role in cognition and learning, language, and social emotional development are highly active now, so this is a critical time for developing these skills, and it is important to make the most of it. A baby acquires knowledge and understanding through thought, experience and their senses. We obviously can't control a baby's thought processes, but we can offer them a wide variety of experiences to stimulate each of their senses and give them multiple repetitions of each experience.

From the age of 6–12 months, the speech centres of the brain become increasingly active. The number of new connections formed between nerve cells depends very much on the amount of stimulation they receive. This is reflected in the fact that from six months, babies show an increasing variation in their developmental achievements and milestones. While this is partly due to their genes, their environment has a huge part to play, e.g. while hearing and deaf children may start babbling at around the same time, the speed at which their sounds subsequently develop will be greater in the children with normal hearing. [89] Similarly, children from deprived backgrounds may say their first word at roughly the same time as those brought up in a highly stimulating environment, but the rate at which they acquire new vocabulary will be vastly different. [90] [91]

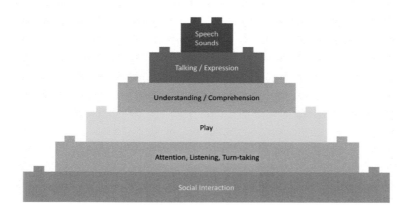

Social Interaction

At this age, babies find other people fascinating, and while someone is talking to them, they will maintain eye contact. They become increasingly skilled at imitating facial expressions and gestures, usually with the aim of encouraging an adult to interact with them. A baby's smile is an utter delight to see and will usually encourage an adult to start a conversation. Mission accomplished!

Social interaction is the best way for a baby to learn; interacting makes them happy and knowing that people are interested in them develops their self-confidence. You will notice that your baby responds more to social interaction and begins to initiate it, not only with familiar people but also often with complete strangers. Babies may appear to be shouting randomly from their pushchair or a shopping trolley, but very often they are trying to catch the attention of anyone passing by in the hope of winning a smile or a brief chat! One of my children used to do this every time we went shopping, from around six months, and it meant that strangers kept him entertained for the entire shopping trip!

The growth spurt taking place in the frontal lobe of your baby's brain is responsible for forming bonds between people. The bonds that they have with familiar people become deeper, and they learn that other people are 'strangers'. For a while, they may find strangers interesting and actively seek attention from them, then suddenly develop a fear of them, along with separation anxiety.

Separation and stranger anxiety

Every child is different and will show a different level of fear of strangers. It will partly depend on their personality and also on how you react when it happens. It is important that they learn that, even though they can't always see you, you will always come back.

These are a few ideas you can try:

- Always tell your baby that you are leaving, where you are going and that you will come back. Try to only leave them very briefly at first and then gradually increase the time you are away.
- Never just sneak off, even if they are very distressed at the thought of you leaving. This will only create anxiety in the baby, as they will never know if you might suddenly disappear.

- Make a point of saying goodbye to other people when they leave and hello when they come back, even if your baby doesn't seem interested. It will help your baby to learn that everyone leaves sometimes but then comes back.
- Play peekaboo or hide-and-seek with toys, or you and your baby. This will help them to learn that even if they can't see someone, they may still be near.
- The first few times you leave your baby to go to another room, keep talking to them so that they will know they haven't been left alone.
- Encourage your baby to interact with as many different people as possible, whether it is a family occasion, mother-and-toddler group or just introducing your baby to different people in the supermarket. Encourage them to be held by people that you know and trust, but that they are not very familiar with. It may only be the briefest of cuddles at first, as you obviously don't want them to become distressed, but each time, they will learn that they eventually find their way back to you. Start by remaining in sight and then go where they can't see you for as long as they are happy.
- Separation anxiety is likely to pass more quickly if you try to help your baby through it and don't treat it as though they are just making a fuss.

Attention, Listening and Turn-Taking

In order to develop good attention and listening skills, your baby must learn which sounds are important and which are just background noise. It takes a lot of practice to filter out distractions, and your baby will already be learning to do this. When you are talking to them, they will be trying their best to listen to your voice and ignore the sounds from the TV or radio, a dog barking, cars going past outside, etc. To give them the best opportunity for listening, try to get rid of as many of the distracting sounds as you can for them.

Your baby will stop moving and making noises when they hear a familiar voice, showing that they are paying attention. They can distinguish between speech and non-speech sounds, and accurately locate the source of a voice. They will focus on different sounds in their environment (e.g. a phone ringing, a washing machine or a dog barking), but they will still prefer the sound of a voice.

Your baby will now already be a good social communicator. Take any opportunity to encourage turn-taking with them, whether it is in play (such as rolling a ball back and forth) or using gestures (so they clap, then you clap and then they clap again).

They may make a noise like a cough, and if you respond with a cough, 'Bless you!' or 'Oh dear!' you will probably find that they end up forcing lots of coughs to carry on the turn-taking game! Join in when they are babbling happily. When they pause, you can repeat some of their babble back to them, then you pause and wait for them to join in again, and so on. By now, they will be leaving more obvious pauses to allow you to have your turn.

Play

When babies play, their whole bodies are involved in reaching, grasping, rolling and touching things. Movement leads to new possibilities for babies' play and learning, and as their physical dexterity improves, it allows them to explore more things within their reach. Once they are mobile, babies like to have some independence to explore their environment, but they have little sense of danger, so they will need a watchful eye for quite some time.

At this stage, a baby begins to participate in adult-led social games (e.g. peekaboo). They will still be happy to spend long periods of time sitting on your lap, copying your facial expressions, sounds and gestures, all of which are an important step towards the pretend play of their toddler years.

Functional play skills also emerge at this age, i.e. playing with an object or toy as it is meant to be used, such as opening and closing a box, emptying containers, pushing a toy car, rolling a ball, or stacking bricks. You can help by showing them how to hold or move things (e.g. show them that if they push a toy car, it will move across the floor), which will give them even more enjoyment than just holding it.

You might find that your child gets absorbed in one functional play activity for quite a long time, but that is fine. As a young baby, they may have held an object, put it in their mouth and moved it from hand to hand; now, using objects and toys in a purposeful way opens up a whole new world for them, and they will get a lot of pleasure from it. You can always play with them and extend their activity slightly, e.g. say, 'Ready, steady, go,' before rolling a ball to them; or put a toy inside the box they are playing with, so that they will peep inside each time, as well as opening and closing the box.

Understanding

Your baby will now recognise their own name and will consistently look when called. They will understand many names of people and familiar objects (e.g. 'ball', 'cat' and 'cup'), and will either give them to you on request or look at them as you name them.

They understand familiar phrases, such as 'bye-bye', 'all gone' and 'come here' when they are used in context and accompanied by gestures. Using gestures when talking to children helps them to understand and learn new words more easily. [92]

Repetition

Repetition is key from now on. Babies and toddlers love to play the same game or hear the same story time and time again. Once they can say the word 'again', there is no going back! Why is this?

We have all heard the saying 'Practice makes perfect', and there are many others like this:

- 'Repetition is the secret of perfection.' (Dr Maria Montessori)
- 'Repetition, repetition, repetition equals results.' (Jeanette Coron)
- 'Repetition rings a bell!' (Ernest Agyemang Yeboah)

This is why repetition is so important:

1. Repetition supports brain development. During the preschool years, a child's brain is especially active and is wired to receive large amounts of new stimulation. The information travels down nerve pathways to the brain. The brain recognises and keeps the pathways containing repeated information as well as automatically pruning the thinner pathways containing information that has not been repeated. The more often information is repeated, the more likely it is to be retained. So, repetition is how children's brains become reinforced for learning, giving them the fastest route to achieving their potential.
2. Repetition leads to predictability. Knowing what to expect and having things happen in a familiar, predictable order means that children feel safe, secure and more confident. A predictable world is the best environment for learning.
3. Repetition also has strong emotional implications for young children. The brain pathways involved in emotional development are strengthened through repeated, loving, day-to-day interaction with parents and other caregivers. For this reason, repetition can help to make children happy.
4. Repetition and practice reduce the amount of effort needed to carry out a task. To learn something new takes a huge amount of mental energy. You can almost see the brain of a baby struggling as they make their first attempts at rolling over, sitting, reaching for toys or saying their first words. With enough practice, these activities become easier and more automatic, so that the baby barely seems to think about them as they do them. They can then focus their mental energy on the next thing they need to learn.

Supporting repetition

This may seem straightforward, but there is, in fact, more to repetition than simply doing the same thing over and over, if you want it to be effective:

1. Provide the opportunity for repetition.
   Give babies and children the chance to repeat activities that interest them and let them continue for as long as they remain interested. Don't be tempted to clear toys away too soon or feel that you must keep directing your child's attention to a new activity. Let them decide when they've had enough.

2. Extend the activity.
   After several repetitions of a favourite activity or story, try extending it slightly. Add a new sound, comment or action that doesn't change the familiarity of the activity but that adds something to it.

3. Use a multisensory approach.
   The best way for children to learn and retain information is to engage all the different sensory pathways to the brain. Using as many of the five senses as possible (vision, hearing, touch, taste and smell) also makes activities more fun and engaging, so that children will want to repeat them. If your child wants to play with the same toy in the same way for a long time, draw their attention to a different sensory aspect of it that they may not have noticed. This also enables you to include a wider variety of vocabulary.

4. Use verbal routines.
   The best way to include repetition in your child's day is to use daily routines as teaching opportunities (see section on *Verbal Routines*, page 7). Routine activities such as mealtimes, nappy changes and bath time are great opportunities for playing, talking and singing, or in other words, learning! Using the same words, phrases, songs or actions during these routines will add another dimension of predictability and ensure that even the most mundane of tasks can be used as a teaching moment.

Expressive Language

Babies of this age soon realise that they have the power to affect the behaviour of other people, and they will use their language skills to do this more and more. Their desire to communicate comes from the knowledge that, when they talk, they can make something happen, and they quickly learn how to use adults as tools to get what they want. [72] Using a sound or action to get what they want means that your child is beginning to understand the concept of cause and effect.

As well as making sounds, babies use their whole bodies to communicate. Your baby will expect you to respond to these movements and gestures as though you know exactly what they mean. Fortunately, you will most of the time, and if not, they will persevere until they get the desired response or until they are distracted by something else.

It is essential that children have the opportunity to develop the concept of cause and effect between the ages of 6 and 12 months, and I have included activities and toys that can be used for this in the *Chatterbox Ideas* section of this chapter.

Before babies use words to communicate, they will use lots of gestures. Some of the first to appear are social gestures such as waving, clapping, nodding and shaking their head. One of the most important ones is pointing. [93] If adults use gestures, particularly pointing, it encourages children to do the same, [94] and the use of gestures can predict their subsequent vocabulary development. Children whose parents point more when interacting with them have faster vocabulary growth than children whose parents point less often. [95] [96]

Gestures and Signs

A gesture is the use of a hand or body movement or action to convey a message. Signs are simply a formal system of recognised hand gestures that are designed to be shared among whole communities. All children and adults spontaneously use gestures in certain situations, usually alongside spoken language. Signs are taught as a long-term means of communication to be used instead of, or as well as, speech. You can choose to use your own gestures with your child or use the recognised signs if you prefer.

Gestures naturally appear before speech in a child's attempts to communicate. From as early as seven months, babies will put their arms up to show that they want to be picked up, reach out for things they want, point at things they want you to look at, wave bye-bye, etc.

Many parents that I have worked with have been reluctant to use gestures or signs with their children because of the worry that if a child can communicate with signs, they will be less likely to use words. *Gestures and signs do not hold back speech development.* Just as crawling is a stage that children progress through before walking, gesturing is a natural stage towards talking. Once a child can walk, they rarely choose to crawl. Similarly, once a child can use spoken words, gestures and signs naturally fade away.

Most parents don't see the point in using extra gestures or signs with children whose speech and language skills seem to be developing normally. However, these are the known benefits, supported by research, of using gestures with your child:

1. A child learning early vocabulary finds it much easier to understand the meaning of a word if it is accompanied by a gesture. [97]

   Using a gesture gives children extra information so that they can work out the meaning of a word. The more information we can give them, the faster they will understand the word. For example, when you know your child wants a drink, you might ask, 'Drink?'; to give them an extra clue, you could show them their cup as you ask, 'Drink?', but if their cup is not nearby, you could use a gesture of pretending to drink, and ask, 'Drink?'

   We don't just do this with children. Adults will naturally use more gestures with each other in noisy environments, such as factories and pubs.

2. The strong connection between gestures and spoken language is supported by MRI scans, which show that they are processed in the same areas of the brain. [98]

3. A child's gesture vocabulary at 14 months old is a strong predictor of spoken vocabulary skills two years later. [99] [94] The more you use gestures with your child, the more they in turn will use gestures [100] [101] and the bigger their vocabulary will be.

4. The use of symbolic gestures by parents not only encourages the earlier and greater use of gestures by children but it also facilitates the better understanding and use of language months later. [102] Children who use a lot of gestures tend to join words together in sentences earlier than those who don't. [96] [103]

5. The use of gestures helps young children to understand and learn spatial concepts such as 'under'. [104]

6. The use of gestures improves children's storytelling (narrative) skills. [105]

7. Gestures can help us to understand and remember mathematical concepts better. [106] [107]

8. Using gestures appears to free up some of our working memory capacity, so that we find it easier to process lots of different information at the same time. [106]

Here are some other reasons to use gestures or signs:

1. Children can use gestures before they can speak. The muscle control required to make a gesture is much simpler than that required to produce a word. Children develop muscle control of their arms and hands before that of their lips and tongue.

2. Using gestures reduces frustration. A child's level of understanding is greater than their ability to express themself verbally. This can lead to frustration and behaviour such as shouting or tantrums. The use of gestures may help prevent some of this.

3. Gestures and signs boost an adult's understanding of what a child is trying to say. They add extra information to the child's attempts to speak, helping adults understand what they are trying to say.

4. Gestures and signs help attention skills. Movement captures and holds a child's attention: there is greater movement involved in gestures than speech, so someone who is talking and signing at the same time is more interesting for a child to look at, and they will pay attention for longer.

5. Gestures and signs help adults to simplify their language. An adult might say something like, 'Do you want another apple?' but if they only know the sign for 'apple' they are likely to just say, 'More apple?' which is easier for the child to understand.

6. Gestures help adults use consistent language. Because the adult will only know a certain number of signs, they will tend to use the same sign for the same word, e.g. instead of using 'lunch, dinner, tea, hungry', etc. to represent eating, if they only know the sign for 'eat' then they will always use that word.

7. A baby can see the gestures and signs they are making. They can watch the shapes that their arms, hands and fingers are making, which isn't the case with their mouth. They can also compare their attempts with yours.

8. You can physically help your child with their gestures and signs. If there is a gesture or sign that you feel would be particularly useful for your child to use – such as one for drink, bottle or dummy – you can help to move their hands and fingers into the right position so that the gesture is clear. This is not possible with the spoken word.

Pointing

Children begin to point between 7 and 15 months old. At first, they use their whole hand, but about three months later they start to extend their index finger to point.

As with gestures, there are two main functions of pointing:

1. **Requesting**
   A child will point to ask for something they want.

2. **Joint attention**
   A child will point to an object to draw an adult's attention to it. This will then encourage the adult to talk about the object the child is pointing at by naming it, describing it and asking questions about it. So, a simple act such as pointing can promote a whole discussion about something the child has shown interest in.

Teaching your child to point

1. One of the best ways to encourage your child to point is to point yourself. Walk around the house, pointing at objects and naming them. Do the same at the park and at the shops. Start with things that are quite close, so that your child knows exactly what you are pointing to and gradually introduce things that are further away.
2. Naming body parts is a useful game. You can point to your own nose, eyes, toes, etc., and your child's, and also a doll's or teddy's.
3. Point at toys that you know your child will be interested in, food that they like or pictures in their favourite books.
4. Reaching is the step before pointing, so encourage your child to reach for things by putting them slightly out of reach. Play any games that involve stretching your arm out and touching something, e.g. line up some dolls and teddies, and then pat each one on the head.
5. Try games that promote using the tip of your child's pointing finger: e.g. popping bubbles; making a fist with one hand, and poking a sock or scarf through the hole in the middle of your fist using your other forefinger; or licking the end of your finger, and using it to pick up some hundreds and thousands or a Cheerio from a bowl.
6. If your child makes no attempt to point or to copy you pointing, take their hand and stretch it towards something that you know they like, and then react as though they have pointed spontaneously themself, to give them the idea of what you want them to do.

7. When your child does start to point, get excited about it! Give lots of praise and reinforcement, and spend time talking about whatever it is they have pointed at. If it is something that they are asking for, give it to them straight away to reinforce the point.

Speech Sounds

Until now, your baby has been experimenting with different kinds of sounds in all parts of their mouth, from cooing and gurgling to smacking their lips together or blowing raspberries!

They will have become adept at producing a variety of vowel sounds, but will now start to produce more consonant sounds, and then they will try to combine them into short syllables such as 'da' or 'buh'.

Babbling really begins when a baby combines a consonant and vowel sound together and repeats this over and over, e.g. 'babababa' or 'duhduhduhduh'. Babbling seems to be a way that a baby practises the sounds and sequences that are later used in speech. As with all of the skills acquired during this period, repetition is crucial for reinforcing the network of neurological pathways in the baby's brain, which, in this case, enable them to decide which sounds they want to make and send the appropriate message from their brain to their speech muscles. Children all over the world begin by using the same set of sounds in their babble, which are usually 'p', 'b', 'm', 't', 'd', 'n', 'w' and 'h'. The variety of sounds used will change as the baby develops greater control of their lip and tongue muscles.

By six months, a baby will produce sequences of the same consonant and vowel repeated (e.g. 'dadadada'), then at around eight to nine months, they will use different consonants in the sequence (e.g. 'badabada'). At around 10 months, they will start using a variety of both consonants and vowels, and this will begin to sound more like adult speech in terms of the variety of sounds plus the rhythm and intonation patterns. It is then called 'jargon' because of its resemblance to adult speech.

The sounds used in babbling will change as the baby's muscle control improves, but the child's social environment also plays an important part in sound development. A child loves playing games that attract attention, and one of those games includes imitating sounds. They pay close attention to the reaction that they get from their parents and go on to repeat the sounds that others take most delight in. Parents tend to react most positively to sounds that appear in their own language, praise their child for using them and repeat them back, thereby reinforcing them further. Babies will gradually drop the sounds that do not appear in their native language, paving the way for a smaller, well-practised set of sounds ready to use when words appear.

The exact link between babbling and later speech development isn't entirely clear. Many studies show that late babbling can predict a speech and language delay. [108] Usually, a good babbler becomes a good talker, but not always. If your child doesn't babble a lot, don't panic, but, equally, if your child babbles constantly, don't assume that they will automatically go on to become a chatterbox.

A baby's control over the muscles of their lips and tongue also improves as weaning begins.

Weaning

There are many good books and websites with detailed information and advice about the stages of weaning and recipes for each stage. Here, I am going to concentrate on the relationship between weaning and speech development.

Stages of feeding development

- **At birth**
  Babies can be seen to suck and swallow, even before birth. The coordination of breathing, sucking and swallowing develops over the first few days.

  Newborn babies have very small mouths and limited tongue movement (in and out, and up and down), so they can only cope with liquids at first.

However, they can adjust their sucking response to the thickness of the milk and to whether they are drinking from a bottle or breast.

Newborns open their mouths in preparation to suck, particularly if they are hungry, and will try to suck anything that touches their mouth. They have a strong gag reflex, which later prevents them from ingesting pieces of food that are too large to swallow. This decreases as they get used to eating foods with different textures.

- **0–6 months**

Public Health England recommends that babies should be given their first solid foods at around six months. [109] However, a Department of Health survey in 2011 demonstrates that 80% babies are given solid food by five months. [110] They can cope with pureed and mashed food at around four months, and they are able to take it from a spoon and use their tongue to move it to the back of their mouth. At this stage, a baby will still have some tongue thrust, which is an automatic response to prevent choking, but it may look like they are pushing the food out of their mouth because they don't like it. This will disappear as their tongue control improves, usually by six months. Drinking milk from the breast or bottle involves an up and down movement of the tongue, which may cause the tongue to protrude slightly. With solids, the tongue needs to stay inside the mouth and move from side to side and diagonally and reach all around the mouth.

- **6–12 months**

By six months, babies are generally able to sit upright and reach out to grasp toys and put them in their mouths. This means that, even if you are not a fan of baby-led weaning, it makes sense to give your baby a spoon or food to hold while you are doing most of the feeding.

As well as pureed and mashed food, it is beneficial to start introducing some lumpy food from six months. Your baby still has a strong gag reflex at this age to prevent them choking, and this will gradually decrease over the next six months as they get used to solid food. As more solid food is introduced, especially lumps, a baby's tongue control develops further to move the food from side to side to allow chewing. Babies who are offered different textures of food from six months old develop a more efficient chewing mechanism sooner. The late introduction of lumpy foods is also related to a reluctance to accept fruit and vegetables later on. [111] [112]

Babies have usually lost their tongue-thrust response by this time, so are able to keep most food in their mouths. From around seven months, they begin to close their mouth around the spoon, so that you won't always need to scrape food that has escaped from around their mouths. Once their teeth start to appear, they can bite into harder food. It is safer to start with 'bite and dissolve' foods at first (such as rusks, cheese straws and sponge fingers) before moving on to foods that require chewing (such as fruit, soft vegetables, bread, pasta and soft cheese, then meat and fish).

How weaning is related to speech development

The muscles of the lips, tongue and jaw enable a baby to eat different foods as well as to learn to talk, and one develops in line with the other. It makes sense that problems with weaning can have a knock-on effect on the development of speech. Exposing a baby to different textures of foods boosts the strength and control of these muscles, which will have a positive effect on their speech development. From six months old, it is also useful to introduce a beaker to your child, to encourage a more mature tongue position and reduce the likelihood of persistent tongue thrust. Choose one with a single small hole to avoid too much water coming out. Start by offering a beaker of water with every meal, and over the next six months, gradually completely replace the bottle with a beaker. Overuse of a bottle has the same implications as overuse of a dummy (see *Dummies* section, page 15). The sucking mechanism for breastfeeding is different and does not have the same implications.

Current guidelines recommend waiting until your baby is six months old before introducing solid food. Obvious signs that a baby is ready to start having something more than milk include these:

- They can sit up well without support.
- They have lost the tongue-thrust reflex, where they automatically push foreign objects out of their mouth.
- They are eager to join in mealtimes and reach for food.
- They imitate eating behaviours such as chewing and smacking their lips.
- They dribble less. As a baby gains more control of their muscles, they learn to swallow saliva rather than letting it dribble down their chin.

Signs that are often mistaken for a baby being ready for solids, but which may be due to other reasons (such as a growth spurt or teething) include the following:

- They start to wake during the night after previously sleeping through.
- They demand feeds more often.
- They still seem hungry after a milk feed.
- They no longer settle easily.
- They constantly chew their fingers or fist.

To begin with, solid food should be about enjoyment and not nutrition, as a baby will be getting most of the nutrients they need from the milk that they should still be having. If most of the food ends up on the floor or in your baby's hair, it doesn't matter as long as they are having a good time. If mealtimes are enjoyable, you are less likely to end up with a fussy eater. Playing with food is a good form of exercise for the speech muscles. Try encouraging your baby to lick food from a plate or egg cup (manners can wait for now!).

Because a baby's mouth is so sensitive, they will learn a lot of valuable information about objects by putting them in their mouth, such as how they taste, whether they are hard or soft, or whether they are hot or cold. At this stage, a baby will also be happy to try most foods, so it is worth making their diet as varied as possible from day one, before they develop any real likes and dislikes.

Babies may need to be offered food many times before they will happily eat it, so don't give up too soon. A baby may reject food because of the texture and temperature as well as the taste, so try varying these before you exclude the food from their diet.

There will be times when your baby will eat more – in terms of quantity and variety – than others, and it is important that any stress you feel isn't passed on to your baby. You don't want every meal to become a battleground. It really is true that when they are hungry enough, they will eat most things!

When introducing solid food, simply offer the food to them so that they must actively take it off the spoon rather than you shovelling it into their mouth. If they don't take it straight away, try resting the spoon on their bottom lip. Also try offering the spoon slightly to the side of their mouth sometimes to encourage a greater variety of tongue movements.

By 12 months, you should be able to introduce the following foods, which will naturally improve the strength and control of specific muscles.

1. Foods that require more jaw movement:

   - Cubes of hard cheese
   - Strips of white meat
   - Strips of cheese on toast
   - French toast
   - An omelette
   - Chips
   - Slices of hard fruit
   - Firm cooked vegetables

2. To encourage babies to use their lip muscles more, try the following:

   - Sucking increasingly thick liquids through a straw.
   - Giving kisses. Kiss a mirror, dolls or teddies. Try putting lipstick on and then make a picture of kisses.

3. To get them to play with tongue movements, encourage your baby to try these games:

   - Lick spots of food from around their mouth (you may need to hold their hands gently to stop them using these to just wipe it away!). Try looking in a mirror together and both doing it.
   - Use the tip of their tongue to catch chocolate flakes, hundreds and thousands, Cheerios, etc. from an egg cup.
   - Draw lines or shapes on a plate with thick yoghurt, chocolate spread, icing, etc., and see if your child can follow the shape with their tongue.

If your baby has any problems with weaning at any stage, talk to your health visitor. They can advise you if it is a developmental or behavioural issue, and if not, they may suggest you contact a speech and language therapist to rule out any problems with the muscles of their lips and tongue. You can, of course, contact a speech and language therapist directly.

Summary

The skills expected by 12 months of age are summarised as follows.

Understanding

- Your baby pays attention to familiar voices.
- They pay attention to sounds around them, e.g. a dog barking or a phone ringing.
- They can work out where a voice is coming from and turn towards it.
- They look at your face when you start talking to them.
- They look at familiar people and objects when their name is mentioned.
- They look at things you point to when you say, 'Look.'
- They recognise their own name and look at the person speaking when they hear it.
- They understand familiar small phrases in context (e.g. 'Up you come' and 'Come here') especially if a gesture is used.
- They smile at lot, often before someone smiles at them.
- They enjoy songs and rhymes, especially those with actions, and show excitement when they hear them.

Expressive language

- Your baby takes turns in little 'conversations' in which you talk, and they babble back.
- They use gestures such as waving and pointing.
- They may have a few single words.
- They initiate favourite games (such as peekaboo) with adults, using gestures, sounds or words.

Speech sounds

- They use long strings of babble, often using more than one consonant, e.g. 'badabada'.
- They use the rhythm and intonation of adult speech, so their babble sounds like they are talking.

Red flags

If any of the following are true for your child at 12 months old, you should consider seeking the advice of your health visitor, GP, or local speech and language therapist:

- Your baby does not turn to look when you speak to them, especially when their name is called.
- They don't respond to and enjoy social games or rhymes such as peekaboo and 'Pat-a-cake'.
- They don't babble using a variety of consonant and vowel sounds.
- They don't look for familiar objects when you talk about them.
- They don't look at things you point to.
- They don't use simple gestures to communicate, e.g. waving bye-bye or putting their arms up to be lifted.
- They don't try to point.

Chatterbox Ideas

All the time

Looking/attention skills

- Continue to follow your baby's focus of attention. Joint attention creates the best opportunities for learning language [113]
- Never try to keep your baby focused on something for longer than they want to. This can impede the development of their attention skills, as your baby's attention will be split between what they want to focus on and what you want them to focus on. It is also very frustrating for you and your baby.
- Use gestures as well as speech to attract your baby's attention and help them to understand what you are saying.
- Use lots of facial expressions to hold their interest when you are talking to them. Use happy, exaggerated facial expressions.

Listening

- Keep background noise and distractions, such as TV and music, to a minimum. Another reason to do this now is because your baby will be making lots of sounds, and it is important that they start to make a link between their lip and tongue movements and the resulting sounds.
- Use your voice to attract and hold your baby's attention. Speak in a lively, animated voice and use lots of interesting sounds.
- Attract your baby's attention by saying their name. Their attention is still fleeting, so have lots of interesting things for them to look at and listen to.
- Choose everyday things that make a noise when you hold and scrunch them, e.g. tissue paper and wrapping paper. Show them to your baby, make noises with them and talk about them. Give them to your baby to make the noises for themself while you describe them.

- Encourage them to listen to different sounds around them. Household objects, animals, instruments and vehicles are all great for this. Start by saying, 'Shhh… listen…' and they will quickly learn that they should be quiet because they are going to hear something interesting. Examples include the following:
  o Show them an object while it is making the sound, e.g. say, 'Look, it's a car. What does the car say? It says "brrm, brrm". Listen to the car. Can you hear it say "brrm, brrm"?' or say, 'Look, there's a dog saying "woof, woof". Listen. Can you hear it say "woof, woof"?'
  o Take your baby to things around the house when they are making a noise, e.g. the washing machine, the kettle boiling or the taps running.
  o Use 'symbolic sounds', which are particular sounds that you link with things that happen, e.g. say, 'shhhhhhh' as the bath fills with water, and 'g, g, g, g, g, g,' as it empties down the plughole. This will attract and hold your child's attention, let them know that voices are fun to listen to, and give them an opportunity to listen to individual sounds on their own, which is important for later speech development.
  o Whenever you are with your baby and you hear an interesting sound, draw their attention to it, e.g. say, 'Listen… What's that? It's a…' Help them to find the source of the sound, e.g. a tractor coming from behind their buggy or a helicopter coming into view. It is useful for them to make the connection between the sound and the object.
  o 'Hide' a noisy object or toy somewhere obvious where your baby can still see it if they are looking in the right direction, e.g. a loud toy clock under a

kitchen chair. Wait and see if your baby can crawl towards it. If they don't do it immediately, it may be that they aren't interested enough in the toy or the game, not that they are not listening. Get down on the floor, crawl towards the toy, and show over-the-top surprise and delight to make them want to play.

- Remember that young babies can only look and listen at the same time if the following are true:
  o There are no distractions.
  o The focus of attention is their choice.
  o What they are looking at and listening to is the same thing, whether that is you talking or a toy that makes a noise. It is useful to play with these toys in groups, e.g. animals or vehicles.

Sounds and talking

- Keep repeating your baby's sounds back to them. They will enjoy the mirroring, and it will make them feel clever. It is the first step in them learning to copy you, which is very important in the language-learning process. It is also helpful for them to have the opportunity to be able to focus on single sounds or syllables, rather than a long flow of connected speech. Always view this as a game where you copy them, not the other way around.
- Interpret your baby's sounds, expressions and body language as though you understand exactly what they mean. For example, if they reach for a ball, you could say, 'Do you want the ball? Ball, please. Here's the ball,' or if they start to make a noise that lets you know they're not happy, you could say, 'Do you want a cuddle? Come to Mummy. Up you come.'
- Use lots of 'symbolic sounds', i.e. sounds associated with the object/thing they represent. Children often use the sound before they use the actual word, because they can be easier to say and fun to use! These include the following:
  Everyday sounds
  o 'Uh-oh' for little accidents
  o 'Shh' for quiet
  o 'Ahh' for a cuddle
  o 'Mmm' or 'yum, yum' for food
  o 'Splish splash' for bath time

o 'Whee' for slides or swings
o 'Tick tock' for a watch or clock
o 'Bang, bang' for a drum
o 'Pop, pop' for bubbles
o 'Pooh' for a nasty smell

Animal sounds
o 'Moo' for a cow
o 'Meow' for a cat
o 'Woof, woof' for a dog
o 'Quack, quack' for a duck
o 'Baa' for a sheep
o 'Roar' for a lion or tiger
o 'Tweet, tweet' for a bird
o 'Oink, oink' for a pig
o 'Cluck, cluck' for a hen
o 'Ribbit, ribbit' for a frog
o 'Hee-haw' for a donkey
o 'Ssss' for a snake
o 'Neigh' for a horse

Vehicle sounds
o 'brrm, brrm' for a car
o 'beep, beep' for a car
o 'choo, choo' for a train

o   'nee naw' for emergency vehicles

- Encourage your child to play with food at mealtimes. Trying different textures and using their lips and tongue to take food from their fingers or a plate is good exercise for their muscles. Manners can wait for now!

Chatterbox time

Music, songs and rhymes

- Continue with the songs and rhymes from Chapter 1 and try using some of them in your baby's routines, e.g. sing 'This Is the Way ('… we wash our hands' etc.) at bath time or 'Head, Shoulders, Knees and Toes' when getting dressed or undressed.
- Your baby will now be familiar with the tunes from their favourite songs, and you can try replacing the original words with ones from your baby's daily routines. This will help to add some enjoyment to things they might not want to do:
  o   'If you're happy and you know it brush your teeth/wash your hair, etc.'
  o   'This is the way we tidy up, tidy up, tidy up. This is the way we tidy up on a cold and frosty morning.'
- Continue using musical instruments. You can now encourage your baby to play along with their favourite songs or rhymes, and play along with them, e.g. have a drumstick each to bang on a drum.

Books and stories

- Have a place where your child knows they can always find some books that they can look at by themself. These should be small and sturdy, so that they can easily turn the pages, and preferably be resistant to a bit of chewing! If you read to your child regularly, they will start choosing books to look at on their own. In this way, they will learn how to handle books, hold them the

right way round and turn the pages from the front to the back. You may find that they will sit and look at a book, and then babble in a way that reflects the way you read to them. [114] You will also find that they start to bring their favourite books for you to share.

- You should now add books with simple stories and rhymes to your child's bookshelf:
  o *Dear Zoo* by Rod Campbell
  o *Oh Dear* by Rod Campbell
  o *Brown Bear, Brown Bear, What Do You See?* by Eric Carle
  o *Where's Spot?* by Eric Hill
  o *It's Mine* by Rod Campbell
  o *Teddy Bear, Teddy Bear, Turn Around* by Penny Dann
  o *The Very Hungry Caterpillar* by Eric Carle
  o *Each Peach, Pear, Plum* by Allan Ahlberg
  o *Goodnight Moon* by Margaret Wise Brown
- Books about daily routines are good at this age:
  o *Little Baby's Busy Day: A Finger Wiggle Board Book* by Sally Symes
  o *My Day: Mealtime* by Alex Ayliffe
  o *My Day: Bedtime* by Alex Ayliffe
  o *My Day: Playtime* by Alex Ayliffe
  o *Baby Days* by Nicola Philp

- Books about things that make sounds are useful and your baby will soon start joining in when you read:
  - *Peppa Pig at the Zoo*
  - *Spot Goes to the Farm* by Eric Hill
  - *Who's on the Farm?* by Julia Donaldson
  - *Garden Sounds* by Sam Taplin
  - *Jungle Sounds* by Sam Taplin
  - *Farm Sounds* by Sam Taplin
  - *My First Things That Go* by DK
  - *Noisy Things That Go (Touch and Feel)* by Libby Walden

Games and activities

- **Turn-taking**
  Make turn-taking a part of playtime whenever possible, e.g. building a tower of bricks, rolling a ball or car, playing with a shape sorter or turning the pages of a book. Encourage your baby to do this by holding the pieces of the toy, giving them one for their turn and saying, for example, 'Harry's turn', then taking one yourself and saying, 'Mummy's turn'. Take your turn quickly at first, so that they don't get frustrated waiting.

- **Social games**
  Tickling games or those involving body parts are good early on, e.g. 'Round and Round the Garden' or 'This Little Piggy'. These also help your baby to learn to anticipate and predict events.

- **Babble bag**
  Make a 'babble bag', which is a set of toys that encourage your child to babble, e.g. a phone, microphone, mirror, tube, noisy book or puppets. Let your baby take the toys out one by one and have some fun making noises.

- **Sound sack**
  Also make a 'sound sack', which is a selection of toys or objects that are associated with particular sounds, e.g. animals, a train, a car or a bell. Again, let your baby take them out one at a time, then you say the name of the toy and make the appropriate sound.

- **Cause and effect**

  Play with cause-and-effect toys, e.g. wind-up toys, toys where you press a button to make a noise, ball popper, pop-up animals or a Frog-in-a-Box.

  You can also play cause-and-effect games with everyday objects:
  - Turn a light or a torch on and off.
  - Turn a tap on and off.
  - Hit a pan with a wooden spoon.
  - Shake a rattle or a bell.
  - Push a ball across the table and watch it roll onto the floor.
  - Build a tower and knock it down.

- **Sticky notes**

  Draw different objects, animals, faces, etc. on Post-it notes and stick them at different heights on a wall or door, or even on parts of you! When your baby pulls off a note, tell them what the picture is. This is good to encourage gross motor skills (pulling themselves up and reaching out) and fine motor skills (peeling off the note). It is also good for vocabulary, for any words for which you can draw the object!

- **Toys tied to highchair**

  Use ribbons, shoelaces, etc. to tie a couple of toys to your baby's highchair. Make the ribbon or lace short enough that your baby can pull them up themself. This is good when you are busy in the kitchen and your baby is at the stage when they keep throwing their toys on the floor. You can use anything that is safe for your baby and that you want to use as new vocabulary.

- **Toys in boxes or bags**

Babies find the most ordinary items very interesting if they are hidden in a box or bag; your child will be motivated to say words as they take each object out.

Use toys, objects from the kitchen, clothes, etc. Have some bags that are easy to access (e.g. a gift bag), but also have some bags with a drawstring, ziplock, etc. that your child will need help with, so that they have a reason to communicate their need for help.

You can use clear bags so that they can see what's inside or colourful bags and boxes. You can put some noisy paper, such as old wrapping paper or tissue paper, inside to add a listening aspect to the activity. A baby loves playing with things that make a noise when they are manipulated and explored. Keep an eye on them in case they eat the paper!

- **Sound bottles**
  Use old plastic bottles. Put a handful of dried food items (such as rice, pasta, cereal, lentils, etc.) inside the bottles. Tape the lids on to make sure that the food doesn't come out. Sit with your baby and encourage them to shake the bottles or slowly turn them upside down and look at the food as it moves from one end of the bottle to the other.

  Don't leave your baby on their own with these as there is a risk of choking.

- **Whisk**
  Thread colourful ribbons, plastic links, shoelaces, etc. through a whisk and give them to your baby to pull out. Talk about the colours, and use phrases such as 'Pull… pull… pull… You did it!' Make a fuss when they manage each one, and they will feel very clever and want to do the activity over and over again!

Chapter 3

12-18 months

Your child will now be well and truly on the move. Their gross motor skills develop from the head down, so they learn to control the muscles of their head and neck first, then their arms and hands, and then their legs and feet. Their confidence will still be beyond their ability, so there will be lots of trips, falls and bumped heads to deal with. You will need to keep a watchful eye as you may find them attempting stairs on their own, climbing up a bookcase or even wandering outside when your back is turned.

Your toddler may seem to yo-yo between being a baby at times and an independent small child at others. They might be keen to try to feed or dress themselves, or to walk a lot when you are out and about, but they will still have a need for lots of reassurance from you, will check that you are nearby, and will frequently seek your affection and help.

This is a time of rapid brain development and it is greatly influenced by the amount of stimulation your child receives. The best way to make sure that they can achieve their full potential is to interact with, play with and talk to them as much as possible.

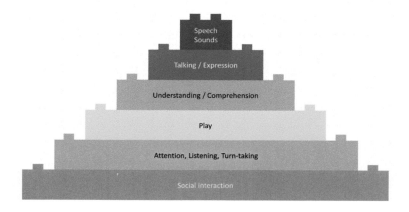

Social Interaction

At this age, your toddler thinks that they are the centre of the world, which is known as being 'egocentric'. They will crave attention and watch for your reaction to their behaviour. They will try to make family, friends and even strangers laugh. It is important to give lots of praise and attention for good behaviour, as problems can arise if they learn that the only way to get attention from you is to do something that they know they shouldn't, such as throwing food or pulling your hair!

The one-year-old is very sociable and enjoys interacting with you and familiar people. Sometimes, slight dips in self-confidence with new people may mean they seem clingy and need extra reassurance in new situations. They will be increasingly curious about other people and will find other children fascinating. They may show affection, chase and cuddle them, but may also push them and snatch toys. They may become very stubborn and show jealousy when you show affection to others. This is all an important part of learning about their own and others' feelings and understanding their relationship with those around them. Giving praise and hugs will let your child know they are safe and that being with others is a good thing.

During this stage, your child will be observing your behaviour closely and will often copy your actions, e.g. pretending to talk on the phone, read a book or brush their hair.

If your baby doesn't try to copy your sounds or words, focus on facial expressions and actions/gestures for a while. Make these as exaggerated and fun as possible. With actions, you can physically help them to make them, e.g. raise your arms and then gently raise theirs, or wave or clap then move their hands to do the same. With a lot of repetition, they will learn that if they copy you, then you will keep playing and having fun with them.

If your baby does not seem interested in copying your actions, then begin by copying theirs. Use a simple action such as clapping or banging on their highchair tray. When they stop, you do the action, then look at them to encourage them to do the action again. Keep your language very simple, e.g. say, 'Clap, clap,' or, 'Bang, bang.' Play the same game with the same actions several times over a period of days. Next, you can try another movement you have seen your baby do before and see if they will copy you, e.g. waving bye-bye.

Attention, Listening and Turn-Taking

Your toddler's attention is very single-channelled, which means they can't focus on what they are doing and pay attention to what you are saying at the same time. Try not to talk when your child is not looking at you, because they are not ready to process your words. They are busy exploring and their attention is on the toy, not on the language you are using. Try to attract their attention and wait until they look at you before you speak.

Your child's attention span will still be very short. However, they will begin to concentrate intently on an object or activity of their own choosing for longer periods of time. When they are concentrating like this, it may seem as though they are ignoring you, but it is simply that they cannot tolerate any adult intervention in what they are doing. They must ignore everything else in order to be able to organise their own thoughts and concentrate. The best thing you can do at this stage is to allow them to focus on what they want and make simple comments on what they are doing.

Your child will now be able to focus on one main sound and tune out some background noise, but they still need the environment to be fairly quiet. If there is a lot of noise, it will be much too distracting. Most of the time, try to keep background noise to a minimum (e.g. no TV or loud music), even when your child is just playing on their own, as they will concentrate and listen more easily in a quiet environment and therefore will learn more.

They will be a lot more interested in speech now and will listen closely to people talking for quite a long time, especially if they can see their faces. It has been shown that toddlers can accurately discriminate word pairs that are minimally different, [115] which is an important skill for the development of speech sounds.

Play

While toddlers play, they are developing the foundations for successful social, communication and academic skills. As they become more mobile and they gain control over their bodies, they enjoy putting things together, such as stacking bricks, posting shapes, or filling and emptying containers.

At this stage, they play mainly on their own. They may watch others playing, but not join in (onlooker play), or play alongside another child, but with no obvious interaction (parallel play). However, they do show a desire to play near other children and pay attention to each other some of the time.

Symbolic play is one of the most important forms of play for helping language development. [116]

When playing, a child will learn that a small chair is still a chair, a box can act as a chair, a picture of a chair represents a chair and is therefore a symbol, and the word 'chair' is another symbol. Symbols are important throughout a child's school life. The ability to use words and to be able to read and do maths rests upon a child's use of symbols.

Pretend play should now be developing, i.e. acting out real-life situations with toys. You will notice that your child acts out things they have seen you do, such as brushing your hair, drinking from a cup and reading a book. You can encourage this in simple ways, e.g. before you pour a drink for your child, pretend to drink from the empty cup; and when you brush your hair or teeth, give your child a brush so that they can copy you if they want to.

Understanding

Your child's understanding of single words continues to increase, mainly of familiar objects, clothes, furniture, body parts and some actions. Between the ages of 12 and 18 months, a child will learn to understand around 20 new words each month.

Your child's understanding of concepts will now be developing, and they will be able to respond to instructions that include words indicating position, such as 'in', 'on' and 'under'; size, such as 'big' and 'little'; and descriptive words, often learned as opposites, such as 'clean'/'dirty', 'hot'/'cold' and 'up'/'down'.

They should be able to pick out two key words in a sentence and respond to these, e.g. when you say, 'Go to the *kitchen* and fetch your *cup*', or, 'Give the *book* to *Mummy*'.

As children learn new words, they need to find ways of storing them in their brain so that they can easily be retrieved when needed. They are stored in groups, with links between them forming networks. [117] The same word can be stored in several different ways, depending on your child's age:

- By their category, e.g. body parts, food or clothes.
- Things with similar features, e.g. those with the same colour, shape and size.
- Words that rhyme, e.g. 'cat', 'hat' and 'mat'.
- By how many syllables they have: one syllable, e.g. 'cat', 'cup' or 'ball', two syllables, e.g. 'yoghurt', 'table' or 'trousers', three syllables, e.g. 'elephant', 'ambulance' or 'strawberry' or four syllables, e.g. 'caterpillar' or 'cauliflower'.
- Words that start with the same sound, e.g. 'cat', 'cup', 'cake' or 'car'.
- Words that have the same vowel sound, e.g. 'tea', 'see', 'peas', 'treat' or 'sleep'.

When words are learned within a category, they are stored better in the brain, so it is useful to spend some time playing with toys or objects that are all from the same category, e.g. vehicles, animals or food. The more information we can give a child about each word, the better. Signing provides children with additional information that makes it easier for them to learn and retrieve the words when they are needed.

Expressive Language

First words

As parents, we are desperate to hear that very first word, and we usually hope that it will be an attempt at 'Mummy' or 'Daddy'! For a child to be said to have used their first word, they need to use the same combination of sounds deliberately and consistently to refer to a particular thing or event, understand its meaning, and want to communicate it in some way.

We don't really know how babies and toddlers choose which words to say first, but there are two main theories:

1. They choose words based on the sounds and syllable structures they can say. This explains why so many children start with one- or two-syllable words using early speech sounds such as 'm', 'b' or 'd' (e.g. 'mama', 'baba' or 'dada'). This is the 'speech-sound dominance' theory. [118]
2. They choose words based on the words they want to say! For example, a child might attempt 'biscuit' because it is something they want to be able to ask for, even though the sounds 's' and 'k' will be difficult individually, and put together, they will be impossible! They may try to produce the word as 'bibi', and if they are lucky, this might be good enough for you to know what they are trying to say! This is the 'word dominance' theory.

Children across many languages show a preference for first words that start with the same early acquired sounds, and words with a simple consonant-vowel or consonant-vowel-consonant-vowel pattern. It is no coincidence that the words for 'mother' and 'father' in all languages are based around early acquired sounds and syllable structures! This suggests that the 'speech-sound dominance' theory is more likely to be correct. However, there are other factors that have also been shown to be important: more frequently heard words are learned earlier, as are words heard in shorter sentences, which are easier to decode and understand as separate words. [119]

We also need to consider that, for a child to use a combination of sounds as an actual word, someone needs to understand what they are trying to say and react in a positive way to it by giving them what they want, praising them or simply saying the word back to them. Obviously, if a child chooses a word that includes sounds they are not yet able to say, then there is less chance of them being understood and of that word being reinforced. So, children may, in fact, be using some words that we simply don't recognise, and it is likely that they will gradually use these less in favour of those that are more easily understood. If the word is particularly important to the child – such as the name of a family member, favourite food or toy –their parents will gradually learn what their child is referring to, even if it sounds nothing like the adult version of the word. These immature, early versions of words are remembered fondly by parents, who may feel quite sad when their child begins to use the correct version. Some of them may continue to be used as special 'family' words that cannot be understood by anyone else! Some of the family words that we still use occasionally include 'Gogo' (Grandad), 'flurious' (furious), 'armblow' (elbow), 'dickifult' (difficult) and 'Mimi' (Mummy).

At 12 months, a child may have one or two words. They will still use a lot of jargon and will communicate a lot of their needs by pointing, accompanied by a vocalisation such as, 'Uh'. They seem to be aware that we talk in sentences, as they will often use a lot of babble with an occasional word thrown in!

They will be a mimic now, copying symbolic sounds, words that they hear adults say or some noises made by other babies. They may start singing to themself and will use more symbolic gestures such as shaking their head to mean no (at this age, 'no' may seem to be one of their favourite words!). [116]

First words are generally a complete accident, just part of the usual string of babble or an imitation of a word a child has heard without any true meaning attached. If these utterances sound like a word parents are desperate to hear, such as 'mama' or 'dada', and they are used in the right context, then parents react as if their baby has knowingly used an actual word. The reinforcement they then give – smiles, clapping and repeating the word back – is a delight to the child, who quickly learns which sounds and words to say to get more praise from their adoring parents.

Reasons to communicate

A baby might be motivated to use words to communicate for any of the following reasons:

- Responding to others, e.g. 'Hello,' 'Bye-bye,' or 'Yes.'
- Asking for something they want, e.g. 'More,' or 'Biscuit.'

- Protesting/refusing, e.g. 'No,' or 'Go away.'
- To get attention, e.g. 'Muuummy.'
- Making comments, e.g. 'Look,' or 'Car.'
- Giving information, e.g. 'Gone.'
- Asking for information, e.g. 'What's That?' or 'Daddy?'
- Thinking aloud and planning, e.g. 'Bath time.'
- Sharing ideas, e.g. 'Park.'

Children are motivated by different reasons to communicate at different stages. Your child may go through a stage of saying 'no' a lot, shouting your name, or asking, 'What's that?' At each stage, use whatever is motivating your child to encourage them to use lots of different sounds or words. I have made suggestions in each chapter under the *Chatterbox Ideas* section and in the section on *Communicative Temptations*.

Although your child may only be using single words (or short phrases learned as a single unit), they can use each of these for one or more of the aforementioned reasons. Typical examples include 'gone', 'more' and 'up'.

- **Gone**
  'Gone' is one of the most common words used at this age, and it can be used to mean each of the following:
    o Your child sees something, but then it disappears.
    o They are searching for something.
    o They are commenting about an empty container in which they were expecting to find something that isn't there.
    o They have noticed a change in something, e.g. a tower of bricks falling down.

- **More**
  This word can be used to mean each of the following:
    o Your child is asking for more food, drink, toys, etc.
    o They are asking for an action to be repeated and are using 'more' instead of 'again'.
    o They are commenting on there being a greater amount of something, e.g. a bowl with one grape and another with lots of grapes.
    o They are commenting on relative size, using 'more' instead of 'bigger', e.g. a little ball and a big ball.

- **Up**
  Again, there are several differing meanings for this word:
    o Your child wants you to pick them up.
    o They see something moving up, e.g. a balloon.
    o They see something getting higher, e.g. a tower of bricks.
    o They are telling you that they are somewhere high, e.g. at the top of a slide.
    o They use 'up' instead of 'tall', e.g. in reference to a giraffe.

The first 25 words/phrases most commonly used by toddlers are these: 'Mummy', 'Daddy', 'baby', 'milk', 'juice', 'hello', 'ball', 'yes', 'no', 'dog', 'cat', 'nose', 'eye', 'banana', 'biscuit', 'car', 'hot', 'thank you', 'bath', 'shoe', 'hat', 'book', 'all gone', 'more' and 'bye-bye'. [120] These are included in the *First-Words Checklist* later in this book (see page 230).

This is not a definitive list, and the words your child chooses will very much depend on their daily routines, experiences and interests.

If you want to help your child learn and use particular words, then it is worth bearing the following in mind:

- Choose words that are easy for your child to say. So, choose words with sounds and patterns that your child already uses, and avoid multisyllabic words (such as 'caterpillar' or 'hippopotamus') or words with difficult sound combinations (such as 'squirrel').
- Think about the words that will be most useful. Choose words that your child is familiar with and that will be helpful for them to get their needs met. Make a list of their favourite people, food, toys and activities.
- Remember that a child must hear a word, in context, around 500 times before they start using it themselves. [36]

When teaching your child new vocabulary, there are four stages:

1. **Looking at objects**
   Play games, read stories and sing songs that include the vocabulary you are aiming to teach. Have as many different visual clues as possible to hold your

child's attention and give them the opportunity to hear the words lots of times in context. This is how they learn the meaning of new words. Aim to teach only a small number of words at a time and choose words from the same category, e.g. family names, social words, foods or animals.

2. **Matching objects**

   This encourages your child to look more closely at objects or pictures introduced in earlier games or stories, so that they can learn to distinguish between them and match and categorise them. Make sure you have two of each item.

3. **Selecting objects**

   Once you have played lots of games using the new vocabulary and have done some matching activities, you can check your child's understanding of the words by asking them to find the objects or pictures as you name them. However, remember that the aim is to teach, not test, so always make it fun.

4. **Naming objects**

   When you are sure that your child understands the words that you are trying to teach and they have experienced many more opportunities to hear the words in context, you can ask them to tell you what some of the objects are. Again, remember to avoid too much testing by making it a natural part of the conversation or fun activity rather than a list of questions asking, 'What's this?' Children will naturally want to tell you the names of things if you hide them around the room or put them in a bag or box.

The *First Words Checklist* (see page 230) can be useful for monitoring your child's first words, but it is not a prescriptive list of words that your child should learn by a particular time or in any particular order. The words that your child decides to use first will be determined partly by their environment and experiences, which will be different to those of other children.

First words are usually names of familiar people, objects, food, toys, body parts, clothes or social words, such as 'hello' or 'bye-bye'. Next, come words associated with an action, such as 'up' or 'gone'. Babies will use the words that are most useful for them to communicate and will use one word to communicate in several different ways, e.g. 'cup' can mean 'That's my cup', 'Where's my cup?' or 'I want a drink'. At first, the child only uses the words in the specific context that they learn them, e.g. they will only use 'cup' to refer to their own cup and no others. This is known as 'underextension'. They may also use 'overextension', where they use one word to refer to several different things, e.g. 'dog' to mean all animals. At the age of 15 months, one of my children used 'Nana' and 'Grandad' to refer to all visitors who came to stay with us!

First words may appear and then disappear for a while as new words are acquired that are more useful to your child, and this is nothing to be concerned about.

There is a huge gap at this age between the speed at which children learn to understand new words and the much slower rate that new words are spoken. This is because a child only has to hear a word a few times before they will recognise it, but they may need to hear it as many as 500 times before they will be able to use it correctly. [36]

Verbal routines are very important at this stage, and your child will begin to take part rather than just listen. If you pause in the middle of a familiar phrase, your child will begin to fill in the gaps.

Communicative temptations

Communicative temptations create a reason for a child to communicate. They are strategies to encourage children to initiate interaction, [121] and are sometimes referred to as communication temptations.

When trying to help your child to actively participate in communication, there must be a *need*, an *opportunity* and a *reward* for their efforts. Communicative temptations are ways to make sure that these three things happen: children need to communicate because there is something they want that you are not giving them; there is an opportunity because you are waiting and giving them time; and the reward is that, when they try to communicate, you give them what they want. Parents and older siblings are often able to anticipate a lot of a child's needs and give them what they want without them having to ask. This meets their need, but also removes the opportunity to communicate and the possibility for rewarding their attempts. If instead, you don't anticipate and let them show you, then your child is more likely to become an active communicator and will start to initiate interaction more often.

There are two main strategies that parents often use to try to get their children to say more words:

1. Ask lots of questions, such as, 'What's that?', 'What are you doing?', and 'What colour is the car?' This is a pointless exercise for the child, because they know that you already know the answers; i.e. you can see what they've got, what they're doing and what colour their car is! We don't very often ask adults

questions that we already know the answer to, because it is a waste of time.

Questions test, but comments teach. The only thing a child learns when asked a question is how to ask a question! Questions can also put pressure on children who may be struggling with their language skills. And many questions only allow for single word answers such as 'yes'/'no', the name of a toy or object, a colour or a number.

2. Saying a word and asking the child to repeat it. Just like asking questions, this teaches a child very little. It doesn't teach the meaning of the word or how to use it to communicate. Even if your child does copy you, it doesn't mean that they understand the words, so that they can go on to use them spontaneously. Also, asking a child to copy you means that they are responding to something you have said, when we are aiming for them to initiate communication.

When using communicative temptations, it is important to remember the following:

*   Communication should always be a positive experience for children, so we never want them to get upset or frustrated. If this seems to be happening, simply model the response that you are aiming for and let them have what they want.
*   Don't use this strategy all the time to the extent that your child starts to feel that you are withholding everything they want. The reward of getting what they want by showing you in some way should motivate them to keep trying.
*   The goal doesn't need to be spoken words. By focusing on words, we may miss other attempts at communication. As adults, we use lots of non-verbal communication as well as words to get our message across. If your child is using a facial expression, a gesture, a point, a grunt, a sound or an attempt at a word to initiate and communicate with you, then accept this. By giving them the chance to become confident at this level, they will be more likely to try something new. Even the best communicative temptation will not help a child to do something they are not developmentally ready to do.
*   Don't make your child wait too long. Even a few seconds may be enough for them to wonder why you are waiting and prompt them to react.
*   As with any interaction with your child, it is best to be face to face. They will initiate communication more easily when they can see your face, and in a communicative temptation situation, your facial expressions let them know that you are waiting for them to react.
*   Maintain eye contact with your child. Eye contact means that they are paying attention to you and are ready to interact and communicate.

- Waiting will motivate your child to initiate. While you wait, show your child that you are expecting them to communicate. Lean forwards and use facial expressions that mean 'I know you're going to say something any minute now.'
- Daily routines are some of the best times to use communicative temptations, because your child will expect certain things to happen, and when they don't, their curiosity may be enough to motivate them to communicate with you. Whatever their response, add one step more to expand what they do or say, to show them the next stage you are aiming for. For example, when you are ready to go out, stand by the door, look at your child, wait and then do one of the following:
    o   If they look at you, point at the door and say, 'Door.'
    o   If they reach or point, then simply say, 'Door,' before you open it.
    o   If they point and say, 'Door,' then reply, 'Open the door.' Try not to ask it as a question – such as, 'Open the door?' – as this only requires a yes/no answer and we are hoping that your child will copy you and use more than a single word.

These are some examples of communicative temptations:

- At mealtimes, give your child an empty cup or plate, and wait. Then give them a small amount of food or drink and wait again for them to show or tell you that they want more.

- When you are about to leave the house, walk to the door, stop and wait.
- If you know your child wants a snack from the fridge, stand in front of it and wait.
- Initiate a familiar game that your child enjoys, then stop and wait for them to show you that they want to carry on.
- Open a jar of bubbles, blow some, then close the jar tightly and hand it to your child.
- Get your child interested in an activity that requires a particular thing to complete, e.g. a crayon for colouring, a spoon for eating or a wand for blowing bubbles. Wait for your child to let you know that they need the item.
- Activate a wind-up toy, let it run down, then hand it to your child.
- If your child needs help with shoes, hand them to them and wait.
- Bend down to pick your child up, but then wait. If they always put their arms up to be picked up, but never vocalise it, model saying the word, 'Up?' and then wait.
- When you are at the park, put your child in the swing and wait.
- With a baby, start an activity that they love, and then wait, e.g. tickle them once, gently throw them up in the air once, bounce them on your knee once, or start 'This Little Piggy' or 'Round and Round the Garden' and wait. When your baby is very young, they may simply kick their legs or make a little sound to let you know that they want you to carry on, and that is enough. As they get older, you will expect them to do more as a prompt for you to carry on.

- Choose a book that your child enjoys, sit down with them and wait. Occasionally, wait a little before turning a page.
- Sit opposite your child with a car or ball and wait.
- If you normally open treats, such as raisins, crisps or chocolate buttons, before you give them to your child, try giving them unopened and waiting.
- At night, walk into a room with your child and wait before you turn the light on.
- Put their favourite food or toys slightly out of reach, so that your child has to let you know that they want it.

Speech Sounds

By 12 months of age, a child's sound-making has changed from babble to what speech and language therapists refer to as 'jargon' but is also commonly known as 'gibberish' or 'gobbledegook'! The change occurs as a child starts to use the intonation patterns, stresses and the rhythm of the language they hear around them, with syllable structures resembling real words. By 16 months old, your child's babble will consist only of the sounds present in the language around them, making it seem even more like they are speaking in their own language, especially when they pause to take turns in conversations with you. Because the overall pattern of the jargon so closely resembles real language, you are more likely to interpret some of the sounds you hear as first words.

Babies' first words tend to include the sounds and syllable structure that they have already practised in babble, e.g. 'mama', 'dada' and 'baba'. However, just because you have heard your child say a sound in their babble, it does not mean that they will be able to use it in their words just yet. Babble is a form of sound play and practice but sounds in words have a system of rules that take several years to master.

Imitating sounds is an important part of speech development. You will already have introduced sound imitation through play without even realising it. Many of the games and rhymes that you will have played with your child will be based on imitating actions, e.g. 'Row, Row, Row Your Boat', 'Head, Shoulders, Knees and Toes' and Peekaboo. Next, you move on to making noises such as blowing raspberries, kissing, yawning and pretending to cough and waiting for your baby to copy you. Doing these with an animated face and making it a lot of fun will increase the chance of your baby copying you. Babies love clowns!

Continue to use lots of symbolic sounds such as those suggested in the previous chapter. You will find that your child uses a lot of these spontaneously now and will take delight in showing off their animal impressions!

Next, move on to simple social words, such as 'hello', 'bye-bye' and other fun words that babies enjoy saying, such as 'no', 'boo' and 'yay'. These contain lots of sounds that your baby can say clearly, which will make them feel very clever!

Once your baby gets the hang of imitation, you will find that they are like a little parrot and will repeat some things that you would rather they didn't! Even when you say quite a long sentence, they will try to repeat the last word back to you.

Summary

The skills expected by 18 months of age are summarised as follows.

Understanding

- Your child understands the names of many familiar objects, toys and people.
- When asked, they can point to parts of their body, such as eyes, nose, ears and toes.
- They can follow simple instructions such as 'Go and get your shoes.'
- They enjoy sharing picture books and can point to a few familiar pictures on request.
- They enjoy simple songs and rhymes and join in with the actions.
- They move or 'dance' in time to music.
- They begin to pretend in play, e.g. talking on the phone.

Expressive language

- They use gestures to make their needs known, e.g. put their arms up when they want to be picked up.
- They copy adult actions, such as waving.
- They imitate animal sounds and can say a few spontaneously.
- They use about 20 recognisable words.
- They imitate a few phrases, e.g. 'All gone milk!' and 'Bye-bye, Daddy.'
- They still use long strings of babble and nonsense words, but with features of real speech, e.g. taking turns or using the intonation of a question.

Speech sounds

- They use the sounds 'p', 'b' and 'm' in words and babble, and may also use 't', 'd', 'n' and w'.
- They still babble when playing.
- You should understand them around 25% of the time. [122]

Red flags

If any of the following are true for your child at 18 months old, you should consider seeking the advice of your health visitor, GP, or local speech and language therapist:

- They do not respond to simple instructions such as 'Where is your cup?'
- They can't point to body parts when asked.
- They don't enjoy simple songs, rhymes and stories.
- They don't take turns with you in making sounds to each other.
- They don't use one or two simple words, e.g. 'mama' and 'dada'.
- They don't use lots of babble with the rhythm and intonation of real speech.

Chatterbox Ideas

All the time

Looking/attention skills

While your child's attention is still single-channelled:

- Follow what they are focusing on, rather than trying to direct their attention. They will concentrate longer if they have chosen the activity.
- When they draw your attention to something they are interested in by pointing to it, or by looking at you and then the object, use this as an invitation to make a comment. Use simple language to describe what they are looking at.
- Try to wait for them to look at you before you speak, so that you know they are listening. At this stage, they can't listen to lots of language at the same time as focusing on an activity. Simply playing alongside them will show them that

you are interested and encourage them to focus for longer. If they want you to say more, they will look at you more often!

Listening

- Help your toddler to learn what 'listening' means: hold your hand near your ear when you want them to listen. Use toys that make a noise, let them look at them, then hold them near their ear so that they can listen to them.
- Hold something that makes a noise near your ear and describe the sound. Then give it to your toddler and encourage them to hold it near their ear. Say, 'Listen', and describe the sound.
- Make every trip outside a 'listening journey', by drawing their attention to any obvious sounds, such as cars, planes, birds and children laughing. Stop and ask them to listen, tell them what the sound is, show them where it is coming from and ask them to listen again. Record some of your journey if you can, then play the sounds back and talk about them when you get home.

- Put small toys, objects or food (e.g. bricks, cars, pieces of biscuit or cheese) into different containers with a lid, and give them to your toddler to shake. Listen to the different sounds that they make, talk about the sounds, then open the container for your toddler to play with or eat what's inside (as appropriate).

- Continue to use play sounds associated with things that happen in daily routines, e.g. 'mmm' as the microwave goes round or 'ooo' as the wind blows outside.
- Encourage your child to listen to stories, songs and rhymes with symbolic sounds, such as animal noises or vehicle noises. This will help them to learn to identify what each of the sounds are, and they will soon start trying to make the sounds themselves.
- Hide a noise-making toy, as in the last stage, but now make it a little more difficult to find than before. You should start by only hiding part of the toy until your child gets the idea and use quite a loud toy. This is meant to be a fun activity, not a hearing test! You can extend this by using a quieter toy and choosing a less obvious hiding place.
- Have a bag full of toys and objects associated with different sounds (e.g. animals, a car, a bell, a clock, a phone or a train), take them out one at a time, and say the name of the object and the sound it makes as you show them to your child.
- Label as many objects, toys, animals, etc. as you can throughout the day. Repetition is key for learning vocabulary, and verbal routines are an ideal way to achieve this. Try to include names of things such as naming body parts and clothes when you are getting your child dressed, names of food items at mealtimes, and names of furniture and household objects when cleaning. Also include descriptive words such as 'clean'/'dirty', 'wet'/'dry', and 'hot'/'cold', and some action words such as 'splash', 'wash', 'dry', 'eat' and 'drink'.

Sounds and talking

- Start little turn-taking 'conversations' with your child throughout the day. When they babble and then pause, repeat the same babble sounds back to them. They will be delighted! They will learn to love these little 'chats', and it will teach them the importance of taking turns. One of the earliest of these that I remember having with my children is when I used to respond to them coughing by saying, 'Oh dear.' Even when the need to cough had passed, they would try a force a cough, just to carry on the game!
- Copy individual sounds that your child makes, even things like blowing a raspberry. This will reinforce the idea that playing with sounds is fun, and

the more practice your child gets making sounds, the better, as it will help the development of their speech muscles. You could spend some time in front of a mirror with them, so that they can watch your mouth make the sounds and watch their own mouth, too.

- Make mealtimes fun! Although your child will be less of a messy eater than six months ago, mealtimes are still a good opportunity to exercise the lips and tongue. Letting your child lick food such as yoghurt from their fingers uses different muscles than those required to take it from a spoon, and it is important to give them a chance to do both. From 12 months old, your child should be drinking from a beaker rather than a bottle, and you can also try introducing a straw. When drinking from a beaker or straw, your child's tongue will be in a better position to practise the muscle movements required for speech, mainly those involving the tip of the tongue. Prolonged use of a bottle will mean that a child has less opportunity to practise these muscle movements, as will prolonged use of a dummy.
- Praise any attempt your child makes to repeat a sound or word that you say to them; repetition is the first step towards learning new sounds and words, even before they know what the words mean.

Chatterbox time

Music, songs and rhymes

Use musical instruments and play them when you are listening to music or singing songs and rhymes. Hold something like a maraca with your child and move their hand in time to the song. You can also help them to clap their hands to the rhythm.

Continue singing lots of the songs and rhymes given in earlier chapters, especially those with actions, such as these:

- 'Head, Shoulders, Knees and Toes'
- 'Here We Go Round the Mulberry Bush'
- 'If You're Happy and You Know It'
- 'The Wheels on the Bus'
- 'Row, Row, Row Your Boat'

Books and stories

Continue with the books used from age 6–12 months. Your child will love these even more now that they are familiar, and they will be able to predict the stories. They will have their favourites by now, which they will love hearing again and again.

Board books are best at this stage, as your child is likely to start picking up a book and looking at it on their own. We want our children to develop an interest in books without worrying that they are going to be scrunched or torn. Between the ages of 12 and 18 months, your child will be more aware of how to handle books, and they will generally hold them the right way round, open and close them, and turn the pages from front to back. With sturdy board books, they may be able to turn the pages one at a time, but with others, they may turn several pages at once. Playing with books should be encouraged, and it is important to teach them from a young age that we play carefully with books, and we don't throw or tear them.

Other favourites at this age include the following:

- *Peepo* by Janet and Allan Ahlberg
- *My Farm* by Rod Campbell
- *Ten Little Dinosaurs* by Mike Brownlow and Simon Rickerty
- *We're Going on a Bear Hunt* by Michel Rosen and Helen Oxenbury
- *There Was an Old Lady Who Swallowed a Fly* by Pam Adams
- *Tabby McTat* by Julia Donaldson
- *I Love My Daddy* by Giles Andreae
- *I Love My Mummy* by Giles Andreae
- *That's Not My…* books by Fiona Watt
- *Wibbly Pig* books by Mick Inkpen
- *Rosie's Walk* by Pat Hutchins

Games and activities

- **Pretend play**
  Use toys that are a miniature version of real things:
    - A toy phone
    - Toy cars and trains
    - Toy household objects, such as a hoover, dustpan and cooking utensils

o   A toy bath, or bed and bedding for a teddy or doll
o   Clothes for a teddy or doll

- **Matching**
  Match pairs of objects. These could be items used in pairs, such as gloves and socks, or just two of the same things, such as two spoons, bananas or balls. To avoid confusion, start with things that are identical. Pick up an object, name it and say, 'Let's find another spoon/glove/ball.'

- **Stacking**
  Toys that can be stacked (such as bricks) or containers to put things in are fascinating for babies at this age. They are very useful for introducing concepts such as 'big' and 'bigger', and 'in', 'on' and 'under'. And, of course, they love it when you say, 'Crash!' as they knock a tower down!

- **Cause and effect**
  Continue with the cause-and-effect toys used from 6–12 months old, but use a wider variety of vocabulary as you play:
  o   'Ready, steady, go.'
  o   'One, two, three, go.'
  o   'My turn… Your turn.'
  o   'On' and 'off'.
  o   'More' and 'again'.

- **Sweeping up**

  You only need a sweeping brush and dustpan and anything that can be swept up, e.g. scrunched-up paper, pom poms, or bits of food such as biscuit crumbs or Cheerios to give the added fun of them being able to eat some as a reward! Make sure the floor, dustpan and brush are all clean before you start, so that they don't eat anything else that isn't good for them!

  Give them a box, bucket or container to put their sweepings in. Show them how to do this and then how to pour them out to sweep again. Use this to add vocabulary, such as 'messy', 'clean', 'dirty', 'sweep', 'full' and 'empty'.

- **Do it yourself (DIY)**

  Give your child a box of toy tools and a list of things that need fixing around the house, e.g. screws that need tightening to make a door close better or a dripping tap that needs tightening with a spanner. This is all pretend, of course, but your child will go along with it and will be proud of themselves for helping you. They will be delighted when you thank them for fixing each thing. You can include the names of anything that needs fixing as well as vocabulary such as 'broken', 'fix', 'loose', 'tight', 'bang', 'hammer' and 'turn'.

  Hammering is always a favourite activity. Wash out empty yoghurt pots, turn them upside down and see if your child can hammer them flat. You can also use old egg boxes. There are also toy hammer sets where a child hammers shapes through a hole, then turns it over and hammers them back from the other side.

- **Tea party**
Best played outside! As well as using just water, try using fruit or herbal teabags. Ask your child what each one smells and tastes like. You will, of course, be required to drink some so make sure to use flavours that you like! Use lots of descriptive words (e.g. 'sweet', 'sour' and 'tasty'), colour words, etc. This is also good for pretend play.

- **Pass the parcel**
Use old wrapping paper or just newspaper to wrap the parcel. In each layer, put in puzzle pieces or toys that you can put together in a game. Include an occasional surprise, such as some raisins, a biscuit or even a banana!
This is good for turn-taking, developing motor skills and for teaching the names of any small items that you care to wrap.

- **Threading**
Use large pasta tubes, toilet-roll/kitchen-roll tubes or curtain rings with shoelaces, string, etc. for threading. This is good for introducing concepts such as 'in'/'out', 'through', and action words such as 'post', 'thread', and 'push'/'pull'.

- **Wallpaper for painting outside**
Lay out the wallpaper on the ground, get your child to lie on it, draw around your child, and when they have got up again, name their body parts and then paint them. You could also do this on a garden path with chalk. Try drawing around objects and then see if your child can match the object to the outline.
This is good for naming body parts and the names of any objects that you can draw around.

- **Long plastic tubes/pipes**
Get these from a DIY or craft shop. Make sure they are wide enough for small toys such as balls, cars and bricks to pass through. Let your child post the toy into the tube, then tip up the tube and wait for the toy to come out of the other end. This is good for developing vocabulary such as 'gone', 'bye-bye' and 'hello'. It is also good for anticipation games, such as saying, 'Where is it?' waiting and then adding, 'Here it is!' Also, for using words such as 'in'/'out', 'through', and 'push'/'pull'.

Chapter 4

18-24 months

Where has your baby gone? They will be getting more independent every day: they will take an active part in routines such as getting dressed and mealtimes, which will usually result in these taking a lot more time! Although they may enjoy making simple decisions about food or clothes, too much choice can be overwhelming, so limit each choice to two or three items. The plus side is that you'll have even more opportunities to promote their rapidly developing speech and language skills. This increasing independence can also show itself in them refusing to sit in their pushchair or car seat, eat a certain food that they have previously enjoyed, or wear certain items of clothing. The negotiations that may be necessary at these times are another opportunity for practising communication skills, and the better their language skills are, the more likely they are to be persuaded to do what you want them to, rather than these situations becoming a battle of wills.

They will be used to the familiarity of their daily routines and may easily become unsettled if these are changed. Try to keep changes in routine as small as possible, and don't make too many at once.

Although your toddler will enjoy becoming more independent, they may still become anxious when you leave them and may demand a lot of attention. Make sure to give them lots of praise for the positive things that they do, because for a toddler, any sort of attention is better than none, and if they can't get it in a positive way, they will use behaviour that they know you won't like.

This is the age when children start to understand other people's feelings, start showing empathy, and try to be kind and helpful. Encourage this, even if it means things taking a little more time or more work for you, e.g. when they try to 'help' you tidy up, sort laundry or prepare food. Your child will offer more spontaneous affection now, giving hugs and kisses to familiar people, pets and toys. It is also a good time to encourage your child to share with others more.

Toddlers haven't yet learned how to control their emotions, and mood swings can be alarmingly rapid and intense. But they are also usually short-lived, with your child moving from screaming in frustration to smiling and playing within seconds. Staying calm, helping them with the source of frustration and using distraction techniques (e.g. saying, 'Oh look, a ladybird!') will help. It is worth reading the section on *Tantrums* (see page 111) as these can start sooner than the typical terrible twos!

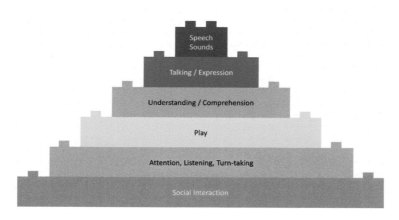

Social Interaction

Separation anxiety tends to peak at around 18 months and then starts to settle down. Some children continue to feel anxious for longer and will go through phases of needing a lot more reassurance. All children are different, and you know your child best. Don't let anyone convince you that 'It's time they grew out of this clingy behaviour.' Trying to force the issue may only prolong it.

At this age, your toddler is probably happier playing alongside, rather than with, other children (known as 'parallel play'), or they may ignore each other altogether. Simply being with other children is important: it is an excellent way to foster your toddler's social and emotional development, and for them to learn how to be kind, how to share and how to resolve conflict.

Now is when your child will probably start fiercely protecting their toys from other children. When organising playdates with younger toddlers, it is wise to keep them short, to have them at a time when the children won't be too tired, and to put away any special toys that your child won't be happy sharing.

It can be tempting to step in when toddlers are tussling over a toy and insist that they share, but they simply don't understand why they should! It is usually better to stand back and let them resolve things themselves. Often, the losing child will simply go off and find something else to play with, prompting the winning one to drop the original toy and start all over again!

It is common to get jealous of others at this age too, particularly when it comes to sharing your attention and affection. Your child still needs to be reassured that they are your number one!

Experts think that babies aged around 18–24 months start to recognise their reflection in the mirror as themselves. [123] Studies have shown that if a small mark is put on a baby's forehead at this age, they will touch their own forehead when they look in the mirror. [124] [125] It is interesting that your child's recognition of themselves as a separate person is revealed in their language: they will begin to understand pronouns such as 'me', 'you', 'yours' and 'mine'.

Attention, Listening and Turn-Taking

Your child's attention will still be very much single-channelled, which means that they can only focus on one thing at a time. If you ask them a question while they are playing, they will probably not respond, not because they are ignoring you but because they are totally absorbed in their play. If you want them to listen to what you are saying, it is best to wait until they are focusing on you rather than whatever they are playing with.

They will now concentrate for longer periods of time on an activity of their choosing, so that you can leave them to play on their own for a while.

Your child will still be easily distracted by background noise, so it is best to keep this to a minimum as much as possible. There may be times when your child seems to be ignoring you, and it is worth considering what the background-noise levels are first. If this happens at the park, the supermarket or when music is playing in the car, it is probably because they cannot filter these sounds out and listen to you. If you need your child to listen to you in a noisy environment, say their name, make eye contact, get face to face if possible, and keep your instructions short and simple.

Your child will now recognise sounds that they hear around them every day, such as the doorbell, a phone ringing and a car outside, and they will anticipate what these mean, e.g. a parent coming home from work or a friend arriving to play. Draw their attention to familiar sounds throughout the day and tell them what is making the sound.

If sharing is a persistent problem, it can help to call it 'taking turns' and set a time limit for playing with a toy before it's their playmate's turn, using a kitchen timer to prompt the swap. Help the child who is waiting for a turn to get involved in something else in the meantime.

At home, you can gently teach the art of sharing by playing turn-taking games with your toddler (play catch, and say, 'My turn… Your turn,' etc.) and sharing food (taking it in turns to take a bite out of a snack). To begin with, each turn should only last a few seconds, but as your child learns that they will always get their turn, you can make each turn a little longer.

Your child will still enjoy exploratory play with things such as sand, water, PlayDoh, and other materials and textures. They will find matching and sorting activities interesting, as these appeal to their newfound understanding of grouping things together in categories. They will like fitting things together, such as bricks, lids on containers or simple inset puzzles. It can be helpful for you to show your child how these things fit together or simply play alongside them so that they can watch you when they want to.

Your child will be engaging in a lot of pretend or pre-symbolic play, where they act out situations and activities that they have seen during their day, such as cooking, cleaning, talking on the phone, reading and working. They will pretend to perform an action using their toys instead of the actual objects, e.g. they might pretend to drink from an empty toy cup or put a teddy to bed.

They will start their play routine quite simply, but will gradually add more detail, e.g. they will put a teddy on a bed; then they will cover it up; next, they might add a pillow; and may eventually include a bedtime story. It is a useful time to introduce miniature animals, vehicles, people, and something that can be used as a farm, zoo, garage or house. Children will usually be happy with something as basic as a cardboard box, especially if you draw on it to make it look more like the real thing.

Your child will now know that a toy represents a real object, so they will use the toy as a symbol for that object. True symbolic play develops when your child uses other objects as symbols, e.g. a brick as a phone, or a box as a boat or bed. This is a very important stage in their development, as words are symbols that represent things such as objects, actions, feelings or concepts. Children with poor language skills often present as toddlers with delayed or limited symbolic-play skills.

It is very important for you to get involved in your child's pretend play to show them how they can extend what they are doing, and so that you can model lots of appropriate language. You will start to hear them using familiar phrases with their toys, and it is surprising how close they will be to things you have said!

Understanding

At 18 months old, your toddler will understand at least 200 words and will learn new ones every day. They will recognise the names of all the objects and actions that make up their daily routines. Their knowledge of categories makes learning new words easier. Every time they learn a new word, they store it within the appropriate category: food, clothes, animals, etc.

They will anticipate familiar routines, and they will get their shoes when they know it's time to go out, ask to go in their highchair when they are hungry, etc.

They will understand some of the different uses of language and will respond appropriately, e.g. replying when asked a question or using a greeting when they meet someone they know.

At this age, they will be able to respond to instructions involving two key words, such as the following:

- 'Go and get an *apple* and a *bowl*.'
- 'Give your *coat* to *Daddy*.'
- 'Where are *Daddy's shoes*?'

By the time they are two, they will respond at a three-word level:

- 'Put your *shoes* and *coat* by the *door*.'
- 'Can *Mummy* have the *big cup*?'

And they will understand some longer and more complex sentences such as these:

- 'You can have a biscuit after lunch.'
- 'We'll go to the park when Daddy gets home.'

Between ages one and two, a child will start to respond to the following types of questions:

- 'Where is the ball?' – They respond by looking at the object or pointing.
- 'Do you want an apple or a banana?' – They respond by looking at, pointing to or saying the one that they prefer.
- 'Would you like a drink?' – They respond by nodding or shaking their head, or saying yes or no.
- 'What's this?' – They respond by naming the object or picture.

Expressive Language

There is now an explosion in your child's vocabulary! At 18 months, they may have 20–50 words, but by two years old the number may be around 200! Bear in mind that there is huge variation in what is considered to be normal, and as long as your child is making progress, anything between the lower and upper figure is what would be considered to be developing along normal lines.

Once your child has around 50 words, they will start to combine them into short phrases (e.g. 'Where teddy?', 'No juice' and 'More biscuit'). Some little phrases – such as 'What's that?' – are learned as a single unit but are still a valuable step in development. By the time they are two, they may be joining three words together, such as 'Me have juice,' or 'Mummy do it.'

Although most of their words will be the names of things (nouns), they will also be using an increasing variety of words including the following:

- Social words, such as 'hello' and 'bye-bye'.
- Action words (verbs), such as 'reading' and 'playing'.
- Descriptive words (adjectives), such as 'big', 'small' and 'hot'.
- Adverbs, such as 'quickly' and 'slowly'.
- Some pronouns – such as 'me', 'you' and 'mine', although there will still be errors with these as they can be very confusing for children.
- Question words, such as 'where'.
- Negatives, such as saying, 'No down' (meaning 'I don't want you to put me down').

- Requesting words, such as 'more', 'again' and 'please'.
- Prepositions/location words, such as 'in'/'out', 'up'/'down' and 'on'/'off'.

It is important to model and encourage your child to use as many of these word types as possible.

Your child may still use overextension: that is, using one label to refer to a variety of things (e.g. using 'cow' to mean all farm animals or 'truck' to mean all vehicles that are not cars). This is a normal stage of language development. Underextension is where your child may only use a word to refer to one particular thing rather than all things that have that name, e.g. they may use 'shoes' to refer to only their shoes and no one else's. Again, this is normal and will disappear as their vocabulary increases.

First sentences/word combinations

We tend to focus on first words as being the most important milestone in early language development but combining words in phrases and sentences is equally, if not more, important. Children are more likely to go on to have a language problem if they are late starting to combine words than if they are just late saying their first words. [126]

The more word types your child has, the greater variety of sentences they will be able to produce. Once your child has around 50 words from different grammatical categories, they will start to combine them into little sentences. Obviously, the more types of words that they have, the easier this will be, so their vocabulary should include all of the types of words listed in the previous section.

It is worth keeping a list of the words your child uses, especially if you are concerned that they are late putting words together. If you find that they say mostly nouns and very little else, then their options for sentence-making will be more limited.

Typical early two-word combinations include the following:

- 'That' plus an object, e.g. 'that cup' or 'that book'.
- 'More' plus an action or object, e.g. 'more juice' or 'more play'.
- 'No' plus an object, person or action to mean no more, gone or don't want to, e.g. 'no biscuit', 'no sleep' or 'no Mummy'.
- A person plus an object, e.g. 'Daddy ball' or 'Grandad drink'. Your child may mean that the object belongs to the person, the person is doing something with it, or your child is giving the object to the person.
- An adjective plus an object, e.g. 'big teddy', 'dirty shoes' or 'toast hot'.

- A pronoun or noun plus an object, showing possession or a connection, e.g. 'my car' or 'Mummy cup'.
- An object or person plus an action, e.g. 'teddy jump', 'Daddy sleep' or 'baby cry'.
- An action plus an object, e.g. 'brush hair' or 'shut door'.
- An action/object/person plus a location word, e.g. saying, 'Get down', or, 'There teddy'.
- A question word plus an object or person, e.g. 'What that?', 'Where Mummy?', or 'Who that?'

Your child will make lots of mistakes in their use of early grammar, which are a perfectly normal part of language development and should be seen as a positive step rather than a problem. Errors are a sign that your child is working out the rules of language. Even very young children can produce correct plurals, past tenses and possessive forms of words that they have never heard before, showing that they are using grammatical rules. This was demonstrated in an experiment by a psychologist where a child is shown an imaginary object and is told, 'This is a "wug"'. Then a second one is shown, and the child is asked what the two are called. Even though the child can never have heard the word before, they can use the rule of making plurals to correctly work out that the plural of 'wug' is 'wugs'. [127]

Speech Sounds

Your toddler may only have a few sounds at their disposal, so at the beginning of this stage, their speech will still sound very immature, and you may be one of the few people who can understand much of what they say. Children tend to produce vowel sounds correctly long before consonants, because they don't require as much precise muscle control. Fortunately, if the vowels in a word are accurate, we can make a good guess what the word might be.

The consonant sounds they will have are likely to include 'p', 'b', 'm', 't', 'd', 'n' and 'w', which are the easiest for their muscles to produce, as they are made either with just their lips or with the front of their tongue. As their muscle coordination improves, they will start to produce a wider variety of sounds. Even when they can produce more sounds, they still have to learn the system of rules that apply to the use of sounds. This may not be complete until they are seven or eight years old.

Phonological processes are patterns of sound errors that typically developing children use to simplify speech as they are learning to talk. Look at the *Table of Phonological Processes* on page 224 to find out which of these are normal for your child's age. Also see the *Sound Wheel* on page 223 and the *Ages and Stages Chart: Speech Sounds* on page 219.

The important thing to remember at any age is to try not to correct your child's attempts at words. Praise their attempts and reply in a way that incorporates what they are trying to say to give them a clear model to aim for next time.

Summary

The skills expected by two years of age are summarised as follows:

Understanding

- Your child understands 200–500 words, including all of the common words (objects and actions) involved in their daily life.
- They find objects when they are named, without being given extra clues such as gestures.
- They can follow two-part instructions, e.g. 'Get your coat and give it to Daddy.'
- They understand two words used together, e.g. 'Where are *Mummy's shoes*?'
- They remember a sequence involving two words, e.g. 'Give me the *cup* and the *spoon*.'
- They understand the different ways that language is used, so they use a greeting when visitors arrive, answer a question, follow an instruction when asked, etc.

Expressive language

- They use at least 50 single words.
- They use some word types other than just nouns, e.g. verbs, adjectives or question words.
- They are starting to put two words together in short sentences, e.g. 'Teddy gone!' or 'Mummy up.'
- They name pictures in books.
- They use their own name, often instead of 'me' or 'I', e.g. 'Harry do it.'
- They join in with nursery rhymes.
- They make lots of animal sounds.
- They ask questions such as 'What's that?' and 'Where we going?'
- They attempt some simple past tense verbs, but often with errors, e.g. 'Mummy goed.'

Speech sounds

- Their speech sounds are immature, but they are understood at least half of the time. [122]
- They use the sounds 'p', 'b', 'm', 't', 'd', 'n' and 'w' in words.
- They miss sounds off the beginning and/or end of words.

Red flags

If any of the following are true for your child at two years old, you should consider seeking the advice of your health visitor, GP, or local speech and language therapist:

- They don't understand the names of lots of everyday objects, such as toys, foods and clothes.
- They can't concentrate on an activity of their own choosing for more than a couple of minutes.
- They can't follow instructions such as 'Go and get your shoes and bring them to Mummy.'
- They don't have at least 25 words.
- They don't use a few simple phrases, such as 'More juice' and 'Where Daddy?'
- They don't copy your actions and want to join in, e.g. reading, cleaning and brushing your hair.
- Their speech is not understood by familiar adults.

Chatterbox Ideas

All the time

Looking/attention skills

- Follow what your child is interested in. Name things that they point to and comment on what they are doing. Describe what they can see, e.g. when they are in a shopping trolley, or where they are going, e.g. when you are getting in the car.
- Comment on what people are doing when you are out and about, e.g. saying, 'Look at the girl running,' 'Look at the man driving,' or, 'The baby's sleeping.'
- Look through family photos and describe who the people are and what they are doing, e.g. saying, 'There's Grandad. Grandad's swimming.'
- Talk about the categories of things that your child can see, e.g. look at fruit and vegetables at the supermarket, name all the clothes when you are sorting laundry, or describe all the vehicles that you can see when you are out and about.
- Print awareness. Read aloud the words that are all around you. Reading road signs, words on food items in shops, names of TV shows, names on letters that you receive, etc. will introduce them to the importance of the written word. It's never too early to draw their attention to the written word, even though it won't mean very much to them for quite a while.

Listening

- Continue with the listening activities from the last chapter. When you are out and about, ask your child about specific sounds that they hear instead of just telling them what the sound is, e.g. saying, 'Listen. What can you hear? Where is it?'
- When playing with toys that have sounds associated with them, try putting a few on the table, make one of the sounds and see if your child chooses the right toy, e.g. some toy animals, a car and a train.
- Hide a noise-making toy, as in the last stage, but now make it a little more difficult than before by using a quieter toy and choosing a less obvious hiding place.

- Try making your own noise-makers with containers of dried pasta, rice, buttons, paper clips, etc. Your child will enjoy shaking them and listening to the sound that they make. They will probably love it even more if the lids come off and it makes a mess on the table or floor!
- Extend your use of play sounds to books and pictures, so if it is a windy day in a story, make the 'ooo' noise that you have used when you have heard the real wind. Encourage your child to join in with these sounds.
- When using your verbal routines throughout the day, try leaving a pause every so often for your child to fill in the word. They will be so familiar with these by now and will love to say the words for you, e.g. saying, 'Splish, splash, it's time for a…' or, 'Time to go out. Let's put on our coats and open the…'
- When reading familiar stories or rhymes, leave pauses for your child to fill in a word or phrase.
- Use different voices when reading stories, which will encourage your child to listen more closely. For some reason, my Gruffalo always had a Birmingham accent!
- Children love rhymes, and they will listen to these more intently and for longer than normal speech. Make up your own little rhymes throughout the day as part of your verbal routines:

> *We're going in the shop.*
> *We're going to skip and hop.*
> *We're going to buy a book*
> *And lots of things to cook.*
> *Fish fingers and some peas*
> *And yoghurt and some cheese.*
> *Spaghetti for my tea,*
> *Then off to bed for me.*

Sounds and talking

- At this stage, it is useful to model a variety of phrases and short sentences for your child. The best way to do this is simply to repeat back what they say and add something extra. This is called expansion. For example, if your child says, 'Car,' then you could reply, 'Yes, it is a car. It's a red car. The car goes "brrm,

brrm". Or if your child says, 'Doggy sleeping,' then you could respond, 'Yes, the dog is sleeping. The dog is tired.'

- This shows your child that you have understood what they have said, and you are interested. By modelling new words and sentences for them to learn, you are staying one step ahead of your child's language level, and you are helping them to get to that level. Remember that a child always understands a level of language that is more advanced than the one they use.

- When giving your child a choice – at mealtimes, for example – make it a choice of two phrases rather than two single words, e.g. asking, 'Would you like more juice or more milk?' or, 'Would you like a big apple or a big banana?' Imitating you is an important step towards making sentences of their own.

- Try to model lots of different types of words at this stage, rather than just giving names of things. While names of things are important, the number of sentences that a child can produce using just nouns is limited. By introducing verbs, adjectives, question words, etc., you are giving your child the building blocks to make an endless variety of sentences.

- If your child is using overextension with categories of words, it may be worth spending a little more time on these throughout your day and modelling the names that they are not yet using, e.g. telling them, 'This one is a cow, this is a horse and this is a sheep…' or, 'That one is a truck, but this is an ambulance. Listen to the sound it makes. What sound does the ambulance make?'

- Similarly, with underextension (e.g. they may use 'shoes' to refer to only their shoes and no one else's), if you notice that they are doing this with particular words, then try to point out all the different shoes, for example, that you see during the day.

There are two main things that you can do to help give your child the building blocks they need to make sentences:

1. Model words from different grammatical categories, so that the emphasis is on these rather than the noun. Do this as often as possible in your daily routines, so that the words are repeated multiple times:

   - **Gone**
     o When tidying toys away, each time you put something away, say, 'Bricks gone,' 'Dolls gone,' etc.
     o Every time someone leaves, after saying, 'Bye-bye,' you can add, 'Nana's gone,' 'Mummy's gone,' etc.

- o At mealtimes, each time your child finishes some food, you can tell them, 'Toast gone,' 'Yoghurt gone,' 'Milk gone,' etc.
- o After bath time, show your child the empty bath and say, 'Water gone.'
- o Play hiding games with toys, and when you hide something, say, 'Ball gone,' 'Teddy gone,' etc., emphasising the word 'gone' each time.

- **More**
  - o Mealtimes are the most motivating for this word! Give your child slightly less than normal, and then when you know they want more, ask, 'More?', 'Would you like more?', 'More toast?', 'More milk?', etc.
  - o When you read a favourite story or rhyme, and they let you know that they want you to do it again, ask, 'More stories?', 'More "Twinkle, Twinkle, Little Star"?', etc.
  - o Put some favourite toys out of reach, and when they ask you for them, start by giving just one. Then say, 'More bricks?' (or similar), and give one more, and so on. Only do this for as long as they find it fun (some children find it hilarious because you're being so silly) and then give them the rest.

- **Up**
  It can be useful to contrast the words 'up' and 'down', and then you are teaching two words at the same time; you can say 'up' with rising intonation and 'down' with falling intonation.
  - o Each time your child puts their arms up to be lifted, say 'Up?' or, 'Do you want to come up?' As you lift them, say, 'Up, up, up you come.' Put them down again briefly, saying, 'Down,' and then pick them up. This will quickly turn into a little game that they will enjoy, knowing that they will be picked up again.
  - o If you have a helium balloon, you could hold it down then let it float up gradually, saying, 'Up, up, up, up.' Then pull it down, saying, 'Down, down, down.'
  - o Play with bubbles outside where the wind will blow them around and keep repeating 'up' and 'down'.
  - o Build towers, and every time you add a brick, say, 'Up,' then a loud, 'Down,' when the tower falls!
  - o At the park, say, 'Up,' when your child is climbing to the top of the slide, and say, 'Down' as they slide down.

- o If your child likes climbing on a step or chair and jumping off, comment each time as they go up and jump down. They will like that you have noticed what they are doing and are commenting, and they will probably do it for a lot longer.
- o When your child has a little fall, comment, 'Oops, you fell down. Jump up.'

- **Action words/verbs**
  - o Throughout the day, make a point of commenting on what you are doing, rather than just naming things. For example, if you are going in the car, talk about driving rather than just saying you are in the car; and at bath time, talk about 'splashing', 'washing' and 'drying', rather than just naming body parts, etc.
  - o Comment on things you see people doing when you are out and about, e.g. saying, 'Look. A man running,' 'The baby's crying,' or, 'The dog is jumping.'
  - o Doing simple activities together such as cooking is a great opportunity to model different verbs, e.g. 'stirring', 'rolling', 'cutting', 'chopping' and 'mixing'.

- o At the park, comment on your child's actions: 'climbing', 'sliding', 'running' and 'swinging'.
- o When looking at books together, talk about what people are doing, rather than just naming things.
- o Take turns telling each other an action to do. Your child will enjoy being the teacher and seeing you do the things that they say.

      o   Use a favourite toy, such as a teddy, and make it do different actions. Take turns choosing an action to ask teddy to do.

2. Extend what they say every time they use a noun on its own by adding a different category of word. For example, if they say, 'Ball,' then you could reply, 'A big ball,' 'Kick the ball,' 'The ball's gone,' or, 'Where's the ball?'

    If you know what they want to say, use a word that will help them get their meaning across, e.g. If they say, 'Car,' they might mean one of these:

      o   'I want to go in the car.' So, you could reply, 'Go in the car? Let's go in the car.'

      o   'I want to play with the car.' So, you could reply, 'Play with the car? Let's play with the car.'

      o   'I can't reach the car.' So, you could reply, 'You want the car? Shall Mummy get the car?'

      o   'I can see a car.' So, you could reply, 'Yes, it's a car. There's the car.'

      o   'I'm playing with the car.' So, you could reply, 'Push the car. Car go!'

Chatterbox time

Music, songs and rhymes

- Use familiar songs and rhymes to encourage your child to use more verbs. You can include these throughout your day. For example, 'Here We Go Round the Mulberry Bush' can be used at bath time ('This is the way we wash our toes…'), mealtimes ('This is the way we eat our yoghurt…') or when getting dressed ('This is the way we put on our shoes…'). Using songs or rhymes will hold your child's attention for longer than simply talking.

- Songs and rhymes are a useful way to introduce the vocabulary for concepts such as colour, size or number. The concepts may still be too advanced, but they will enjoy the songs and will learn to recognise the words. These are some songs and rhymes that will help with this:

      o   'One, Two, Three, Four, Five, Once I Caught a Fish Alive'

      o   'Five Fat Sausages'

      o   'Three Little Monkeys'

      o   'Sing a Rainbow'

      o   'If You're Wearing Red Today'

Books and stories

- If you have books freely available for your baby to look at, you may now often find them pretending to read them on their own. They may repeat words and phrases they have heard you say when reading, or they may simply name the pictures that they recognise.
- Make a photo album with pictures of family and friends. Talk about who is in the photos, where they are, what they are doing, what they are wearing, etc. These are often a child's favourite books.
- Continue reading your child's favourite books and try leaving an occasional pause for them to fill in a word or phrase, e.g. when reading *Oh Dear* by Rod Campbell, try saying, 'No eggs here…' Even very young children with only a few words will quickly try saying, 'Oh dear.'
- Books with rhyming text are still very appealing at this age and learning to recognise words that rhyme is a very important part of a set of pre-reading skills that are known as 'phonological awareness'. It is never too early to start teaching these to your child.
- Lift-the-flap books are useful for encouraging your child to try to join in the story. You don't need to stick to the text, you can just talk about the pictures and say to your child, 'I wonder what's under the flap,' then wait for a response, or lead them in by saying 'It's a …'

- It is useful to introduce books with concepts of colour, size, shape and number to familiarise your child with the vocabulary. Don't expect them to understand what the words mean yet, but the books will be appealing at this age. Here are some examples:
  - o *Oh Dear* by Rod Campbell
  - o *Where's Spot?* by Eric Hill
  - o *Dear Zoo* by Eric Hill
  - o *It's Mine* by Rod Campbell
  - o *First 100 Words* by Roger Priddy
  - o *Peep Inside the Garden* by Anna Milbourne
  - o *Tales from Acorn Wood* by Julia Donaldson
  - o *My First Gruffalo. Who Lives Here?* by Julia Donaldson
  - o *Baby Touch and Feel Colours and Shapes* by DK
  - o *Numbers, Colours, Shapes* by Roger Priddy
  - o *My First Colours* by DK
  - o *First Book of Colours* by Roger Priddy
  - o *Big and Little* by Margaret Miller
  - o *Big Shark, Little Shark* by Anna Membrino

Games and activities

- **Expand the environment for play**

Now the environment for play becomes more important. Your child will already have vocabulary reflecting things in their immediate environment, so if we want to help expand their vocabulary, we need to expand their environment:

- o Try to spend more time playing outside, in the garden or the park.
- o Travel on a bus as well as in the car.
- o Visit the countryside if you live in the town (and vice versa).
- o Try attending a mother-and-toddler group, soft play or a music group.
- o Take turns with friends to visit each other's homes.
- o Go swimming.

- **Categories**

Spend some time playing with categories of toys and objects, such as animals, vehicles or a toy kitchen.

Let your child help you when sorting laundry, emptying the dishwasher, etc., so that they are learning to sort things into groups or categories.

Use words such as 'in'/'out' or 'clean'/'dirty', as well as just the names of things. For example, as you put the dirty clothes in the machine you could say, 'Daddy's socks are dirty. Dirty socks in.' Then when you take them out say, 'Daddy's socks are clean. Clean socks out.'

Hide toy animals around the room, then ask your child to find the one that says 'moo', 'baa', 'meow', etc.

Go on a treasure hunt around the house and look for the following:

- o Things that are different colours.
- o Things that are hard or soft.
- o Things that are big or little.
- o Things that are a particular shape.

- **Flashcards**

You child will enjoy looking at pictures now, so a set of flashcards is useful. These can be enjoyed in lots of ways:

- o Sorting things into categories, as mentioned previously, or ask your child to find the ones you eat, drink, wear, drive, etc.
- o Hide the cards around the room and see how many your child can find. Ask them to tell you what they have found, modelling this by saying, 'I see a ball', 'I've found a glove', 'I've got a car', etc.
- o Put some cards on the floor and ask your child to find the ones that you tell them to and then post them in a postbox. Let them have a

turn telling you. As you post them, you could say, 'Bye-bye ball,' 'Ball gone,' etc.

- o Put a paperclip on the pictures and use a magnetic fishing rod to take turns catching a picture.
- o Put some pictures on the floor and tell each other which one to jump on next.
- o If you have two sets of cards, you could ask your child to find ones that match.

- **Social phrases**
  Use the time when you get toys out and put them away to model little phrases such as, 'hello teddy', 'bye-bye dolly', 'bye-bye monkey', etc.

- **Body parts**
  Take a doll with you when you bath your child, so that you can encourage understanding and use of two-word phrases that include your child's name or 'dolly' plus a body part. For example, ask, 'Where is dolly's nose?' Then point to your child's toes and ask, 'What are these?' If they just say, 'Toes', you can then ask, 'Are they dolly's toes or Henry's toes?'

- **Turn-Taking**
  When you are playing turn-taking games, such as rolling a ball or car between you, try modelling by saying, 'Mummy's turn… Henry's turn…' and, occasionally, ask, 'Whose turn is it now?'

- **Match containers with lids**
  Using any safe containers with lids – such as tins, Tupperware, boxes, etc. – take the lids off and mix them up on the floor. Encourage your child to match the right lid to the right container.
  This is useful for vocabulary such as 'big'/'small', 'big', 'bigger' and 'biggest', and shape vocabulary.

- **Hide toys**
  Hide miniature toys or objects inside balls of PlayDoh or, wrap them up in tissue paper. Unwrapping is good for motor skills and makes simple naming tasks more interesting. This is good for teaching the name of anything small enough to wrap.

- **Mud kitchen**

Use old kitchen items to make an outdoor mud kitchen. Mixing, mashing, stirring, etc. takes on a new dimension outside. Use this for teaching verbs such as 'stir', 'mash', 'roll', 'chop' and 'wash'; opposites such as 'clean'/'dirty' and 'wet'/'dry', food vocabulary, pretend play routines, etc.

- **Make a den**
Children love dens! Use chairs, cushions, blankets, etc. A child will find toys that they may have tired of to be exciting again if they can play with them in their own private place. Don't forget to put some books in there too and be prepared to be invited in for story time!

- **Use toys to accompany story time**
Have a selection of toys or objects that appear in some of the stories you read with your child. Let them hold the items and see if they notice when each one appears in the book. After sharing the book, talk about the story again using the toys.

- **Paint with water**
Give your child a bucket or container of water and a selection of brushes with which to paint various surfaces outside such as paths, fences, garden

furniture, toys, etc. This is good for teaching concepts such as 'wet'/'dry', shapes, 'up'/'down', etc.

- **Pre-writing skills**

  It's never too early to encourage the development of pre-writing skills. Don't focus too quickly on forming letters, try to make drawing fun!

  Your child will need a lot of help at first, and you may need to take their hand in yours to guide them, but they will gradually learn better control, and then you can just give occasional verbal prompts.

  These are some of the activities you can do to develop pre-writing skills:
  - Go outside and draw with your fingers in sand or mud.
  - Draw on cakes with tubes of icing.
  - Sprinkle some flour or icing sugar on a plate or tray, and draw lines, swirls and different shapes.
  - Paint together. Copy what your child does and encourage them to copy you. Make marks on the paper, moving from top to bottom and left to right, telling them that is the way we write.
  - Try holding your child's hand while they hold a crayon and draw together. Then let them hold your hand and do the same.

  - Encourage large movements when making marks; this encourages use of the muscles of the whole arm and shoulder against gravity, and it helps to reinforce the child's 'mental picture' of the pattern. This is recommended at the early stage of learning letter formation.

o   Start to make a link for your child between pre-writing shapes/marks and letters, e.g. a circle is the same as an 'o'.
o   Experiment with different colours of chalk, markers, crayons, pens, pencils and paints, and different surfaces to draw on.
o   Make shapes with noodles or spaghetti.
o   Use stencils.
o   Practice doing dot-to-dots. Encourage your child to stop on each dot. Use arrows to indicate which is the next dot to improve their planning and direction. Make letters or numbers out of dots.
o   Make shapes and lines out of rolled up PlayDoh.

Chapter 5

2-3 Years

This stage of your child's development is characterised by an insatiable curiosity about everything! They will want to investigate their physical environment but have no sense of danger or the boundaries of their own abilities, so accidents are very common. They will often run so fast that they trip themself up or will climb or balance on something that is not steady enough to take their weight, so they will still need a lot of supervision. They will be able to move and chat at the same time – saying, 'Mummy, Daddy, watch me!' – rather than having to focus fully on their physical movements and balance.

At this age, toddlers are developing an increasing sense of their own identity; they will have their own ideas and will want to assert these more and challenge rules. They will not always understand why their artwork on floors, walls or furniture may not be to your taste! They may use the word 'no' on a regular basis and come across as bossy a lot of the time, when they are trying to assert their wishes. Routines and rules that they have previously accepted may now be greeted with asking, 'Why?' Your child will like an ordered, predictable routine to their day, and they may get upset by unexpected changes. Pre-empt the 'why' questions by explaining the reasons behind your requests, rules and limits. Your child is more likely to do what you ask if they understand the reason, and it will help them to learn about the consequences of their actions, both positive and negative, e.g. saying, 'If you help me tidy the bricks away, we will have enough time to read a story,' or, 'If you throw the car, it might break, so if you do it again, I will have to put it away.' Most important rules need very little explanation, e.g. 'We do not hit. Hitting hurts.' After 100 'why' questions, you may resort to stating, 'Because I said so,' but this doesn't teach your child anything, will not satisfy them and may simply prompt another 'Why?'

Your child will start to experience new emotions – such as anger, frustration and possessiveness – and these can seem overwhelming at times; it can be useful to label these and talk about them whenever the opportunity arises to enable them to deal with them. They will now be able to tell you when they are experiencing more familiar feelings, and they may say that they feel happy or sad.

The world is a very big place to a two-year-old, and it is quite a task to make sense of it. Because they have only experienced a tiny bit of it, the rest will be made up largely from their imagination. They will rely on their parents to help them understand what is real and what isn't. This is one of the reasons why it is important to answer a toddler's questions as fully as possible, because the bits that go unanswered will be filled in using their imagination. Examples of a child's misunderstanding at this age include the following:

- They may give human characteristics to objects, e.g. believing that the moon can see them.
- They may think that everything they see on TV is real. This is another reason why it is important to watch TV with your child, so that you can answer any questions they may have. A child can be left worrying for days about something small that they have seen on TV, e.g. if they see a person roaring like a lion, they may worry that someone they meet may actually turn into a lion!

- They believe that everyone thinks and feels the same as they do.
- They think that everything is black or white, with nothing in between, e.g. good or bad. This is why it is important to be careful about how you handle your child's behaviour. Labelling a child as 'bad' because they have done something naughty may make them feel that they are a totally bad person, rather than being a good person who has done one small thing wrong.
- They don't understand the fact that accidents happen, and often need to find a reason why. So, if they fall down, they may say that the pavement tripped them up, or if they spill their juice, they may tell you that the cup jumped off the table! Children are usually not deliberately lying at this age; they are just trying to make sense of a part of life that they don't yet understand. At this stage, one of my children felt the need to blame me for every accident he had, even if I was nowhere near him! Once I had apologised, he was happy again! Perhaps he felt that the world was out to get him, and it was more comforting to know that it was the fault of someone who he knew would never hurt him deliberately.
- They take things very literally, e.g. when a friend told one of my children that she wanted to 'eat his toes', he made sure to keep his feet away from her for the rest of the day!

The terrible twos are a stage when your child is coping with a lot of emotional changes and developing a sense of their identity and a desire to become more independent. It is perfectly normal for your child to test the boundaries of what is acceptable. They may start to whine to get their own way, throw food or toys, stamp their foot in anger, or shout at you. Never give in to these methods of your child trying to get their own way or simply getting attention. Experiencing new emotions such as anger, frustration and possessiveness can be overwhelming at times, and one possible result can be the dreaded tantrum!

Tantrums

Tantrums are uncontrolled outbursts of anger and frustration, and they are distressing for a child as well as their parents.

Tantrums usually occur between the ages of one and three but are most frequent during what are commonly known as the 'terrible twos'. They happen for three main reasons:

1. Your child doesn't have the language skills to understand what is happening or why, and they are either taken by surprise, confused or frustrated. This is often due to their limited understanding of time concepts. Young children want everything now and don't understand why they have to wait. Phrases such as 'in a minute', 'after lunch', or 'when we've been to the shops' are difficult for two-year-olds to understand and they feel as though they are never going to get what they want. They also don't like unexpected changes to plans or routines. Even if you have tried to explain to them why, for example, they can't go to the park today or why you have to go shopping on the way to a favourite place, they may not understand what you have said, feel taken by surprise and react with a tantrum.

2. They are experiencing new feelings – such as anger, frustration, jealousy and embarrassment – and don't know how to cope with these or express them in a more appropriate way. One of the few feelings that adults get to experience for the first time is grief and, even though we know what it is, why we are feeling it and that it won't last forever, it can still feel overwhelming for a while. We need those around us to understand and support us and accept that we may not behave as normal for some time. While the negative feelings of young children are much more short-lived, they don't know that at the time, and can feel equally overwhelmed.

3. They don't have the language skills to express what they want, what they need or how they feel, and the resulting frustration becomes too much. If you know what has caused the tantrum, you can use simple language to try and put their feelings into words. This will let them know that you understand and can help them to express this feeling the next time.

During a tantrum, try to do the following:

- Keep your language simple and clear. Your child will be feeling overwhelmed and out of control, and they can't process long, complicated sentences while they are in a full meltdown. For example, if you are in a busy shop, you could say, 'Let's move,' if you want to go somewhere more quiet. Saying, 'We need to move out of the way because people can't get past us with their trolleys, and someone might bump into you,' will be way too much for them to process. If they can't understand what you mean, they will only get more frustrated, and it will be harder for you to remain calm.
- Don't feel embarrassed or guilty as though a tantrum makes you a bad parent. Most children have the occasional tantrum, and the looks that you get from

other parents will usually be those of sympathy because either they know what it's like or they are relieved that it's not their child today! Disapproving looks from those who don't have children should simply be ignored!

- Make sure that your child cannot hurt themself or anyone else. Move them if necessary.
- Stay calm (or pretend to!). The noise, fuss and possible embarrassment that goes with a tantrum can make this difficult. The worst thing you can do is to shout back or punish your child in some way. This is more likely to make the tantrum louder and longer!
- If all else fails, ignore your child until they are calm enough to listen. Simply wait it out. Stay close, so they know you are there, but don't try to reason with them or distract them once the tantrum has started, as it is probably too late. Giving them attention during a tantrum simply reinforces it.
- Don't accidentally reward the tantrum. If they have a tantrum because they want something and you have said, 'No,' then if you let them have what they wanted after they have calmed down, they may think you have given in to the tantrum and try similar behaviour as a means of getting their own way in the future.

Ignoring your child can work in the short term, but it doesn't help to prevent the next tantrum. If your child knows that you will be there to listen and help them to work things out, then next time, they may turn to you instead of having a meltdown.

If you sense that a tantrum is building, or immediately after a tantrum has occurred, try doing these things:

- Empathise. If you know what the last straw was that triggered the tantrum, tell them so, e.g. saying, 'I know the tower keeps falling down. It's annoying, isn't it?' or, 'I can see that the big boys won't let you have a turn on the slide.'
- Ask them what is wrong. It is better if they can work it out for themself. If they still can't explain, you can try giving them a choice, such as 'Are you fed up waiting or do you want the big boys to play with you?'
- Ask if they know what they want to do to make things better. If not, you can offer some suggestions, e.g. asking, 'Shall we take turns or shall I help you with the last few bricks?' or, 'Would you like me to come down the slide with you?'
- Work through the solution with them and praise any attempt they make to sort things out for themself, such as persevering with building the tower or asking the older boys if they can have a turn. Helping them to work through a problem is much more helpful than just solving it for them every time.

Try these things to avoid future tantrums:

- Help your child to learn how to recognise, understand and respond appropriately to their feelings (see section on *Feelings*, page 147). Tantrums are often a result of a child becoming overwhelmed by strong feelings and being unable to talk about them or react in a more appropriate way.
- Help your child to develop an understanding of time (see *Understanding* section on page 154, which discusses time concepts). Tantrums can be as a result of them having little understanding of what 'in a minute', 'later', 'after' and 'tomorrow' mean, and they want everything *now*!
- When your child reacts well, be specific with your praise so that they recognise what they have done right, e.g. saying, 'That was good waiting,' instead of simply, 'Good boy.' They are then more likely to respond in this way again.
- Try to have a strategy ready. Decide on how you might handle the next tantrum, rather than waiting until it happens. It is impossible to think clearly in a busy shop when your child is screaming. You may have a distraction technique that always works, such as a favourite toy or snack, and you want to make sure you have it available with you at all times.
- Be aware of situations that are likely to trigger a tantrum, and if possible, build in some extra time to allow you to diffuse things. Trying to rush your child has the potential to be the last straw.
- Be aware of danger signs, especially tiredness, hunger and irritability, e.g. it may be necessary to leave a party early if your child is getting grumpy, to keep walking trips short to avoid them demanding to be carried, or to go to the checkout armed with a healthy snack to avoid requests for sweets.
- Accept that you can't control your child's emotions or behaviour directly. All you can do is watch for triggers and step in to guide their behaviour, which will hopefully avoid a tantrum developing. It may take some time before their tantrums disappear altogether.
- Pick your battles. You don't have to win every time, and making your child do every small thing that you want may backfire in the form of more tantrums. Rules are important but keep them for things that matter.
- When you want them to do something, keep it simple and positive, e.g. saying, 'Please shut the door,' rather than, 'Don't leave the door open.'
- Don't make promises you can't keep. A broken promise about a treat that your child has looked forward to may cause problems. If you must go back on a promise, don't wait until the last minute to let them know. Be honest about why this is and discuss how things can be rearranged.

- Rather than saying no and making your child feel like they have lost, give them a choice of two options that you are happy with, and then everyone wins.
- Children get things wrong constantly because they are just learning. They will remember criticism more than encouragement, so we have to overdo the positive to get the balance right. They need to hear around six positives for every negative. Try to give your child little tasks that make them feel helpful and provide a natural opportunity for praise.
- Children don't want to be annoying! Sometimes, we accidentally train them to whine by giving in at the last minute. Be clear and firm, and then move on.
- Use active listening in which you repeat back to them what you think they might be feeling. Knowing that you are trying to understand will help your child feel comforted and calm.

While your child is riding this emotional rollercoaster for the next year or more, it is important that they know that you will understand and support them. Their relationship with you will give them comfort, encouragement and confidence, and it will help them to learn to develop strategies of their own to solve problems, which will be even more important once they are at school and you are not there to do it for them or with them.

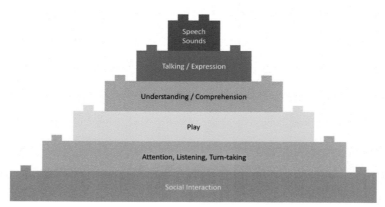

Social Interaction

In their desire to explore the world, toddlers gradually learn the social skills necessary to get along with other people. A strong attachment to a parent or carer gives a child an anchor from which they can confidently explore at their own pace. A lot of their behaviour will be influenced by watching what other people do, so they will learn a lot through observing their parents, carers and siblings. I have often found that, when I meet a child who is very kind, polite, patient and generally friendly, their family members show the same characteristics. Other important factors include your child's personality and temperament, their position in the family, the opportunities they have to play with other children, and, of course, their communication skills.

Shyness can be an issue at this stage, when you are trying to encourage your child to make friends with other children and don't want them to miss out. Trying to force a toddler into social situations can make this stage last even longer, so it is best to just be patient and let them interact at their own pace. Often, making one special friend – especially one who is more extrovert – will give them the confidence to join in play opportunities more readily.

Your child will now enjoy the company of children their own age and will enjoy group activities as well as playing with individual children. They will still like to have a parent or familiar adult nearby, but will go off and play for increasingly long periods of time. They will keep coming back for a reassuring cuddle every now and again. Because they are spending more time away from you, new fears may appear, such as a fear of the dark or monsters under the bed.

They will still be possessive of their toys, but they may be willing to share for short periods of time. They will start to show more empathy and concern for other people's feelings. They may put a comforting arm around a friend who is upset, or they may even cry if they see another child cry.

Attention, Listening and Turn-Taking

At this stage, attention is still single-channelled, but your child will start to be able to pay attention to what you are saying. They will have to stop what they are doing, listen to you and then carry on. Therefore, you will need to make sure that you have their full attention before giving them an instruction or asking them a question. Say their name to attract their attention, and then make sure they are looking at you before you start talking.

Your toddler will still be very easily distracted by noises and visual events such as someone coming into the room, and they may be unable to listen to you until these events have passed. It is therefore important that, when you are trying to improve your child's attention skills, distractions such as the TV are kept to a minimum. Some children never have the opportunity to develop their attention skills, because their environment is far too distracting, and they may get stuck at this stage for several years. They may start school being able to focus for only short periods of time and are unable to follow instructions, particularly those given to the whole class. Parents often wonder why it is necessary to limit TV or screen time, and this is one of the most important reasons. By giving your child the opportunity to play and interact while there are no distractions, you are enabling them to develop skills that are essential for learning throughout their whole school life.

It is important that your child's listening skills continue to develop. They need to be able to work out which sounds are important and which they can ignore. They also need to be able to pick out the important words in the endless stream of language they hear around them. All these things improve with practice, so the more you do now, the easier you will make it for your child to learn language.

Your child will now listen to longer stories, particularly if they are about things they are interested in. While living in the countryside, we used to see busy farmers every day, and at this age, one of my children would happily listen to a long, made-up story about a farmer every night until he fell asleep!

Your child will soon start taking turns during play with other children without being asked to do so. Encourage this by making toys available that are easy to play with in turns, e.g. bricks, puzzles, cars and balls.

Never expect them to take turns with a favourite toy. Also, if you often take turns with your child during the day, they will understand earlier how this works, e.g. stirring a cake mix, rolling PlayDoh or blowing bubbles. Make your turn short at first so that they will know their turn will come soon. Remember that there is a difference between taking turns and sharing. The former usually involves short, back-and-forth exchanges; the latter is more about being kind and involves longer periods of waiting, or giving something to another child to keep, such as food. With sharing, a child is never sure when or if they are going to get their toy back, and at this stage, you may need to keep an eye on the situation to make sure that the quieter, more passive child doesn't always lose out.

Play

Your child will be aware of their gender, and they may start to prefer playing with children of the same gender and with typically boys' or girls' toys, no matter how many friends or what variety of toys they have available. A classic example is to give your child a stick and watch what they do with it. Boys are more likely to treat it as a gun, and girls are more likely to treat it as a baby or a flower. I have tried this with my own children, and they did exactly that! Infant monkeys behave in exactly the same way, with females being more likely to treat a stick as a baby than males, [128] so it does appear to be an instinct rather than a learned behaviour.

Your child may still prefer to spend a lot of time playing alone or with you but will watch other children play and join in with them for increasing periods of time.

They will enjoy imaginative or make-believe play, such as playing 'house', which reflects the things that they do in their daily life, e.g. having a tea party. They will enjoy dressing up and like to pretend they are someone else from time to time.

This is important in helping your child to develop their own ideas and stories, and to share these with others through language.

They can now play with other young children, but it's still best to keep playdates fairly short, as they can end in tears, usually because someone isn't sharing or because someone else wants to direct the play. When having to share or take turns causes problems, make sure that playdates include some activities where the toddlers can play at the same time, such as a tub of bricks, painting a picture, dancing to music or listening to a story. With other activities, if you know that one of the children has difficulty sharing, put out two of each toy, e.g. shape cutters for PlayDoh, musical instruments, cars or sandpit toys.

Your toddler may have favourite toys or games, and they may spend a large portion of their day with these. While you can offer a wide selection of things to tempt them, it is important not to try to force them to spend less time on their favourite activities. They will learn far more from playing with their favourite toys than something you have chosen that they have little interest in. As before, follow their lead, comment on what they are doing and try to extend the activity to include other things. It is up to you to be inventive, e.g. if they are obsessed with trains and spends most of their time playing with Thomas the Tank Engine, you could read books about trains, make a larger-scale train using chairs and pretend to go on a trip, take them to watch some trains at a local station, or even go on a short train ride and talk about what you can see out of the window, the sounds you can hear, etc.

Understanding

Your child's ability to follow increasingly long and complex instructions and answer different types of questions will improve significantly over the next few months. It will depend on several aspects of comprehension: receptive vocabulary, working memory, concept development and understanding of specific question words. It is therefore useful to look at these separately:

a. **Vocabulary**
   Your child will now understand the idea that words can be grouped into categories, both general categories (such as names of things and action words) as well as an increasing number of sub-categories (such as names of people, clothes, foods and toys). Every time they learn a new word, they will store it in the appropriate category. Familiar categories will include more-detailed words, e.g. in the category of body parts, they may have understood terms

such as 'arms', 'legs', 'eyes', 'nose' and 'tummy', but will now begin to learn words such as 'knees', 'elbows', 'eyebrows' and 'back'.

b. Concepts

Concepts are tools that help a child make sense of the world. Both things in a child's environment and their experiences have certain features that can be classified using concepts. Knowledge of basic concepts is an essential component of language development. Basic concepts include terms that define position, time, number, description (colour, size, etc.) and feelings.

This is a good time to introduce concept vocabulary, as it is when children start to take an interest in the more detailed features of objects and will naturally start to classify them by size, shape, colour, etc. You may find that when they are playing, they start sorting their toys into groups, even if they don't always have the vocabulary to describe them.

Concepts such as colour and shape are best taught in a certain order, as follows:

1. **Colour** – Primary colours (i.e. red, blue and yellow) should be taught first, followed by the secondary colours (i.e. orange, purple and green).
2. **Shape** – Start with the basic shapes of circle, square, triangle and rectangle, followed by oval, heart, star and diamond.

3. **Number** – Start by keeping it as simple as 1, 2, 3! Play lots of games where you count things, sing songs and rhymes with numbers, etc. Once you are sure your child can cope with these, then go up to five, then to 10 and so on.

Children often learn other concepts in pairs, usually opposites, and tend to understand the meaning of one before the other. Between the ages of two and two and a half, your child will learn concepts such as these:

- o 'Up'/'down'
- o 'In'/'out'
- o 'On'/'off'
- o 'Big'/'little'
- o 'One'/'many'

c. **Memory**

Memory helps us to process, store and recall information, so it is vital in all areas of language development.

There are three types of memory:

1. **Short-term memory**

This enables us to hold information in our memory for around 15–30 seconds. We may need to repeat or rehearse the items to prevent them being lost from our short-term memory, e.g. repeating a phone number until we can write it down.

2. **Long-term memory**

This refers to the storage of information over an extended period, whether that is hours, days or years.

3. **Working memory**

This provides a 'mental workspace' in which we can hold information while we engage in other mental activities. This would include simple tasks such as remembering two numbers while adding them together, remembering a shopping list while looking for a pen and writing it down, and remembering directions you have been given while you are driving.

There is an auditory and a visual component to working memory. The term 'auditory memory' refers to this part of working memory, and it is the one that is usually referred to as the most important part for language development. However, it makes sense that using visual prompts to aid auditory memory will result in better learning.

Working memory is an active process that allows us to use new and learned information while we are in the middle of an activity.

Because working memory refers to a child's ability to store and use information, it follows that it will be related directly to their learning potential. It has been demonstrated to be an important predictor of later school attainment. [129] [130] If parents help their child to develop strong working memory skills at home, it can have a positive impact on their later achievements in school.

Children aren't born with good memory skills; they develop and improve the more they are used.

Ways to improve your child's memory include the following:

o   Using songs and rhymes about an event can help your child to remember, as our brains are wired to remember patterns such as those found in music.

o   Make activities interesting and exciting. Children are more likely to remember information that is presented in a fun way.

o   Active learning (i.e. play) is the best way for young children to learn, so try to involve your child in everything you do, rather than just expecting them to sit and watch you or listen to what you are saying.

Even when you are reading a story, encourage them to turn the page at the right time, leave pauses for them to fill in a word, talk about the pictures rather than just stick to the text.

- o Attention, listening and memory skills are very closely connected, and by working on one, you will be helping the others. Attention allows us to take information in, listening skills enable us to make sure that the information we are focusing on is accurate, and working memory helps the brain make sense of it.

- o Children are more likely to remember information that they understand, so it is important that we use age-appropriate language and reinforce it in as many ways as possible to aid comprehension and learning, e.g. if a toddler visits a farm, the adult should name the animals, make the noises for each one, and use simple sentences to talk about what the animals are doing and the differences between them. Afterwards, the parents can help the child to draw a picture of what they saw at the farm, look at photos that were taken, recreate it with toy animals, sing 'Old MacDonald Had a Farm', read a book about a farm, etc. Each of these will help the child to understand and store the farm vocabulary more accurately in their memory.

- o Visual aids help a child to remember information, so do things such as drawing pictures and reading stories about their experiences.

- o Use as many of the senses as possible when you are engaged in an activity with your child. Our own memories of childhood (e.g. holidays, Christmas and school) are often triggered by a smell, taste or sound, so try to draw your child's attention to as many of these things as possible.

- o Limit your child's TV time. When a child is watching TV, they are not actively using the information they are presented with, and their working memory is not involved. If they do watch TV, try to watch with them and then use what you have seen in an activity afterwards.

- o Encourage questions. Understanding something is the first step in remembering, so always encourage your child to ask questions about their environment and experiences.

- o Try to make sure your child gets enough sleep, as it has been shown to be important in the consolidation of new memories. [131]

d. **Understanding question words**

This is another important stage in the development of verbal comprehension.

Your child will now start to respond to questions such as these:

o 'What are you doing?' – They will use a verb in the answer.

o 'Where's teddy?' – They will give a full response such as, 'He's in bed,' rather than just pointing.

o 'Who' questions – These are often introduced when family members come home from work or school, or when visitors knock at the door and we say, 'Who is it? It's Grandma!', etc.

Expressive Language

Your child will start this stage with around 200 words, and some children will continue to learn as many as 10 new words a day. For most children, the rate that they learn new vocabulary starts to slow down and grammatical development seems to take priority. There are four main ways that this happens:

1. The number of main parts in your child's sentences increases, such as in these examples:

o 'Daddy ball.' → 'Daddy kick the ball.'

o 'Do bubbles.' → 'Do bubbles in the garden.'

o 'Mummy car.' → 'Mummy's driving the car.'

o 'Me garden.' → 'Me play in the garden.'

o 'Toast hot.' → 'My toast is hot.'

o 'Go bed.' → 'Not go to bed.'

o 'Juice.' → 'No more juice.'

This means that your child can create a wider variety of sentence structures, each of which is now longer.

2. Each of the main parts of the sentence, which were limited to a single word, are now expanded to short phrases, such as in these examples:

o 'Ball.' → 'My ball.'
'Big ball.'
'The ball.'

o 'Play.' → 'Playing.'
'Am playing.'
'Played.'

o 'Car.' → 'Mummy's car.'
'Fast car.'

		'The red car.'
o 'Park.'	→	'In the park.'
		'At the park.'
		'To the park.'

Typically, the types of words that are learned during this stage that help to create these phrases include:

- o Pronouns, e.g. 'me', 'my', 'you', 'he' and 'them'. Your child will start referring to themselves using 'I'/'me' rather than their name.
- o Prepositions, e.g. 'in', 'on', 'under' and 'by'.
- o Adjectives, e.g. 'big'/'small', 'happy'/'sad', 'hot'/'cold', 'fast'/'slow' and 'tired'.
- o Auxiliary verbs, e.g. 'Me *can* do it', 'Ball *has* gone,' and 'He *is* sleeping.'

3. Your child's sentences will include more of the small grammatical markers that indicate features such as these:
   - o Verb tenses, e.g. 'play' → 'plays', 'playing' and 'played'.
   - o Plurals, e.g. 'brick' → 'bricks'.
   - o Possession, e.g. 'Daddy shoes' → 'Daddy's shoes'.

Errors are quite common at this stage and are perfectly normal. The English language has so many exceptions to the rules of grammar, which children have to learn as they go along. They begin by applying the same rule to everything.

Typical errors would include these:

- o Verb tenses, e.g. 'me goed' ('I went') or 'she singed' ('she sang').
- o Plurals, e.g. 'mouses' ('mice') or 'foots' ('feet').
- o Possession, e.g. 'that is him's' ('that is his').

At age two, a child's language is often described as 'telegrammatic' or 'telegraphic', which refers to the wording of a telegram where any word that can be left out is left out. Over the next six months, the little words that make the meaning of sentences clearer are added, and they will gradually sound less telegrammatic and more adult-like.

4. As well as the previous examples of how children's sentences develop, they also start to produce more questions and commands, which increases the variety of their language as well as the complexity, such as in these examples:
   - o 'Where Mummy going?'
   - o 'What them doing?'
   - o 'Put the brick there.'
   - o 'Give me the ball.'

Stammering

Around half of children between the ages of two and five will have a period of temporary stammering, [132] which is sometimes also known as 'developmental dysfluency'; with younger children, many speech and language therapists refer to it as 'bumpy speech'. [133] This often coincides with a period of rapid development of physical, language and cognitive skills. This age is a particularly crucial time for speech and language development, with lots of new demands being placed on the child as they learn new sounds and words, use longer sentences, express new ideas and feelings, and ask lots of questions. [134]

What is stammering?

Stammering occurs when normal speech is interrupted, usually by the repetition or extension of certain sounds or words. Stammering, which is also called stuttering, can range in frequency and intensity from mild to severe. The stammer may come and go, it may last for a period of weeks or months, or it may persist for longer. For some children, it starts gradually, but for others it can begin quite suddenly and sometimes quite severely. This can be worrying, for both the parents and the child.

A child's fluency may be worse when they are tired, ill or stressed, and it may vary depending on who they are talking to.

Causes of stammering

Up to 11% of children under the age of four are thought to go through a more prolonged period of stammering. [135] We don't know for sure what causes stammering in a child, but it is believed that a variety of factors are involved. [136] These may include the following:

- **Genetics**
  The tendency towards stammering has a genetic component. [137] Around 60% of all people who stammer have a close family member who also stammers. [138] A child is also more likely to stammer if there is a family history of other speech and language problems. [139]

- **Neurological factors**
  There appear to be structural and functional differences in the brains of children who stammer. [140] Research indicates that people who stammer appear to process language differently than those who don't. [141] [140]

Other risk factors

- **Age**
  Children who begin stammering before they reach the age of three and a half are more likely to outgrow it.

- **Length of time stammering persists**
  If your child's stammering lasts longer than six months, it is less likely that they will outgrow it.

- **Gender**
  Twice as many preschool boys will stammer than girls. [142] By age five, this increases to three to four times as many. [143]

- **Other speech and language difficulties**
  If your child has a speech and language delay or disorder, they are more likely to develop a stammer, and it is less likely to improve without additional support. [144] [139]

Features of stammering

- Repetition of whole words, e.g. saying, 'And... and... and... and another one.'
- Repetition of single sounds or syllables, e.g. saying, 'Mu-mu-mu-mummy.'
- Prolongation of sounds, e.g. saying, 'Ssssssometimes.'
- Blocking of sounds, where the child seems to open their mouth to speak but no sound comes out.
- Obvious muscle tension, especially in the face, neck or upper body.
- Extra body movements, which are used as an attempt to force the words out, e.g. head movements or stamping a foot.
- A change in breathing, such as holding their breath or taking an extra-large breath before talking. This can then affect the flow of speech.
- Avoiding eye contact during a moment of stammering.
- If children start avoiding certain words or situations because of their stammer, it is worth seeking advice from a speech and language therapist. Watch out for your child doing any of these:
  - o Avoiding or changing words, or frequently resorting to saying, 'I've forgotten,' or, 'I don't know.'

o   Avoiding situations when there is an expectation to speak, e.g. getting upset at circle time or show-and-tell at nursery or school.

o   Becoming a lot less chatty than normal for more than a day or so.

Treatment for stammering

Around 75% of children who start to stammer will resolve their problem without the need for direct intervention. [142] The challenge for speech and language therapists is to identify the other 25% and determine the most effective form of intervention. There is no one way of treating stammering that works for all children. Early intervention is the most effective, so if your child has a persistent stammer, it is advisable to seek an assessment sooner rather later. The efficacy of the therapy should be measured by the child's confidence and ability to use speech in different communicative situations as well as by their level of fluency. Whatever the outcome, therapy should help to improve your child's confidence as they learn to manage their stammering and improve their communication skills.

Tips for parents of a dysfluent or stammering child

Parents can have an enormous effect on how a child views their stammer and on how comfortable they feel in their ability to express themself and to be heard by those around them. Here are some steps you can take to help your child:

- Try to maintain a calm, quiet atmosphere at home.
- As often as you can, try to model language that your child will find easiest to use; i.e. short, simple sentences.
- If everyone around your child speaks slowly, they will feel that they can do the same.
- Use lots of pauses for thinking time to show your child that this is okay.
- Pay attention to what your child is saying, not the way they are saying it. Showing interest in what they are talking about will take the focus off their stammer.
- Try not to offer suggestions such as, 'Slow down,' 'Take a deep breath,' or, 'Try again.' This will only draw attention to the stammer and make your child think they are doing something wrong.
- Try not to finish their sentences for them. This may make them feel as though you have given up. Simply wait for them to finish, maintaining eye contact to show them that you are still listening.

- If your child becomes upset by their stammer, say something like, 'Good try. That was a really tricky word, wasn't it?' and then distract them with something that they enjoy or are good at.

- If your child is very aware that they are struggling with speech, and it feels right for them, you can say something like, 'Lots of people get stuck on their words, and that's okay. You're doing really well.' You can even draw attention to times when you forget a word or stumble when talking, and then say, 'Mummy/Daddy got stuck on that word, didn't they? I'll just keep trying.'

- Try to minimise the pressure on your child when talking with them by not interrupting and by using fewer questions.

- Try to make time each day for one-on-one 'talking time' with your child when there are no distractions, and they know they have your full attention. Even five minutes can make a difference. During this time, let the child choose what they would like to do. Let them direct you in the activities and decide themself whether to talk or not.

- Give extra praise for things that your child does well, so that the stammer does not affect their confidence. Try to praise something about what they have said if they have stammered while saying it, e.g. stating, 'That was a lovely story,' or, 'That was a kind thing to say.'

Obviously, we do not always have time to give a child our full attention every time they speak, and their needs must fit in with the rest of the demands of family life. Sometimes, it may be necessary to say, 'I can't listen right now, but I will when I have finished what I'm doing.' This is better than pretending to listen, as children may become very sensitised to our responses, and they will recognise when we are impatient, bored, embarrassed or just not listening.

Speech Sounds

Your child's sound system matures quickly during this year, and you should be able to understand what they say at least 50% of the time. [122]

They should already have the sounds 'p', 'b', 't', 'd', 'm', 'n' and 'w', and in the next few months, 'f', 's' and 'h' will appear.

Some of the immature features or processes will gradually disappear, which will mean that this happens:

- 'Dada.' → 'Daddy.'
- 'Tat.' → 'Cat.'

However, other features such as these may persist during the next few months:

- Unstressed syllables are deleted, e.g. 'banana' is 'nana', and 'spaghetti' is 'getti'.
- 'p', 't' and 'k' may continue to be replaced with 'b', 'd' and 'g', e.g. 'pea' is 'bea', 'toe' is 'doe', and 'car' is 'gar'.
- Difficult sounds continue to be replaced by those that are developmentally easier to pronounce, e.g. 'sea' is 'tea' and 'jump' is 'dump'.
- Sounds are missed off the end of words, e.g. 'up' is 'u' and 'pig' is 'pi'.
- Where there are two consonants together in a word, they continue to be reduced to one, e.g. 'spoon' is 'poon' and 'blue' is 'bue'.
- The sound 'th' is said as 't', 'd' or 'f'; e.g. 'that' is 'dat' and 'think' is 'fink'.

Summary

The skills expected by three years of age are summarised as follows.

Understanding

- Your child follows more complex instructions, e.g. 'Get the ball from the box and give it to Daddy.'
- They recognise some colours and shapes.
- They understand some basic concepts, such as 'big'/'little', 'in'/'out' and 'up'/'down'.
- They respond correctly to 'what', 'where' and 'who' questions.
- They understand the functions of objects, e.g. being able to answer when asked, 'What do we sleep in?'
- They understand and remember simple stories.
- They understand the concept of quantity, e.g. 'more', 'a bit' and 'a lot'.

Expressive language

- They have around 200–300 words, including lots of action words (verbs).
- They use sentences of three main parts, e.g. 'Daddy kicked the ball.'
- They use lots of phrases including words such as prepositions, e.g. 'in', 'on' and 'under', and adjectives, e.g. 'hot'/'cold', 'happy'/'sad' and 'big'/'small'.
- They use pronouns, e.g. 'him', 'her' and 'it', and refer to themself with 'I' or 'me' rather than their name.
- They ask lots of questions using question words such as 'what' and 'where'.
- They give instructions during play, e.g. saying, 'Put that brick on the floor,' or, 'Give me the car.'
- They start using word endings for things such as plurals and different verb tenses.
- They enjoy having a chat but may often change the subject.
- They chat to other children as well as adults.

Speech sounds

- Their speech is still immature, but they should be understood at least 75% of the time. [122]
- They use the sounds 'p', 'b', 'm', 't', 'd', 'n', 'w', 'k', 'g', 'ng', 'y' and 'h'. The sounds 'f' and 's' may also appear.

Red flags

If any of the following are true for your child at three years old, you should consider seeking the advice of your health visitor, GP, or local speech and language therapist:

- They move quickly from one activity to another and cannot concentrate on one for 5–10 minutes.
- They don't enjoy listening to longer stories.
- They don't engage in pretend or imaginary play a lot of the time, such as feeding a teddy or putting it to bed.
- They don't show interest in playing with other children.
- They don't like you joining in with their play.
- They often have trouble understanding what you say or just repeat what you have said.
- They don't not use smaller grammatical markers, such as plurals ending in 's' and pronouns ('me', 'mine', etc.).
- They don't ask lots of questions.
- A lot of their speech is difficult to understand.
- They can't follow two-step instructions, e.g. 'Get the ball and put it in the box.'
- They are not learning new words every week.
- They don't use lots of phrases, e.g. 'Go shops,' 'Car gone,' or, 'Where teddy?', and some sentences, e.g. 'Let's go to the park.'

Chatterbox Ideas

All the time

Looking/attention skills

- Draw your child's attention to facial expressions in books, on TV and people that they know, and discuss with them how expressions show what people are feeling. Start with basic feelings such as being happy, sad, angry and scared. Having the vocabulary to describe how they are feeling and knowing that all these different feelings are normal will help them learn to deal with and express their own feelings.

- Take every opportunity to use the things that your child is looking at as chances to talk about the concepts of size, shape, colour, number, etc. For example, on a walk to the shops, talk about the vehicles that you see:
  - o 'Look, there's a tractor. It's got two big wheels and two little wheels. The wheels are round. It's a blue tractor. There's another tractor. One tractor, two tractors.'
  - o 'There's a bus. It's a big, red bus. It's got round wheels. Let's count the wheels… One, two, three, four.'

Listening

- Throughout the day, include ways to help your child to shift their attention from what they are doing to what you are saying. Instead of simply commenting on what they are doing, say their name, wait for them to look at you and then comment. Don't be tempted to give too many directions or ask lots of questions, however, as this can be very frustrating for a child. Having to make the effort to shift their focus of attention is still not easy for them. Imagine how you feel when you are talking on the phone and your child is interrupting you constantly; they feel like this when they are focused on an activity and they are asked questions or given instructions.
- Try to make all comments or directions relevant to their activity, so that they don't need to change what they are thinking about as well as shifting their attention.
- Continue to draw your child's attention to everyday sounds, and see if they know what might have made the sound, e.g. if the doorbell rings, or you hear a car horn or a dog bark, ask them what they think it is.
- Try to include some concepts when doing listening activities, so as well as talking about what is making a sound (such as a bird, a car or a dog), talk about the features of the sound, e.g. saying, 'The bus went "beep, beep". That was loud, wasn't it?'

Sounds and talking

- Introduce words to describe feelings, starting with 'happy', 'sad' and 'cross'/'angry'. Once a child can label an emotion, they are able to talk about how they feel rather than just reacting. Try to put their feelings into words (e.g. stating, 'I know you were cross when they knocked your tower down.'), describe your own feelings (e.g. saying, 'I am frustrated that I can't find my car keys.') and ask them how others may feel (e.g. asking, 'Emma has been left out of the game. How do you think she feels?').

- Use everyday activities and jobs to talk about concepts:

- **Sorting laundry**
  - o Compare long and short socks or sleeves.
  - o Sort pairs of socks using the words 'same' and 'different'.
  - o Play I spy, e.g. saying, 'I spy something red.'
  - o Say things like, 'Put the socks in the drawer,' or, 'Put the pyjamas under the pillow.'

- **Bath time**
  - o Use the words 'clean' and 'dirty'.
  - o Use the words 'wet' and 'dry'.
  - o Say things like, 'Let's wash under your arms,' or 'Let's wash behind your ears.'

- **Tidying toys**
  - o Sort toys into colours, shapes, whether they are hard or soft, etc.

- **Mealtimes**
Talk about the colour and shape of different foods in terms of the following words:
    o 'Hot'/'cold'
    o 'Fat'/'thin'
    o 'Long'/'short'
    o 'Hard'/'soft'

Chatterbox time

Music, songs and rhymes

- Music and songs can be used to help your child's memory skills:
    o Play simple rhythms on an instrument and ask your child to copy you. Start with something very simple, such as a single shake of a maraca or a bang on a drum, and when your child can copy you accurately, make it gradually more difficult. Ask them to play a rhythm for you to copy.
    o Sing simple songs and rhymes together. Learning the words will help your child's memory.
- Sing lots of nursery rhymes that have prepositions, such as the following, and do the actions:
    o 'Ring a Ring O' Roses' (down)
    o 'The Grand Old Duke of York' (up and down)
    o 'Hokey Cokey' (in and out)
    o 'Jack and Jill' (up and down)
    o 'Hey Diddle Diddle' (over)
- Sing songs and rhymes with colours and numbers, such as these:
    o 'One, Two, Three, Four, Five, Once I Caught a Fish Alive'
    o 'One, Two, Buckle My Shoe'
    o 'Five Little Monkeys'
    o 'Five Fat Sausages'
    o 'Five Little Ducks'
    o 'Alice the Camel'
    o 'Ten in the Bed'
    o 'Sing a Rainbow'
    o 'Lavender's Blue'
    o 'Roses Are Red, Violets Are Blue'

Books and stories

When reading familiar stories, try missing an obvious word out and see if your child can fill it in, or make an obvious mistake (e.g. saying 'The dog says, "Moo".') to check whether they are paying attention and listening to the words.

Introduce books with concepts such as colours, shapes and numbers, such as these:

- *Numbers, Colours, Shapes* (board book) by Roger Priddy
- *My First Shapes* by DK
- *My First Colours* by DK
- *My First 1, 2, 3* by DK
- *Shapes* by Roger Priddy
- *Lift-the-Flap Colours, Numbers, Shapes* by Usborne

Opposites are a useful way to teach concepts, and some good books to use for this are as follows:

- *The Picture Book of Opposite Words* by Wise Cube
- *Touchthinklearn: Opposites* (board book) by Xavier Deneux

- *Opposites* by Roald Dahl
- *Lift-the-Flap Opposites* by Usborne

Include books with prepositions, such as 'in', 'on' and 'under':

- *Where's Spot?* by Eric Hill
- *We're Going on a Bear Hunt* by Michel Rosen and Helen Oxenbury
- *Where Is Baby's Birthday Cake?* by Karen Katz
- *Bear and Hare: Where's Bear?* by Emily Gravett
- *Pop-Up Peekaboo* book series by DK

Games and activities

1. **Parallel play and sharing**
   At this stage, when having to share can cause conflict, make sure that playdates include some activities where the toddlers are not required to share or take turns, such as a tub of bricks, painting a picture, dancing to music or listening to a story. With other activities, if you know that one of the children has difficulty sharing, put out two of each toy, e.g. shape cutters for PlayDoh, musical instruments, cars or sandpit toys.

2. **Memory games**
   These are some memory games you could play:

   - Have a treasure hunt around the house or garden, and give your child two or three clues to find each object or prize, e.g. telling them, 'Go to the kitchen, open the fridge and look behind the milk.'
   - Play games that use visual memory, e.g. finding matching pairs or Kim's game: put some objects on a tray, just three or four to begin with, and talk about what they are. Cover the tray with a tea towel and ask your child to close their eyes while you take one thing away. Get them to open their eyes again and see if they can spot which thing is missing. Choose items that start with the same sound, things that rhyme, or things that are the same colour or shape.
   - Give your child a list of instructions to remember for a mini assault course, either inside or outside, e.g. saying, 'Jump over the cushion, roll the ball to

Mummy, and then run to the kitchen,' or, 'Jump up and down, run around the tree, and bring me the watering can.'

- At any time during the day, e.g. when you and your child are both in the car, when your child is in the bath or when they are at the table waiting for a meal, play a quick game of 'I went to the shop and I bought…' or 'I went to the farm/zoo/school/seaside and I saw…' Take turns adding something to the list and see how many your child can remember.
- When you go shopping, give your child a few items to remember. Start with two or three things that they like so that they are more likely to remember.

3. **Craft**

This is a good time to introduce craft activities if you haven't already. Crayons, paints, PlayDoh, etc. will help to develop a child's fine motor skills, but this is also an ideal opportunity to work on colours, shapes and numbers:

- When colouring or painting, it is useful if you also have some paper. Talk about the colours you are using and the shapes you are making. It will not always be easy for your child to draw or paint a recognisable circle, square or triangle yet!
- Don't introduce too many concepts at once. To begin with, stick to red, blue and yellow; circle, square and triangle; and one, two and three.
- With PlayDoh, you can make shapes then stick them together to make different things, e.g. a square and four circles can make a car, a square with a triangle on top can make a house, and a circle with a triangle on top can be a clown's head!

4. **Pretend play**

Encourage as much pretend play as possible. Your child will love to copy what you do, so they will enjoy activities such as these:

- **Washing up**

Prepare for a lot of mess! Put a towel on the floor, stand your child on a chair next to the sink and stand with them while they wash up a variety of plastic cups, bowls, plates and cutlery. This is a good opportunity to talk about colours, shapes, and concepts such as 'clean'/'dirty', 'wet'/'dry' and 'hot'/'cold'.

- When you are doing other jobs around the house, let your child join in with their own cloth, feather duster, and dustpan and brush. Toy versions of a hoover, a cooker and pans, a table and chairs, etc. are useful, but are not essential. They will allow your child to pretend whenever they feel like it, and you will find that they are occupied for increasing amounts of time in their own little world. This is when you will start to hear your child talking to themself a lot more during play, and you will often hear them repeat little phrases that they have heard you say, e.g. saying, 'Be careful with the knife,' 'Try not to spill the juice,' or, 'Let's tidy up!'
- Encourage your child to include a doll or teddy in their daily routines, so when they are getting ready for bed, let them get teddy ready; when they are having a bath, let them take a plastic doll in the bath. It will give them the opportunity to practise words and phrases that they have heard during the day.
- Playing shops is another activity that toddlers love, and it offers opportunities for including lots of vocabulary, concepts and memory, such as these:
  o Sort items of shopping into different colours or shapes.
  o Give your child a basket and a short list of things to remember to buy.
  o As well as the basic foods, toy food sets often include a variety of items such as an aubergine, kiwi fruit, sweetcorn, watermelon, bagels, pretzels and prawns. This gives your child an opportunity to learn the names of food that they may not have heard of or eaten yet.

5. **Sound lotto games**

These are useful for helping to develop your child's listening skills. These come in the form of picture boards and a CD or app with various sounds, e.g. sounds around the house, animal noises and voices to match to facial expressions. You play each sound and see if your child can find the matching picture.

6. **Teddy's birthday**

Pretend it is teddy's birthday. Save old wrapping paper and let your child try to wrap up some presents for teddy with Sellotape. Talk about what might happen at teddy's party, what they will eat, who they will invite, etc. Turn snack time into party time, and have toys as guests, play party games and let your child help teddy to unwrap their presents! Later in the day, make time to talk about the party, and let your child tell you everything they can remember about it. This is a great opportunity for them to practise their narrative skills.

7. **Matching colours**

Use bags or boxes of different colours. Give one to your child and ask them to collect things of that colour from around the house. Empty the bag together and talk about what you have found.

8. **Washing line**

Put a 'washing line' of double-sided sticky tape across a door or the side of a table. Have to hand a selection of small items that will stick to the tape. Use any plastic objects, toys, letters, numbers, etc., and let your child stick them on the line and take them off. Use this for vocabulary regarding colours, shapes, numbers, etc.

You can also stick some photos on the line and talk about the people or events. You could use them to make up a story together, which will help your child's sequencing and narrative skills.

9. **Paint with water**

Give your child some water and brushes to paint different surfaces outside, such as paths, fences and garden furniture. You can also draw things with chalk and see if your child can guess what they are, then show them how to copy the outline with their brush to make them disappear. This is good for any vocabulary you choose to use and for pre-writing skills.

They can also paint with water inside, on pieces of card. When the card dries, the picture will disappear!

10. **Magic pictures**

Draw an object on a piece of card with a marker pen and cover it with a piece of kitchen roll. Let your child dab a wet paintbrush on the kitchen roll to make the picture soak through. See how quickly they can guess what the picture is as it soaks through.

11. **Foam shapes**

Use foam shapes to make pictures. They will stick to surfaces when wet, so they are perfect for bath time, but they will also stick to windows or doors when wet. Talk about the colours and shapes, and then see if you can guess what the other person has made.

12. **Play farming**

Save some leftover raw vegetables, e.g. carrots, potatoes, a piece of cauliflower or broccoli. Bury them near the surface of an area in the garden and ask your child to be the farmer and dig them up. Name each one, count how many you have, wash them and even try cooking them. Your child may be more willing to taste them if they think they have grown and harvested them themself! This game is great for food vocabulary.

13. **Sieving**

Use a pack of old flour, semolina, sugar, etc., and mix some small toys in it. Give your child a bowl and a sieve to see what they find. They are more likely to try to say the name of an object if they are surprised to find it.

14. **Fishing game**

Attach paper clips to pictures and take turns to use a magnetic fishing rod to catch them. Choose themes such as animals, colours, words beginning with a particular sound, etc.

15. **Posting game**

Children love posting. Use a toy postbox or make one from a cereal box. Have a selection of pictures, then ask your child to find one by giving them a clue, e.g. saying, 'Where's the one that says "moo"?', and let them post it. Again, use categories and themes for the pictures and clues.

16. **Skittles**

Stick pictures to plastic cups and take turns to roll a ball and try to knock down as many as you can. Say the words that are on the cups you have knocked down and count them. Or you could put a small toy or object on top of each cup and say what it is if you manage to knock it off the cup. Both are good for learning names of things, counting, and fun words such as 'crash'.

17. **Shopping game**

Use toy food or a selection of real food items to make a shop. Draw some of the items on pieces of paper to make shopping lists then take turns to be the shopkeeper or the customer. When your child is the shopkeeper, ask them for two or three items at once and see how many they can remember. This is good for vocabulary and memory skills.

18. **Catch the rat**

Tape a cardboard tube to a door. Choose some toys or objects that will fit through the tube. Let your child choose a toy, drop it into the tube and see if they can catch it. This is good for vocabulary and for motor skills.

19. **Paper aeroplanes**

Draw a picture on several pieces of paper and make paper aeroplanes. Take turns to throw them to each other and say what picture is on the plane. This is good for vocabulary and comparison words such as 'high', 'higher' and 'highest'.

20. **Hide-and-seek**

Hide toys, pictures or puzzle pieces around the room for your child to find. Use this for any vocabulary. Children will happily name things that they find, and it is a more natural alternative to simply asking 'What's this?'

Chapter 6

3–4 Years

Your child's curiosity about the world continues as a three-year-old, and now they are able to verbalise this with an endless list of questions! This seems to consist largely of 'Why?', to which there is rarely a response that they are satisfied with! It takes great patience to avoid resorting to saying, 'Because it just is,' or, 'Because I said so,' but most parents do at some point to try to end the interrogation. Remember that part of the reason they keep asking the question is because they want you to keep talking to them. Some of their questions may be genuine, but many are just a strategy to keep the conversation going.

As well as asking questions, your child will now be chatting confidently about anything and everything. Remember that it was your aim to 'raise a chatterbox', and by now, you probably have one! They will be using longer and more complex sentences, asking lots of different questions, making up stories, telling jokes and telling the occasional fib.

Telling Lies

It is quite a revelation for children when they realise that parents can't read their minds! Telling lies is a normal stage that most children go through at this age, for several possible reasons:

- To get attention.
- To make something they are telling you sound more exciting or interesting.
- To avoid getting into trouble, e.g. denying that they have broken or eaten something.
- To get something that they want, e.g. by telling one parent that the other usually lets them have a treat!
- For a three-year-old, there is still a fine line between reality and imagination, and they may sometimes pretend that part of a story is real.
- To avoid hurting someone's feelings; i.e. telling a white lie. These sorts of lies don't tend to develop until a child is older. At age three, most children are brutally honest!

How to handle lying

- Make sure your child understands the difference between a lie, which may have consequences, and telling a tall story for a bit of fun. You can distinguish these from each other by using the labels of a 'lie' for one and a 'story' for the other, respectively. Using their imagination in stories is an important stage of development. You can let them know that making up stories is okay, and you can even help them to develop their story further.
- Praise your child when they own up for doing something accidentally, e.g. spilling a drink. Let them know that accidents happen to everyone and encourage them to help you clear up the mess. They are then less likely to lie about things like this in future.
- Be a good role model. If you do something wrong, own up. If you tell a lie or pretend to, then admit to it soon afterwards.
- Explain some of the possible consequences of lying, such as getting people into trouble who haven't done anything wrong.
- Never call your child a liar, but make it clear when you know they are not telling the truth and give them the opportunity to own up, e.g. if they deny eating some cake, but the evidence is around their mouth, take them to look in the mirror! Let them know that they won't get into trouble as long as they tell the truth. You should obviously then keep your promise as a child won't own up again if they are punished as a result.

    Friends of ours used to tell their young children that when they told a lie, little lights flashed on their forehead! For a while, their children would then put one of their hands on their forehead each time they were going to lie!

Your Child's Sense of Humour

Another development in a child's use of language at this age is humour. Finding words, rhymes, songs, etc. funny shows a more advanced level of understanding. Having a good sense of humour can help children both emotionally and physically:

- Children with a well-developed sense of humour are happier and more optimistic. [145] They have higher self-esteem and are more well-liked by their peers. [146]
- A good sense of humour has been shown to alleviate stress and reduce mental health problems. [147]
- Children who laugh more are physically healthier. They have better immune function, so they can fight off illness more easily. [148] They have lower blood pressure and better digestion, and they sleep better. [149]

Never feel that it is a waste of time to just be silly and have fun with your child.

Possibly the best sound in the world is a young baby laughing. Parents will do anything to encourage that giggle: blowing raspberries, tickling or making silly sounds, preferably including an element of surprise. It is important to continue this as your baby grows. The best way to help develop their sense of humour is to show them your own. Be silly, tell jokes and funny stories, and find humour in everyday things, e.g. if you spill something, trip (without hurting yourself) or mix up your words.

At this age, children tend to delight in slapstick humour, so the more you play the role of a clown, the funnier your child will find it. They will try to make you laugh by doing the same, doing things such as putting their clothes on wrong (e.g. when you ask them to put their shoes on, they might put them on their hands), deliberately giving the wrong answer to a question (e.g. if you ask, 'What does a duck say?' they reply, 'Moo'!). They will delight in your laugh as much as you do in theirs, and once they know you find something funny, they will repeat it over and over again.

Sharing humour is important socially, for developing friendships and close bonds between people, which is why laughter is contagious. We laugh more with other people than we do on our own. Sharing funny experiences as a family lasts a lifetime: you ask, 'Do you remember the time when...' and you laugh all over again. What seems like a small funny moment that you share when your child is young may end up being a memory that stays with them forever.

Feelings/Emotions

Young children deal with many of the same emotions as adults do – they get angry, sad, excited, happy, frustrated, nervous, etc. – but they often don't have the words to express these things. Instead, they may act out these emotions in physical (and often inappropriate) ways. For example, a child may get frustrated when they can't build a tower without it falling down, and they may throw the bricks; or they may want to stay at the park longer than is possible, and they may throw themself on the ground and scream.

Children can easily be overwhelmed by their feelings, and this is one of the reasons they may end up having a tantrum. As adults, it is rare that we get to experience an emotion for the first time. Even when we do, such as feeling grief following the loss of a loved one, we recognise the feeling, can label it and we understand that we are not going to feel it as intently forever. Children don't have this knowledge or understanding and at first need adult support to help them manage their emotions. Gradually they learn and can express their feelings in more appropriate ways so that tantrums become less frequent.

Recognising and understanding emotions is an important skill, both for your child's own emotional wellbeing and also their relationships with others. By the time they are three, your child will be able to recognise and label basic emotions – such as 'happy', 'sad' and 'angry' – in themself and others. [150] There is a substantial increase in the recognition of emotions between ages three and four. [151] It is important to make the most of this because the ability to recognise and label emotions has been demonstrated to help develop positive social interactions, and difficulty recognising and labelling emotions can contribute to later behavioural and learning problems. [152]

There are lots of things you can do to help your child understand and express their feelings from an early age:

- Use simple vocabulary to give names to feelings. The first emotions that children recognise and understand are 'happy', 'sad' and 'cross'/'angry'. Once your child is confident with these labels, you can introduce words such as 'bored', 'confused', 'disappointed', 'excited', 'fed-up', 'frustrated', 'jealous', 'lonely', 'shy', 'worried', 'scared' and 'surprised', and then 'brave', 'curious', 'embarrassed', 'impatient', 'proud', 'relieved' and so on.
- Label your child's feelings for them at first, e.g. saying, 'You wanted Daddy to play, but he's gone out, so you're sad. Daddy will play when he gets back, then you'll be happy.' By giving a label to each emotion, you enable your child to develop a vocabulary for talking about feelings.
- Express your own emotions, e.g. if rain prevents a planned activity, you could say, 'I'm sad that we couldn't go to the beach and I'm a bit bored now. How about you? What shall we do instead?' or, 'Do you remember this morning when Mummy's laptop wasn't working? I got cross. Can you remember what my face looked like? Can you make a cross face?'
- Give your child lots of opportunities to identify feelings, both in themself and in others, e.g. telling them, 'It's your birthday, and we're having cake. I can see you smiling. Are you happy? I'm happy too,' or, 'That little boy has just dropped his ice cream. Oh dear, he's crying. How do you think he feels?'
- Use books, pictures and TV shows as examples.
- Teach your child about different ways to respond to specific feelings, using your own feelings as examples, e.g. explaining, 'When I get cross, I take a deep breath, count to five and find someone to talk to.' Teach in the moment (though avoiding times of extreme emotion), by saying, 'You look cross that you can't fit the puzzle piece in. Shall we take a deep breath and count to five? How can I help?'
- Always make clear the distinction between how they feel and how they act on that feeling. It is always okay to feel something, but it is not okay to hit out: tell them that they should 'say it, not do it', e.g. say, 'I'm cross,' rather than hitting out.
- Talk about how to express emotions in acceptable ways, point out examples of what is and isn't acceptable, and discuss alternatives, e.g. 'Freddie knocked

Henry's tower down, and Henry threw a brick at him because he was cross. What else could he have done?'

- Suggest strategies such as taking a deep breath, going somewhere quiet, asking an adult for help, asking for a turn, asking for a hug, etc. Also encourage your child to work out strategies of their own by talking about situations that they might remember or that happen often, e.g. saying, 'You seemed cross when Sophie wouldn't share her toys yesterday, and you shouted at her. What could you do next time?'

- As well as thinking of ways to make themself feel better, encourage your child to think about others' feelings, e.g. if a friend is poorly and can't go to a party, ask your child how could they cheer them up.

- Praise your child when they talk about their feelings, e.g. explaining, 'I'm really happy that you told me you were cross. Now I can help you.' Children need to know it is okay to say how they are feeling.

- Praise your child when they express an emotion in an appropriate way, e.g. if they knock down a tower accidentally, and then say, 'Aaaaaargh!' and ask for help instead of throwing the bricks.

- Help your child to practise expressing their feelings. The more you practise, the easier your child will find it to use these in real situations.

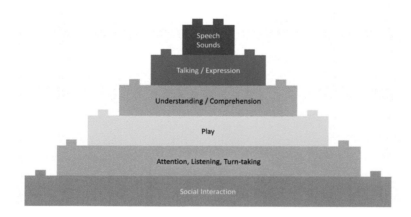

Social Interaction

You will find that your child's confidence in social situations will increase over the next year. They will actively seek out the company of other children and will make lots of new friends. If they don't already mix with other children regularly at a nursery, playgroup, etc., now would be a good time to give them the opportunity. Starting school with a group of your friends is a lot less daunting than doing it alone. Regularly spending time in a group will help them to develop the ability to follow group instructions and play in small groups, rather than with just one or two other children. Both of these are skills that are very useful to have for their first day of school.

We all want our children to have lots of friends, and be popular at playgroup, nursery or school. One particular study finds that children's popularity with peers can be predicted by the level of their understanding of spoken language. [5]

If you worry about your child not having enough friends when they start school, use some of the time you have left with them at home to model ways that show your child how to be a good friend.

These include the following:

- **Being a good listener**
  We all like to have a friend who listens, but it isn't always obvious to a child what is involved in being a good listener (see the *Attention, Listening and Turn-taking* section on page 152).

- **Asking to join in with a game**
  When your child wants to join in an activity with a friend, do they just stand by and wait to be asked or do they confidently start playing? It can help if you show your child by saying, 'Can I play?' when they are in the middle of an activity, or make a suggestion that might improve their game, e.g. if they are

bouncing a ball, suggest, 'How about throwing the ball to me, and I'll throw it back?'

- **Showing empathy**
Talk about feelings with your child. When you are sharing a book or watching TV, pause from time to time and see if they can work out how someone in the book or TV show might be feeling by their facial expression. Then, if it is a negative feeling, discuss ways they could help that person to feel better. We all like to have friends who help to cheer us up.

- **Turn-taking**
This is important for all social interaction whether it's a conversation, a game or waiting in the queue for lunch. It is difficult being friends with someone who never lets you have your turn, tends to monopolise a conversation or activity, or who often pushes in front of you. Give your child lots of opportunities to practise within the family (see the *Listening* section within *Chatterbox Ideas* on page 162).

- **Following the rules of games**
Children must adapt to the school environment where there are lots of new rules, and not only those set by the staff. Children often make up their own games with rules on the playground and are more likely to welcome children into the game if they stick to the rules. Practise this by starting with simple turn-taking games, then try games such as Simon says, tig or hide-and-seek, which have simple, obvious rules.

- **Being kind**
This includes things such as sharing toys, encouraging someone who is struggling, and being aware of other people's feelings. Show lots of small acts of kindness to your child and give them lots of praise every time they are kind.

Attention, Listening and Turn-Taking

This is an important age for the development of attention skills. Your child should now start being able to shift their attention from one thing to another, without adult help. They may be playing and hear a noise outside, listen, comment on it, and then carry on playing; they may be drawing a picture and answer questions about what they are drawing without you having to get their direct attention first. If you need your child to listen to something important, it is still best to make sure you have their attention first, though.

A child's attention span is roughly three minutes per year of their age. [153] [154] You may find it is less if there are distractions in their environment, or if they are hungry or tired; it may be more if they are particularly interested in an activity.

Attention problems are common among preschool children. There has been much research focusing on the increased number of preschool children presenting with concerns about attention problems. [155] By four years of age, as many as 40% of children have sufficient problems with attention to be of concern to their parents and preschool teachers. [156] There has also been increasing concern regarding the amount of screen time spent by young children and its relationship with early attention problems. Some research finds that the number of hours of TV watched per day at ages one and three years is associated with attention problems at age seven years. [157] There is also evidence of some immediate negative effects that TV has on attention, showing that children perform poorly on tests requiring focused attention after they have watched a fast-paced TV show compared with those who haven't. [158]

Attention and listening skills go hand in hand, and if children start school struggling with one, they will have problems with the other.

There are so many routines and rules to be learned during their first few weeks, and teachers find themselves having to repeat the same information and instructions over and over again. Even then, there will always be a few children who don't do as they are asked; very often, this is because their attention and listening skills are still not where they should be by then. 'Children should ideally develop listening skills before starting primary school. The ability to listen is a major element in the attention skills that children need for all school-based learning,' states Sue Palmer, a former primary headteacher. [159] Often, a negative cycle develops when a child is a poor listener. Parents get frustrated when they think they are being ignored, and they resort to shouting, which then rewards the child's poor listening, because as far a child is concerned, any sort of attention is better than none. It is obviously better to give praise when your child does listen well and follow an instruction, as this will encourage them to do it more.

One of the best ways to help your child's listening skills is to show them how it's done! (See the *Listening* section within *Chatterbox Ideas* on page 162).

Just about everything your child does at school depends on their ability to listen: following instructions in the classroom, sitting quietly in assembly, learning the words to a song for the Christmas concert, joining in a game in physical education (PE) and listening when a friend is telling them something. Children struggle to multitask, and it is important that a child is expected to focus on only one thing at a time and be given information in manageable amounts. Also, a child's listening skills will always be better when they are interested, but the hard part is helping them to listen when they are not particularly interested. This is something that we all struggle with at times!

Being a good listener is important when making new friends too. A child who doesn't listen to what other children say, who talks over them or who doesn't follow the rules of a game may be excluded from play, as they are seen to be domineering or uncooperative.

Your child should now be tuning in to the finer details of the speech they hear around them, and they may start to notice when words rhyme, when you make a mistake saying a word, or when you miss a word out of a familiar rhyme or story. Continue to use the suggestions for attention and listening activities, and always praise your child when they have listened well or concentrated successfully for long enough to complete an activity (see the activities in the *Listening* section within *Chatterbox Ideas* on page 162).

At age three, children may still find it difficult to take turns, but may only need a little encouragement or prompting. If they have good listening skills, they will probably also be good at taking turns. Both involve pausing and waiting while the other person has a turn, whether that is in talking or playing a game. The best way to encourage good turn-taking is to model it as often as possible.

Play

By now, your child will enjoy playing with other children, and one of the main functions of play at this age is as a social activity; i.e. they like to play simply to be in the company of other children. They will usually choose to play with others, rather than by themself. The best play is chosen by children rather than adults and is motivated by fun, not prizes, with rules that can be changed through negotiation and with themes that can be developed using the children's imagination.

Children use language to plan, negotiate and agree rules for their games, and they often like to change the rules as the game goes along. Different types of play require different rules:

- In constructive play, children must agree on exactly what they are making with the materials, e.g. building a castle from bricks.

- In pretend play, when acting out a story, each child must stick to their role and not keep changing character.
- With any symbolic play, all of the children have to accept the use of certain objects to represent others, e.g. if they are playing 'garages', they all have to accept that one child may use a brick as a toy car. Anyone saying, 'That's not a car; it's a brick,' would obviously spoil the whole game.
- In rough-and-tumble physical play, children must agree not to hurt each other.
- Common traditional games such as tig and musical statues have agreed rules that children must stick to, even if it means that they are out of the game temporarily.

Imaginative play forms a large part of children's play at this age. They engage in pretending about familiar experiences, such as going to the doctor's or going to a café, and they act out even the smallest details of their experience. They also act out stories they have heard or roles purely from their imagination. They use language to set the scene, describe their character and feelings. They change roles frequently, depending how it fits in with the developing story, e.g. saying, 'I'm not a mum; I'm the teacher now.'

At this age, children don't always need props to inspire and guide their play. All they need is imagination, so the sky's the limit! It helps if you sometimes do the same, e.g. pick up a brick as though you are answering the phone or walk into the kitchen as though it were a shop. This will encourage your child to use their imagination even more and will give them some new ideas for play.

It is important that children get lots of opportunities for free play without adult intervention, as this is a time when they apply their knowledge of language more fully. The language used by children sharing pretend play is far more complex than that used in structured activities led by adults or when they are doing routine activities, such as sitting and eating together at a table. [160]

Understanding

Your child will be able to respond to longer and more complex instructions, e.g. those containing words such as 'and' or 'then'. Their understanding of concepts will be increasing all the time, including those such as colours, shapes, position, e.g. 'in front', 'behind', 'next to' and 'between' and more abstract concepts such as 'same'/'different'.

An understanding of time concepts has a big impact on a child being able to sequence events. They need to understand the difference between past, present and future events, and the fact that the order that they are expected to carry out tasks can be changed by using concepts such as 'before'/'after'. Time concepts can completely change the meaning of an instruction, e.g. '*Before* you go outside, put on your coat.' The level of a child's concept development will therefore affect their ability to follow certain instructions, and this is important from their first day at school onwards.

Think about a typical instruction that a child might hear in the classroom: 'Listen, everyone. It's nearly playtime. Now, remember, before you go out to play, first I want you to go to the toilet, wash your hands and then put your coat on.' A child might misunderstand this for several reasons:

1. They may not understand some of the concepts or vocabulary, e.g. 'first' and 'and then'.
2. They may have poor auditory memory, so they may only remember parts of the instruction.
3. They may have poor sequencing skills, so they may remember all the parts, but then do them in the wrong order.

Usually, if a child doesn't understand an instruction like this, they will either do things in the order that they hear them or do the thing that they heard last. In this case, doing either will be wrong: they will either go straight out to play or they will put their coat on. In the first few weeks of school, teachers make allowances for children getting things wrong, but if a child continues to do this, especially if they do not have any obvious language difficulty, they may start to be labelled as a poor listener.

Your child is now at the age where they can understand simple number concepts. They will quickly learn to count to ten and will understand 'first', 'second', 'third', etc., so you can introduce books and simple games involving numbers and letters.

A child's understanding of questions becomes more advanced at this age, and they will start responding appropriately to the following:

- 'When' questions, as their understanding of time improves.
- 'Why' questions, and 'because' to explain cause and effect.
- 'How' questions, which require more critical-thinking skills.

It is important to give your child more opportunities to listen to stories without pictures, to encourage them to focus on the language they hear without having any visual clues. Try to use expressive intonation to hold your child's attention; check their understanding as you read by pausing regularly to allow them to comment or ask a question; and ask them about what they think might happen next, how a character might be feeling or why a particular event happened. They may only give simple, obvious responses, but the important thing is that they are thinking about the story in more detail. Once they are at school, the most difficult part isn't learning the mechanics of reading individual words but is learning to understand what they have read. Encouraging them now to think about a story as you go along, to make inferences and predictions, to ask and answer questions, and to summarise the story at the end will put them at an advantage when they are expected to do this when they are the one reading the story.

Expressive Language

Your child should now be using full sentences with only occasional grammatical errors, such as 'goed' instead of 'went' or 'sheeps' instead of 'sheep'.

Complex sentences

'And' is an important word that appears this year. Once your child works out how to use it, you will hear it all the time! They will start by using it to join two words into a phrase, such as 'Mummy and Daddy' or 'Me and you', and they will gradually add on more and more. For example, when asked what food they would like at their birthday party, they might say, 'Sausages… and crisps… and cake… and biscuits… and cheese…' Next, your child will learn to use 'and' to join two sentences, e.g. saying, 'We went to the park, and I went on the slide.' This means that by adding this single word, children's sentences double in length! Next, they will learn to link sentences together with other words, such as 'then', 'but' and 'because'. When my youngest child discovered 'and', her three older brothers found that they suddenly had far fewer opportunities to join in family conversations! While she had our attention, she would simply add 'and' or 'and then' to carry on talking for another ten minutes! It was then that we had to be stricter about everyone getting an equal share of talking time!

This stage of grammatical development, moving from simple to complex sentences, is a time when you might see the first signs of non-fluency/stammering/bumpy speech. Don't panic! Just as a child is more likely to stumble and fall when they first learn to run, so they may stumble over their words with a sudden increase in the length and complexity of sentences (see section on *Stammering* on page 126).

Narrative skills

Your child's narrative skills will be developing, and they will be able to retell a story, either one based on their own experiences or one that they have read with you. They will be able to sequence these in the correct order so that the stories make sense. Encourage them to talk about anything! They will start to use past, present and future tenses correctly to tell you what they have done, are doing or are going to do. They will be able to express their opinions and talk about their feelings. Remind them of experiences you have shared, and talk about feelings, thoughts and plans. Talk about anything that involves organising their thoughts into a sequence that makes sense. Encourage them to tell you about things they have done each day. Or if you have been with them, it is useful if they can tell someone else, and you can check whether they are telling the events in the right order and prompt them when necessary. You can use words such as 'first', 'then' and 'and then' to help your child put events in the right order. A child's narrative skills are a good indicator of their understanding and feelings about events in their life. It can be useful for your child to take a favourite toy with them when you are out and about, then when you come home, they can retell the story with the toy as the main character.

Cooking with your child is a good opportunity to help them practise their narrative skills. Read out the sequence of steps in the recipe, and after each one, ask your child to remind you what you have done so far; when you have finished, go over all the steps again, in the right order, ending with 'And now we can eat it!'

Problem-solving and questions

At this age, children start to use language to solve problems, usually out loud. You can encourage this by doing the same thing and asking for your child's help, e.g. explaining, 'I can't find my keys. I wonder what I should do? I need to look in all the places I usually put them, then ask Daddy if he's seen them. If I can't find them, I'll have to use the spare set until I find them.'

Your child will be asking lots of questions now, using 'what', 'where', 'when', 'who', 'why' and 'how'. The list may seem endless, but it is an important skill to enable your child to make sense of the world; it will be particularly useful once they start school, as it will enable them to ask when they don't understand something.

Your child will understand the social aspects of communication more by now, and they will speak differently to strangers than to familiar people, to younger children than to adults, etc. This is another skill that will be important at school, when they will be expected to talk differently to their teacher than to their friends.

Speech Sounds

Between the ages of three and four, your child will develop several new sounds, and their speech will sound a lot more mature. They will start using 'f', 's', 'z', 'l', 'sh' and 'y', and consonant blends such as 'sp', 'st', 'br', 'tr', 'pl' and 'kl'.

You should now be able to understand them most of the time.

Most of the residual immature features or processes, such as the following, will disappear during this year:

- Deleting unstressed syllables, so 'nana' will become 'banana', 'getti' will become 'spaghetti', and 'tato' will become 'potato'.
- Sounds will no longer be missed off the end of words so 'du' will become 'duck', and 'ca' will become 'cat'.
- The appearance of consonant blends will mean that, where there are two consonants together in a word, both will be used, so 'poon' will become 'spoon', 'bue' will become 'blue', etc.

There will still be a couple of immature features that may persist for at least another year:

- Mixing up the sounds 'w', 'y', 'r' and 'l', e.g. 'leg' is 'yeg', and 'run' is 'wun'.
- 'Th' will still be difficult, e.g. 'thing' is 'fing', and 'that' is 'dat'.

You may find that your child is able to use a sound in one word position but not in another; for example, they may be able to use a sound at the beginning of a word but not in the middle or at the end. This is perfectly normal. Parents sometimes think this is due to laziness, but as I have said before, children are never lazy with their speech: there is simply no point, and to actually choose to say a sound in one word position but not in another would be almost impossible. Carry on giving lots of models to help your child learn; correcting their speech will not achieve anything other than frustrating everyone.

Summary

The skills expected by four years of age are summarised as follows.

Understanding

- Your child responds to an instruction without stopping what they are doing.
- They understand position concepts, such as 'in front', 'behind', 'next to' and 'between'.
- They understand most colour and shape names.
- They understand the concepts of 'same'/'different'.
- They listen to a story and answer questions about characters and events.
- They predict what might happen next in a story.
- They follow more complex instructions that include words such as 'and' and 'then'.

- They understand time concepts of 'past', 'present' and 'future', and can respond to questions about 'yesterday', 'today' and 'tomorrow'.
- They respond correctly to 'why' questions.

Expressive language

- They use full sentences with only occasional grammatical errors, such as plurals or past tense errors.
- They link sentences together with words such as 'and', 'then', 'but' and 'because'.
- They use past, present and future tenses.
- They use pronouns correctly, e.g. 'I', 'you', 'we' and 'they'.
- They can use thousands of words.
- They ask lots of questions, including those starting with 'who', 'where', 'what' and 'why'.
- They often start conversations with others.
- They make up long stories, sometimes confusing fact and fiction, but often not as deliberate lies.
- They use language to problem-solve, e.g. they can work out a response to the question 'What shall we do if it starts to rain?'
- They tell simple jokes and enjoy the attention they bring.
- They understand the social aspects of communication, e.g. will whisper secrets, will be more polite with strangers and will use baby talk with younger children.

Speech Sounds

- They use the sounds 'p', 'b', 'm', 't', 'd', 'n', 'w', 'k', 'g', 'ng', 'h', 'f', 's', 'z', 'l', 'sh' and 'y'.
- They start to use consonant blends, e.g. 'sp', 'st', 'br', 'tr', 'pl' and 'kl'.
- They can be understood almost all the time. [122]

Red flags
If any of the following are true for your child at four years old, you should consider seeking the advice of your health visitor, GP, or local speech and language therapist:

- They don't understand the things you ask them to do.
- They don't want to play with other children most of the time.
- They don't respond to 'who', 'what' and 'where' questions.

- They still show poor concentration.
- They don't ask lots of questions.
- They can't tell you about the things that they have done.
- They don't use lots of grammatical markers, such as plurals, verb endings, tenses and pronouns.
- They are not starting to use more complex sentences, e.g. 'I got up *and* I went to nursery.'
- They still have unclear speech.
- They are very non-fluent and struggle to get their words out.

Chatterbox Ideas

All the time

Looking/attention skills

- Your child's skills of observation will be improving, and this is a good way to motivate them to talk. You can buy or download picture scenes where something is wrong or silly. A child who normally describes a picture using lots of single words or short phrases will suddenly need to use their language skills more fully to explain to you what is wrong with the picture.
- Funny TV shows will appeal to your child's sense of humour and may prompt them to come and tell you about what they have watched.
- When looking at books or watching TV together, point out facial expressions that characters are using and see if your child can tell you what they think the person is feeling and why.
- Sit with your backs to each other and take turns to choose an object, describe it to the other person and see if they can guess what it is. This will encourage your child to look at features in detail and choose the best information to give as clues. It will also make them try to link pieces of information together to work out an answer.
- Look at family photos to prompt your child to recall events and tell you about them using their narrative skills.
- Use photos or action pictures to make a story, then mix them up and see if your child can put them back in the right order and retell the story.

Listening

1. One of the best ways to teach good listening is to model it:

   - Look at the person who is talking.
   - Maintain eye contact.
   - Don't interrupt. Stay quiet and wait until it is obviously your turn to speak.
   - Use encouraging gestures and facial expressions, such as smiling or nodding.
   - Respond appropriately, e.g. respond with surprise if you hear something unexpected.
   - Try to keep still. Fidgeting suggests a lack of interest and an eagerness to get away!
   - Listen to all the words so that you can understand what is being said.
   - Occasionally, repeat back some of what you hear, in your own words. This lets the speaker know that you have listened and understood. This can be one of the most important things you can do with a young child, as they have a lot of different things they want to say, but only a limited amount of language with which they can do it. For example, 'Mummy door' can mean any of these:
     o 'Mummy, there's someone at the door.'
     o 'Mummy, will you open/close the door?'
     o 'Mummy, that's a door.'
     o 'Mummy, I trapped my finger in the door.'

     If your child isn't sure whether you have understood what they mean, the conversation may get stuck at this point. If you repeat back what you have understood, they can move on to the next thing they want to say.
   - Ask relevant questions. This lets the speaker know you are interested, that you have understood what they are saying and that you want to hear more.
   - Always praise your child when they show good listening skills, e.g. when you have read a story to the end. This will encourage them to keep trying.

2. Read a favourite story and ask your child to do an action every time they hear a particular word, e.g. to growl like a bear when they hear the word 'bear' in *We're Going on a Bear Hunt* (by Michel Rosen and Helen Oxenbury); to hee-haw like a donkey when they hear the word 'donkey' in *The Wonky Donkey* (by

Craig Smith); or to move like a monkey when they hear the word 'monkey' in *Night Monkey, Day Monkey* (by Julia Donaldson). At first, if they don't do the action straight away, pause when you have said the word to let them know that it's time to do it, or do the action with them the first few times.

3. Read a favourite story and make a deliberate mistake to see if your child can spot it. Children love correcting adults, and this is fun for them as well as helping to develop their listening skills.

4. Ask your child to close their eyes while you make a noise that they hear every day. Ask them to identify the sound, e.g. boil the kettle, open and close the fridge door, or shake a box of cereal.

5. Cook together. This is great for improving listening and memory skills, and for following instructions:

   - Read out the list of ingredients to your child and see how many they can remember and repeat.
   - Give your child a few ingredients or utensils to remember and get out for you. This will require using working memory, as they must remember the list while they are looking through the cupboards.
   - Use a YouTube recipe; let your child watch it and then tell you the next step. This will encourage them to listen to the details and then summarise the information into an instruction for you.

6. Send your child to pass on messages around the house, e.g. asking, 'Will you ask Daddy if he'd like a cup of coffee and tell him we need to leave at four o'clock?' or, 'Will you ask your brother if he is ready for school and tell him to bring his book bag?' Check how much of the message they have understood, and use this information to modify your next message, making it easier or harder if necessary.

7. Sit with your backs to each other and take turns to describe a picture for the other one to draw. Compare the pictures afterwards and see if you can work out why the instructions that were given didn't work.

8. Play Chinese whispers when you are sitting around the table.

9. Play Simon says.

Sounds and talking

At this age, children love to chat! Every conversation is a bonus and will do the following:

- Help your child's turn-taking skills.
- Encourage them to listen.
- Develop their use of questions.
- Extend their vocabulary.

- Give them an opportunity to practise using newly acquired grammar and sounds.
- Encourage them to use their sequencing and narrative skills to talk about events.

Feelings

Use any opportunities throughout the day to talk about feelings, including those of other people:

- When you are doing something that you are both enjoying, ask your child how they feel. Prompt them if necessary, by telling them how you feel.
- If you see someone expressing an obvious emotion, talk to your child about it, e.g. if you see another child crying, discuss how they might be feeling and why.
- Brainstorm strategies to deal with negative emotions after the event, e.g. if your child is pushed by another child at the park, and your child lashes out, when you get home, ask if they can think of other things they could do if it happens again.
- Take turns to make a face and see if the other person can guess what you are feeling. Then talk about all the things that make you both feel that way, e.g. a smile shows you are happy, and the things that make you happy are parties, Christmas, story time, going to the park, etc. Use a mirror so that your child can see your face and their own. Make up a little rhyme such as, 'Mirror, mirror, what do I see? I see a happy face looking at me!' to make it more fun.
- As well as talking about feelings throughout the day, have a special time when everyone shares the feelings they have had during the day, such as dinner time. Avoid bedtime, as you don't want your child to be thinking about bad feelings just as they are trying to go to sleep. Each person could share their worst and best feeling of the day, and then talk about what happened. The family can then brainstorm their ideas to deal with any negative emotions.

Chatterbox time

Music, songs and rhymes

Learning songs and rhymes by heart is a powerful tool for developing auditory memory. Children love doing this, so it is a particularly good way of achieving a goal with very little effort. These don't have to be traditional songs or rhymes; songs that they hear on the radio are fine, as well as those on children's TV. Action songs will still be popular at this age, and if your child attends a nursery or playgroup, they will probably come home singing songs they have learned there and will expect you to join in!

Encourage your child to use simple musical instruments such as a drum, maracas, a tambourine or a triangle to play along in time to music.

Dance at every chance! Dance around the room with your child. As well as being a fun way to get some exercise, moving to music and keeping to a rhythm is known to help language development and pre-reading skills (see section on *Music*, page 193).

Sing songs about feelings, e.g. use songs such as 'If You're Happy and You Know It':

If you're happy and you know it, clap your hands.
If you're cross and you know it, stamp your feet.
If you're sad and you know it, cry a tear.

Books and stories
Listening to stories of increasing length is a great way to improve a child's attention span, and asking questions, leaving gaps or making deliberate mistakes can be a

useful way to check how well your child is listening. You can ask your child what they think might happen next or why something happened.

Use familiar stories to encourage your child to use their narrative skills to retell the story. You can collect some props, which are objects that will prompt your child to talk about the next thing that happened in the story. Look at where the props fit in when you are reading the story, then put the book away and see if your child can tell the story with just the props. Help your child with prompts such as, 'First…', 'Then…' and 'And then…' to help them retell the story in the right order.

When sharing books, pause regularly to encourage your child to make comments or ask questions. Share your thoughts about what has happened, how the characters might feel and what might happen next and give them the opportunity to do the same. Ask them to work things out from clues in the text. For example, if a character has done their homework and is getting tired, ask what time of day it might be, or if a character says they need an umbrella, ask what the weather is like.

Look through a photo album together and encourage your child to tell you about their memories of the events, prompted by the photos.

Have a 'story bag' of random objects. Take turns to pull out three or four objects, and then make up a story around them. Use things that you think will prompt an interesting story, such as a toy plane, a lion, a torch or a key.

Make a scrapbook to prompt stories. Include photos, postcards, pictures that your child has seen online, and things they have found such as a leaf, a flower or a penny.

Share books about feelings such as these:

- *The Selfish Crocodile* by Faustin Charles
- *The Huge Bag of Worries* by Virginia Ironside and Frank Rodgers

Share books about lying. These can be useful if your child's lying seems to be getting out of hand:

- *Hippo Owns Up* by Sue Graves
- *I Didn't Do It* by Sue Graves
- *There's a Lion in the Library* by Dave Skinner (this may be a bit scary for some children!)

Your child will now be able to appreciate funny pictures and silly rhymes, so it is worth introducing books with an element of humour:

- *Bananas in My Ears* by Michel Rosen
- *Pirate Pete and His Smelly Feet* by Lucy Rowland
- *Poo in the Zoo* by Steve Smallman
- *Oi Dog* by Kes Gray
- *My Dad Thinks He's Funny* by Katrina Kermein
- *Mixed-Up Nursery Rhymes* by Hilary Robinson
- *You Can't Take an Elephant on the Bus* by Patricia Cleveland-Peck
- *Timmy on the Toilet* by Peter Lemon
- *That's Not Funny* by Jeanne Willis
- *The Wonky Donkey* by Craig Smith
- *The Story of the Little Mole Who Knew It Was None of His Business* by Werner Holzwarth

Games and activities

- **Play 'schools'**
Your child will now be excited about the thought of starting school and will love any games associated with a typical school day. This will be good practice for when they have to do the real activities. Try some of these:

  o Make a register of family members, and let your child take the register every morning.
  o Play show-and-tell. Take turns to bring an object to the table at the end of a meal and tell the rest of the family about it. Encourage everyone to ask questions.
  o Play getting changed for PE. Make sure you have plenty of time, as your child may struggle with some things such as buttons or zips at first. Once they are changed, let them stay in their PE clothes to go outside for a while and then get changed back again when they come in.
  o Take turns being the teacher and reading a story. Use teddies, dolls, etc. to make extra classmates. Playing the role of the teacher can help your child feel better about starting school and it gives them the opportunity to practise their narrative skills.
  o Have a school lunch, by putting their lunch in a lunchbox or on a tray, and then see how well your child manages.
  o Put your child's name on their bedroom door or where they hang their

coat. Although they won't need to recognise their own name straight away, it will be something they are expected to do soon after starting school.

o Encourage your child to persevere with activities that they find difficult and to try to work out different ways to approach them. However, you should let them know that they can always ask for help if they need it.

o Make a few trips to school at the beginning and end of the school day, so that your child can watch how the other children behave. Talk about what you see and hear: the bell ringing, the children lining up, the teacher coming out to collect her class, parents waving goodbye, etc. Talk about how the children might be feeling to encourage your child to bring up any worries.

- **Shapes**

o Put some pieces of paper on the floor, each with a shape drawn on it. Ask your child to look around the house to see how many things of each shape they can find, then put them on the piece of paper and work out how many of each shape they have found.

o Using chalk, draw some shapes on an outside wall. Give your child a ball or beanbag and see if they can hit the right shape when you shout it out.

- **Numbers/counting**

o Any game using a dice is useful at first, as your child will only need to count to six.

o Write the numbers one to five on paper bags or cardboard boxes. Ask your child to look around the house to find things with each number on, and then put them in the right bag or box. It may be a puzzle piece with a number on, a shoe of that size or a book with a number in the title.

o Hopscotch is good for recognising numbers and counting.

o Play bingo, but only use low numbers that your child can recognise.

- **Letters/sounds**
When introducing phonics (letters and their corresponding sounds) to your child, remember to check that they are developmentally ready to produce those sounds before you expect them to be able to say them. If they struggle to say particular sounds accurately, remember just to provide a good model of the sound, rather than correcting them (see the *Sound Wheel* on page 223).

o Give your child a bag and a piece of paper with a letter written on it. Ask them to look around the house to find anything with that letter on, e.g. a book, a tube of toothpaste or a packet of crisps. You simply want them to match the letters at first.

o As they become more confident with letters and sounds, you can tell them a sound and ask them to find things starting with that sound.

o Look at books together and see if your child can find particular letters. Have some plastic letters that they can hold and refer to while they are looking.

o Match three-letter words. Write some three-letter words on pieces of paper or card, e.g. 'cat', 'man' or 'dog'. Give one to your child and then see if they can find the same word from a choice of three.

o Give your child a three-letter word plus the individual letters that make up the word. See if they can put the letters in the right order to make the word.

o Write each family member's name on some used envelopes and ask your child to sort and deliver the 'post'.

- **Writing**

o If your child doesn't enjoy doing writing activities on paper, let them draw with other things. Try letting them use their finger to draw lines and shapes in shaving foam, body lotion or bath crayons on the wall tiles at bath time; use chalk to draw outside and then use a spray bottle of water to clean it off; or roll out some PlayDoh and use their fingers or utensils to mark lines or shapes.

o   Draw some letters with chalk on the path outside, then let your child use a paintbrush and water to paint over them and make them disappear. This will help them understand how letters are formed.

o   Make dot-to-dots of letters or numbers. Joining the numbers in the right order will help your child see how to write the letters and numbers in the correct way.

- **Memory**

  Use the memory games from the last chapter (see page 122) but increase the number of things you ask your child to remember.

- **Craft**

  Your child's ability to manipulate creative materials will be much more coordinated by this age, and they will enjoy drawing, painting, cutting, sticking, and using kitchen rubbish (such as boxes, yoghurt pots and tubes) to make imaginative constructions such as robots or castles.

  Continue the craft activities from the last chapter, but try to extend these to include other skills:

  o   Draw a large letter on a piece of paper and ask your child to decorate it to look like something that starts with that letter, e.g. make a B look like a butterfly, an S look like a snake or a T look like a tree.

  o   Draw around some objects using dots. Ask your child to join the dots and then find the object that matches what they have drawn.

  o   Write your child's name on a large piece of paper and let them decorate it with stickers, glitter, etc. to turn it into a piece of art.

  o   Paint some tubes of dried pasta, such as penne. Once they are dry, let your child thread them onto string or a shoelace to make jewellery.

- **Miniature play**

  Miniature toys allow your child to extend their pretend play. You will find that they will play with their favourite toy farm, house or garage for long periods of time. They can make up much more elaborate storylines with miniature toys, as they are usually much more detailed.

- **Dressing up**

  As well as acting out familiar experiences, your child will start to use their imagination a lot more and make up stories beyond their own experiences, with fairy-tale characters, spacemen, explorers, etc. Simple props and dressing-up clothes can help to spark your child's imagination, and you may find that they want to stay in character all day long and may even insist that you use their character's name and not their own! Talking about what their character has been doing at the end of the day is a good way to practise narrative skills.

- **Construction**

  Your child's fine motor skills will now allow them to create more elaborate structures with smaller bricks, such as Lego, and instead of just being a simple building task, this will become one of the ways that they express their imagination. This will mean that they use their language skills a lot more too, by talking to themself as they build, creating a story around the structure that they are building.

- **Jigsaw puzzles**

  Your child will be able to complete simple jigsaw puzzles now. Some children love them and will spend a long time doing one after another, but other children have little interest in them, so it is worth trying one or two first to avoid wasting money. These are good for fine motor skills and vocabulary.

- **Card Games**
  Simple card games such as snap, pairs games or picture lotto will appeal to your child now. Because these involve an element of chance rather than just skill, it means your child will genuinely be able to win, which is always a confidence boost! There are lots of games available to buy, which are usually based on a theme such as animals, foods, etc., so choose ones that your child will be interested in or that includes vocabulary you want to focus on.

- **Board games**
  Start with simple games such as snakes and ladders and ludo. There are lots of others available, which are based on different themes that may appeal to your child. Make sure you check the age level on the box, as it is very frustrating for a child to find a game that they are excited about only to find that the rules are beyond their level of understanding. There are many printable versions available, or you can make your own. These are good for practising turn taking and learning to follow the rules of a game.

- **Memory box / scrapbook**
  Create a memory box or scrapbook of things that you have collected with your child, such as a plane or train ticket from a holiday, a leaflet from a visit to a farm or zoo, or shells from the seaside. Look at them together from time to time and talk about your memories. If they can't remember the actual event, encourage them to make up a story about the items.

Chapter 7

4-5 Years

Your child will start school at some point in the next year, and you will be hoping that everything you have done with them over the past four years has given them the best chance of thriving in the classroom. You may already have a little chatterbox, but there are still things that you can do before and after your child's first day at school, so that they can make the most of every learning opportunity that comes their way. Believe me, the time will fly by, and there will be times where you are too busy or too tired, or when you feel that you no longer have a role to play in your child's learning journey. Even if you have given them the best possible start over the past four years, you still have a huge part to play in their achievements throughout the rest of their school life.

Here are some more statistics from the Department of Education (for the years 2017–2018) that show just how important it is for children to start school with good speech and language skills, and how the effects of poor skills can follow a child throughout their time at school:

- For those children identified as having SLCNs, only 28% reach the expected levels of progress at the end of reception, compared to 72% of all pupils.
- Just 15% of pupils with identified SLCNs achieved the expected standard in reading, writing and mathematics at the end of their primary school years, compared with 61% of all pupils.

- Only 15% of children with SLCNs achieved five GCSEs at grades A*–C, compared with 57% of all pupils.

It is worth looking back at the previous chapter to check whether there are any obvious gaps that need filling before you carry on with the suggestions in this chapter. Keep the communication pyramid in mind. It is essential that your child's skills are solid at each level, and those at the bottom of the pyramid will have a bigger impact on their ability to learn and make friends than those at the top. A child with a minor speech problem will find it easier to learn to read and to make friends than a child with poor listening or turn-taking skills.

If you feel that your child's skills are where they should be, there are still many things that you can do to help prepare them for school:

- Keep to a good routine. Once your child is at school, it is important that they can cope with a strict routine of getting up early enough to have time to get ready, eating a good breakfast to set them up for the day and going to bed early to make sure they are getting enough sleep. Try to introduce this routine as soon as possible if you haven't already.
- Practise some practical things that your child will need to know how to do, e.g. getting undressed and dressed again for PE, tidying up toys when they have finished playing, and putting their hand up when they want to speak. You could try this one at mealtimes and encourage the whole family to join in!
- Play 'schools' whenever your child asks, and have circle time, work time (when they draw or practise writing skills), play time (when they go outside), PE, lunch time, art and craft, story time, etc. If your child has friends round to play with, take the chance to do this with them all to make it feel more realistic. They will all then have the opportunity to practise waiting for their turn at lunch time, listening in a group, cooperating when doing craft, etc.
- Help your child's phonological awareness. Phonological awareness is a child's ability to pay attention to, identify and manipulate sounds in words. As well as being important for speech, it is a very important pre-reading skill. It includes the following elements:
  o Rhymes (e.g. 'cat', 'hat', 'mat' and 'sat')
  o Stress patterns in words (e.g. the stress is placed on the first syllable of 'water' and on the second syllable of 'begin')
  o Syllables or 'beats' (e.g. 'elephant' has three syllables: 'el-e-phant')
  o How words can be broken down or segmented into individual sounds

(e.g. 'dog' ['d-o-g'] is not the same word as 'dot' ['d-o-t'])

o   How individual sounds can be put together or 'blended' to make words (e.g. d + o + g = dog, a four-legged canine.)

This is not the same as trying to teach your child to read. You can have fun with activities that will make learning to read easier for them without having reading as an implicit goal. Even after your child has started school, it is still useful to continue with these activities. If you are unsure about any of the activities, check with your child's teacher.

If you decide to progress to phonics (letters and their corresponding sounds) with your child, remember to check that they are developmentally ready to produce those sounds before you expect them to recognise and read them (see the *Sound Wheel* on page 223). I have included specific activities for phonological awareness in *Chatterbox time* at the end of the chapter (*page 186*).

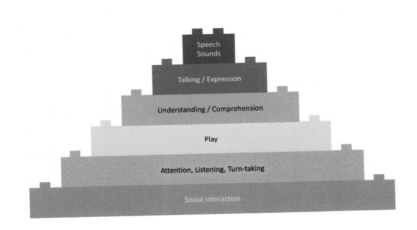

Social Interaction

Your child will now feel comfortable in most social situations. It is important that they have as many different social experiences as possible before starting school, especially if they don't routinely attend nursery or playgroup, so take up any opportunities for playdates, parties, trips to soft-play centres, etc. In new situations, they will still be guided by your response, so show that you are positive in a new situation and keen to have fun.

They will enjoy the company of other children and will make lots of new friends when they start school. They may have one or two special friends that they particularly like, but they should be encouraged to keep a wide circle of friends. Your child's friends will now be more than just someone to play with: they will also influence your child's thoughts and behaviour. Behaving like their friend to try to impress them is normal, but it may not always be in a positive way, and you may find that they are cheeky or rude, and they may answer back for the first time. It is important to discuss unacceptable behaviour with your child as soon as it starts and explain that there are things that their friends do to make them laugh, but that they are not acceptable to you. School is a whole new world for your child; it may seem scary at times and having consistent routines and discipline at home will help your child to feel safe.

Your child will now understand more about the feelings and needs of other people, and they will play more cooperatively, but may occasionally seem bossy or get upset if their wishes are not considered.

Toilet humour will still be popular with your child, and they will often resort to this to make their friends laugh. You will need to have clear boundaries in terms of the people and situations where this is acceptable but remember that it is a normal stage and your child will seek out someone to share it with, often Dad or Grandad!

Attention, Listening and Turn-Taking

One of the biggest challenges that your child will face when they start school is the increased demands made on their attention and listening skills. This is the area where spending some extra time in the pre-school years will have huge benefits for them once they are at school. They are expected to filter out all of the new distractions around them, to shift their attention at short notice within a group situation, to listen to longer and more complex instructions, and to pay attention for far longer than has ever been expected of them.

Your child's attention will now be more flexible and dual-channelled, which means they can listen to what is being said without having to stop what they are doing or look at the speaker. Now that they can shift their attention on their own, you can start to increase the complexity of the language that you use. However, remember that, at first, they can still only pay attention to more than one thing at a time for a short period, so if they aren't looking at you or responding, they probably aren't listening. You don't need to help them shift their attention any more, but wait until you know they are listening before asking questions or giving instructions.

Your child's attention span is still relatively short, but they should now be able to focus on one activity on their own for at least 10 minutes, and even longer when you play with them. Gradually increase the length of time you expect your child to concentrate for. If they start to get distracted, you may need to be more animated in your responses to help hold their attention.

Your child's turn-taking skills will be a lot more mature now, both in play and in conversations. Once they start school, they will be expected to take turns in group situations as well as in pairs. All the simple turn-taking activities you have done with them since they were a baby will have paid off, and this skill will engender huge benefits for them at school, both socially and academically.

Play

Imaginative play will now form a large part of your child's playtime. Being with other children most of the time opens up a whole new world of play opportunities. Your child will expand on the themes that they have been exploring by adding more detail in terms of the storyline, props and language that they use. They will still use a lot of imagination, but now understand the difference between reality and fantasy, e.g. when playing 'doctors' and bandaging a broken arm, they may reassure someone watching by saying, 'She hasn't really broken her arm!'

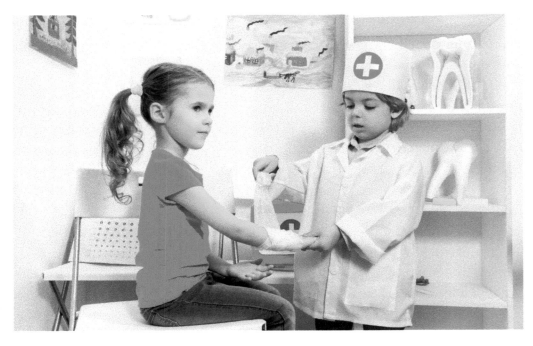

A child's ability to use their imagination is an important cognitive skill, and it shouldn't be underestimated. It allows a child to think creatively, plan, problem-solve and understand other people's points of view: they have to use language to think about what game to play, negotiate what role each person will have, consider the rules of the game, think about what toys or props are needed, and work out solutions when something doesn't go to plan. All of these are important skills for life.

You might find that your child's play becomes more physical and action-packed now, especially for boys. They will act out roles of good guys and bad guys, chase each other, play-fight, and safely work through negative feelings such as frustration and anger. Girls tend to act out these feelings in a more subtle way, using language more than rough and tumble, but this is just as important, as it is a rehearsal of how to behave when they experience these feelings for real. It is good to encourage this form of play and to avoid stepping in unless someone is genuinely hurt or upset. Children will slowly learn what behaviour is acceptable and develop better self-regulation as a result.

By introducing props with words or numbers – such as home-made shop signs, menus, a till, coins or train tickets – you will help your child's literacy and numeracy skills while they are playing. They will naturally want to use these as an extension to their play, and it is an easy way to encourage learning without your child even being aware that is what they are doing! If you want to encourage exploring other subjects, try making a cardboard telescope for them to look at the stars, use a magnifying glass for looking at bugs, or bake some 'dinosaur bones' from dough and hide them in a sandpit or in the garden for your little archaeologist to find!

Once your child is at school, they will have a lot more opportunities for physical and creative play, and they will often come home and want to continue these with you. You won't need to think of many new ideas for play, but you will need to have materials available.

Understanding

Your child will now be able to follow long and complex instructions that are given to them in a group. They will be expected to carry out instructions in a particular order: 'First… Next… And then…'

They will understand detailed responses to the questions that they ask, including words such as 'because', 'otherwise' and 'instead of'.

They can now follow stories without pictures, and they can answer questions about events and characters, remembering a lot more detail and using it in their responses. They can simply tell the story back to you, recalling the main events in the right order. Encourage them to do this with events in their own life: give them time after school each day to tell you what they have done. Check whether the events are in the right order and how many details they have remembered.

They should now be able to make some inferences, where they will combine information from the language that they hear with knowledge that they already have to come to a new conclusion. [161] This can also be thought of as reading between the lines or making an educated guess. They need to look for clues in the information they have, to work things out that are not stated outright.

Inferencing

Inferencing is a critical skill for understanding what we read. Authors only provide us with a certain amount of information about characters and events, and they leave us to infer the rest. There is a strong association between a child's ability to make inferences and their understanding of stories. [162] [163] This, in turn, predicts later reading ability. [164] [165]

It is not only literacy that is affected by a child's ability to make inferences. Reading comprehension is a fundamental prerequisite of children's success in school, not only in literacy but as a means of accessing the rest of the curriculum, including maths and science. [166] It therefore makes sense to encourage your child to try to make inferences as early as possible. I have given some examples in the following *Books and stories* and *Games and activities* sections (see pages 187 and 188).

Expressive Language

By now, your child will have mastered the fundamentals of language: they will have a very large vocabulary and will learn new words at school almost every day; they will use all the basic sentence types, both simple and complex; and they will only make occasional grammatical mistakes, usually with structures that are exceptions to the rules.

They will regularly use language to do all the things that they need it for. They give information; ask and answer questions; make requests and suggestions; offer, state and express their own ideas and opinions and enjoy long discussions about anything and everything!

They can retell stories in a logical order and sequence their own ideas in a way that makes sense. They will use words such as 'and', 'but', 'then', 'because', 'so' and 'while' to express things such as these:

- A sequence of events, e.g. saying, 'We went in the hall, and then we sang some songs, and then we went outside, and then we had our lunch.'
- Cause and effect, e.g. explaining, 'I gave Jack my apple *because* he was very hungry,' or, 'It was cold outside, so we put our coats on.'
- A contrast, e.g. 'Miss said it was raining, *but* it wasn't,' or, 'I like cheese, *but* he doesn't.'

The journey home from school or when sharing an after-school snack is an ideal opportunity to allow them to use these skills to tell you about their day while the events are fresh in their mind. At mealtimes, you may notice the improvement in their conversational skills: they will be better at waiting for their turn and listening to what other people are saying. However, some children who are quiet and shy at school may have so much to say when they get home that they can monopolise family conversations!

You may not notice much change in the length of your child's sentences or a noticeable increase in their vocabulary, but they will use their language skills in new ways. You may hear them being very polite, the way they may talk to their headteacher, or using slang expressions or even swear words that they have learned in the playground. You may need to explain what is and isn't acceptable for them to say at home!

Speech Sounds

Your child's speech will now be almost fully mature. They may still have difficulty with a few sounds, notably 'r', 'th', and clusters of three sounds such as 'spr' and 'scr', which may not be clear for another year or more. You should be able to understand what they are saying almost all the time.

Most of the immature features of their speech will have disappeared, and their use of sounds will be a lot more consistent. You may even notice that they are able to correct themself when they make a mistake with their sounds.

Summary

The skills expected by five years of age are summarised as follows.

Understanding

- Your child can follow simple stories without pictures.
- They understand nearly everything that is said to them at home.
- They understand a sequence of instructions, e.g. 'First… Next… And then…'
- They understand more concepts such as 'first'/'last', 'above'/'below', 'light'/'heavy', 'front'/'back', 'near'/'far', and 'first', 'second' and 'third'.
- They understand comparative and superlative, such as 'big', 'bigger' and 'biggest'; and 'tall', 'taller' and 'tallest'.
- They ask when they don't understand what a word means.

Expressive language

- They use long, complex and complete sentences with only occasional grammatical errors.
- They use lots of descriptive words, e.g. 'wet'/'dry' and 'hard'/'soft'.
- They tell stories with the events in the correct sequence.
- They tell stories using the past, present and future tenses.
- They use language to solve problems, thinking them through out loud.
- They use language to negotiate and agree the rules of games.
- They are skilled at taking turns in long, complicated conversations, and are less likely to interrupt or change the subject when someone else is talking.

- They can share their feelings and opinions.
- They can make up stories from their imagination.

Speech sounds

- They are easily understood.
- They use most sounds, apart from 'r', 'th', and clusters of three consonants (e.g. 'spr' and 'scr'), which may not be clear until age seven.

Red flags

If any of the following are true for your child at five years old, you should consider seeking the advice of your health visitor, GP, or local speech and language therapist:

- They can't follow an instruction or answer a question while focusing on an activity.
- They can't follow a sequence of instructions in the right order.
- They can't answer questions about a story they have heard.
- They make lots of grammatical mistakes.
- They can't organise their thoughts to retell a story or recount an event.
- They are non-fluent and struggle to get their words out.
- They make mistakes with a few particular sounds.
- They can be difficult to understand at times.

Chatterbox Ideas

All the time

Looking/attention skills

Observation is recognised as an important skill in early years and primary science. [167] When they explore, children observe using their senses; by noticing details by sorting, grouping and classifying objects, or by sequencing events. [168]

You can help your child to develop their skills of observation by doing the following:

- Encouraging them to use all their senses. Observation in young children is tactile and involves the senses of touch and hearing as much as sight. [168]
- Helping them to look for details.
- Helping them to look for similarities that will help them to sort things into groups or categories.
- Encouraging your child to draw their observations: the sketching of details has been found to improve observational skills by facilitating the focusing on important features that a child then remembers. [169]
- Helping them to maintain their focus. While young children can make very sophisticated and detailed observations, they can get distracted easily and may need support to refocus. [170] As children mature, they begin to engage in more close observation and for longer periods of time. [168]
- Encouraging your child to use their observational skills when playing with friends. One of the most important factors supporting the development of observational skills appears to be social interaction. [171] Interaction with others seems to challenge children, and also leads to new ideas and more scientific thinking. [172]

Listening

- Model good listening when your child tries to talk to you, and you are busy. If you can, pause what you are doing, look at them, show interest and wait for your turn to speak. If you often just ignore them and carry on with your task, it will take them longer to learn how to be a good listener.
- Gradually increase the length of time you expect your child to concentrate for. If they start to get distracted, you may need to be more animated in your responses or use gestures to help hold their attention.
- When you give your child a longer instruction, try to break it down into smaller parts, and give them enough time to process it. If they don't respond straight away, they are probably trying to work out what you have said and how they are expected to respond. The more distractions there are around them, the longer it may take for them to respond.
- Turn-taking activities are a good thing to use to extend a child's attention span and to improve their ability to keep shifting their attention from one thing to another and back again. Once your child has good attention and listening skills, help them to learn to wait a little longer by looking at them to show that

you are listening and then pause before you respond. When children start school, they spend a lot of time waiting for their turn with a teacher, and it is useful if they have some practice first.

- If you have something important to say to your child, say their name and tell them it is time to listen. In the classroom, each teacher has a strategy for letting the class know that it is time to stop and listen, and it is useful to start doing this at home.

- Make sure your child's activities are age-appropriate. Your child's attention won't last very long if an activity is much too easy or too difficult for them, and they will either get bored or just give up.

- Have lots of activities with an obvious end to them. Your child is more likely to keep going with a puzzle where they can see that they will have completed it in a few more pieces, or a book with only a couple of pages to get to the end, than an activity that seems like it might go on indefinitely. The success of simply finishing will also boost your child's confidence.

- As discussed in the section on *TV/Screen Time* (page 197), screens can have a negative effect on attention span. Probably the worst time to ask a child to do an activity requiring good attention is following a long period of screen time.

- Don't expect your four-year-old to sit still for long periods of time. They will need lots of movement breaks, and these will benefit their concentration.

- If you want your child to stop a favourite activity, make sure it is to move on to something else that they might enjoy, such as a meal or bath time. You will struggle to persuade them to put away their favourite toys to go shopping! Teachers often time free-play activities just before break, lunch or home time.

- Having a good daily routine will help your child to predict how long activities may last, and it will help them settle more quickly into each one. If a child thinks they may have all day to play, they may spend a long time wandering around their toys and deciding what to do. However, if they know that they have an hour to play, they are likely to focus their attention more quickly, knowing that there is an end to the time they have available.

- Be aware of how your child learns best and use this to boost their attention when needed. Some children are visual learners, others need things to be explained, but most learn best by having a go. If your child is struggling to focus on an activity, especially if they are simply expected to watch or listen, think of ways you can make it more interactive for them: 'Tell me and I forget, teach me and I may remember, involve me and I learn.' [173]

Sounds and talking

Your child will develop some awareness of immaturities or 'mistakes' in their speech, and it is important not to draw attention to these. Show them that it is what they have to say that is important, not how they say it. Praise them when they explain something well or tell you a story about something that has happened to them; notice when they use vocabulary that you have never heard before, e.g. say, 'That's a good word. Where did you learn that? Can you tell me what it means?'

When talking or reading to your child, try making a few deliberate mistakes to show them that we all get things wrong from time to time. If they notice and point out your mistake, you can ask them if it matters and whether you need to try again. If they don't notice, just carry on.

Chatterbox time

Music, songs and rhymes

- **Syllable recognition and syllable blending**
  It might be easier to use the word 'claps' or 'taps' when introducing syllables to your child, e.g. asking, 'How many claps are in it?'

  You need to model syllables first for your child to begin to understand how you are breaking up words:

  o   Try clapping out people's names, e.g. 'Char-lotte'.
  o   Tap out the number of syllables in objects around you, e.g. 'pen', 'pen-cil' or 'mic-ro-wave'.
  o   Point out items in books/catalogues and identify the syllables e.g. 'aer-o-plane' or 'sun-shine'.

  When your child is ready to start identifying the syllables themselves you could try:

  o   Sorting pictures into separate piles according to the number of syllables (one, two, three or four).

- Saying 'one', 'two', 'three' or 'four', and ask your child to find a picture of something with that number of syllables.
- Using a large-sized picture (e.g. an elephant), ask your child how many syllables the name of the thing in the picture has, then let them cut the picture into that number of pieces.
- Your child will become more aware of how syllables blend together if you repeat the whole word back after they have identified the syllables.
- For another blending task, you can say a word with two or three syllables, leaving big gaps between them, then your child should say the word, e.g. 'cow... boy' = 'cowboy'.

- **Tongue twisters**

  At this age, children love to have a go at tongue twisters, such as these:

  - 'Peter Piper'
  - 'She Sells Seashells'
  - 'Red Lorry, Yellow Lorry'

  Most of the fun of these is from getting them wrong! Adults find them just as difficult as children, and it's good for your child to know that we all make mistakes sometimes when we speak.

Books and stories

Your child should now be happy to sit and 'read' familiar books on their own. Encourage them to tell you the stories. With less familiar books, you can read them first and then ask them to tell you what happened.

Introduce some non-fiction books about your child's favourite subjects, whether it's space, trains, dinosaurs, nature, etc.

Continue reading bedtime stories but try to use some books without pictures so that they get used to just listening.

When reading to your child during the day, try to give them opportunities to make inferences. Ask them questions about how characters might be feeling, what they think they are doing, where they are, etc.

The *Where's Wally?* books are good for developing observation skills and can keep a child happy on a long car journey.

You can include some fantasy books now, as your child will understand the difference between fantasy and reality.

If you are not always able to read to your child, try audiobooks. Most popular authors have audio versions of their books, e.g. David Walliams, Julia Donaldson, Cressida Cowell, and classics such as C.S. Lewis, Roald Dahl and Enid Blyton. It is better for your child to listen to an audiobook as they fall asleep rather than watch TV or look at a Kindle or tablet. Some examples include:

- *James Herriot's Treasury for Children* by James Herriot
- *How to Train Your Dragon* by Cressida Cowell
- *Topsy and Tim Start School* by Jean Adamson

Games and activities

- **I spy**
  As well as being good for phonological awareness, this is a good game to play to improve observation skills. As well as using sounds, you can say, 'I spy with my little eye, something…' followed by one of these examples:

  o 'blue', 'red', 'yellow', etc.
  o 'round', 'square', 'triangular', etc.
  o 'that says "woof"/"moo"/"baa"'
  o 'that you can eat'
  o 'that flies in the sky.'

- **Car journey clues**
  This is a variation of I spy. Give your child some verbal clues while you are driving, which will help develop their inferencing skills. See if they can link the pieces of information together and spot the answer. Here's an example:

  o This thing has wheels, but no engine.
  o You can eat and sleep in it.
  o People stay here on holiday.
  o Answer = A caravan.

Then, ask your child to have a turn giving you clues.

- **Surveys**

  These are particularly useful on a long car journey. Give your child a clipboard with a page each of pictures of animals, vehicles, buildings, colours, etc. Each time your child sees one of the items on a list, they will put a tick next to the picture. When you arrive at your destination, you can help them to add up the ticks and work out which animal, vehicle, building, colour, etc. they saw the most of.

  This is good for improving observation skills and working on vocabulary and categories.

- **Number and letter recognition**

  These are a couple of ideas for helping with number and letter recognition:

  o When you are at the shops or in the car, give your child a number or letter to spot. They can carry a plastic letter or number with them so that they can put it next to the one they have spotted to show that they match.

  o Use chalk to draw some numbers and letters on a wall or path outside. Give your child a ball or bean bag and ask them to aim for a particular number or letter. Then give them a spray bottle full of water and ask them to clean off all the number fives, all the S's, etc. If your child recognises all letters of the alphabet, write some easy three-letter words (e.g. 'cat') several times around the garden, and ask them to spray away all the cats!

- **Word matching**
  Write a three-letter word on a piece of paper and give it to your child. Ask them to go around the house and see if they can find that word written anywhere, e.g. 'dog', which they might find on the cover of a book, a tin of dog food, dog shampoo or the dog's water bowl, or 'hot', which they might find on a tin of hot dogs, a packet of hot chocolate or a tap. Leave a few where your child will find them easily.

- **Playing 'post office'**
  Save old letters and birthday cards with each member of your family's names on, including the envelopes. Play 'post office' with these, putting letters inside the envelopes, using stickers as stamps, and getting your child to look at the names and sort them into piles to deliver to the right people. Give them a bag to be the postman and get them to give the 'post' to the right people in the family. They may need help with some of the names, but they should recognise their own.

- **Rhyming**
  Use a selection of objects or pictures of things that rhyme or look for ready-made, age-appropriate rhyming games. Play lots of games with these and point out to your child when you find words that rhyme. Once your child has begun to recognise rhyming words themself, then you can move on to activities where they must decide if words rhyme or not.

  Remember to always sit facing your child so that they can see your face and hear you well, and make sure you have their full attention before saying the words.

  Have a bag or box containing the items, the names of some of which rhyme with others. Ask your child to pull two things out and say the words; then ask them if they rhyme or not, e.g. ask, 'These say "dog" and "frog"; do they rhyme?'

  If they say, 'Yes,' and so get it right, give them lots of praise and repeat the words, to confirm that "dog" and "frog" do rhyme.

  If they get it wrong, say the words again, putting emphasis on the rhyming section, e.g. say, 'Listen again. Dog. Frog. Do they rhyme?'

  You can also do this with pictures of the items. There are many pairs games available that have rhyming words, or you can print off your own. Simply put the pictures face down and take turns to turn a pair over and see if they rhyme.

- **Alliteration/words that start with the same sound**

  Your child will need to have some letter-sound awareness to play alliteration activities. Make sure that they know what individual sounds look and sound like. Only use sounds that your child can already use in their speech. Try some of these:

  o Play 'pairs': put a selection of pictures face down on the table, take turns to turn over two at a time and find ones that start with the same sound.

  o Write down the names of items around the house that start with the same sound, e.g. 'bed', 'bath' and 'bowl'. Choose one word, say it, point out the sound at the beginning, and then go around the house trying to find another thing that starts with the same sound. If they aren't sure, use another written word to prompt them. See how many things you can find that start with that sound.

  o Play odd-one-out games, explaining that you are going to be listening to the sound at the beginning of the words, e.g. show your child three pictures – such as for 'boy', 'bear' and 'cup' – and ask which word is the odd one out.

  o Play the game 'I went to the shop and I bought…' but only thinking of words that start with one sound, e.g. 'bin', 'bed' and 'box'.

  o Put a selection of written letters in a box, take turns to pull one out, then say as many words as you can think of starting with that letter.

  o Give your child a shopping list of different sounds. Ask them to go around the house and find one item that starts with each of the sounds. Let them tick the sounds off the list as they go.

- **Story sequencing**

  Encourage play that promotes story sequencing. If your child crashes two cars together, you could say, 'Oh, oh, I think I can hear a police car coming. I wonder what the policeman will say. And here comes an ambulance. What will happen next?' Then, when your child has finished playing, ask them to tell you the story of what happened.

- **Inferencing clues/riddles**

  Let your child be a detective and hide some clues for them to find. Read the clues to them and see if they can link them together to solve the riddle:

  o 'I am round. I bounce. You can kick me. What am I?' (Answer = a football) o   'I am sitting at the table. I have a plate of food. I am using a knife and fork. What am I doing?' (Answer = eating)

o   'I am wearing wellies. I have an umbrella. The ground is wet. What is the weather like?' (Answer = raining)

o   'Yesterday, I was four. Today, I am five. I have a cake with candles on. What special day is it?' (Answer = birthday)

- **Fantasy play**
  Fantasy play is well established by now, with your child making up great adventures. They may want to pretend to be an explorer, a pirate or a superhero, but they will love it even more if you join in with them. You won't need toys at all, just a great imagination! All children like to use cushions on the floor as stepping stones across 'hot lava', to build dens with blankets, etc.

Chapter 8
Across All Age Groups

Music

Using music and songs with babies and young children is something that parents have done for generations. As well as being a relaxing, enjoyable experience that provides important bonding time, there are other significant benefits to be gained from sharing music with your child. Many of these have been the subject of increasing amounts of research in recent years.

The benefits of music

- Young babies listen to their mothers for longer when they sing than when they just speak. [174] [175] [176] The longer your baby listens to you, the more they will learn.

- Listening to music promotes the listening and discrimination skills required for speech and language development. Just as physical exercise tones the body, it is suggested that listening to music 'tones the brain for auditory fitness'. [177] Listening to music can improve auditory attention, discrimination and memory. [178]

- The ability to move to a beat has been linked to language development. [179] [180]

  Rhythm is an integral part of both music and language. The ability to keep a beat is fundamental for the understanding and production of language as well as for music. [181]

- Regular exposure to music enhances speech and language processing.

  Language skills and musical ability have long been known to be closely connected. Increasing amounts of research reveal that the areas of the brain responsible for processing speech and language and for music overlap. [182] Because of this overlap, any stimulation of one area will have a beneficial effect on the other. Music can be a useful way to reinforce the brain connections necessary for speech and language development. [183]

- Before birth, babies can hear the more musical features of speech.

  Features of speech such as pitch, rhythm and low-frequency vowels are able reach the ears of babies before birth. [184] Once they are born, babies are then able to recognise these features, not only in the voice of their mothers, [88] but also in familiar pieces of music. [185] This is one of the reasons why, for generations, mothers have soothed their babies by singing lullabies or using pieces of music that they relaxed to during their pregnancy. [186]

- Babies are thought to perceive sounds and words as a form of music.

  For the first few months of their lives, babies respond to the intonation patterns, melody and rhythm of the speech they hear. Before they can understand the individual words and sounds, they seem to perceive speech as a form of 'vocal performance'. [187] This seems to be why we naturally use sing-song intonation patterns when we talk to babies. Baby talk (motherese/parentese/child-directed speech) is found in almost all languages [49] and has the musical features that infants respond to best. Because babies respond to these musical features, it makes sense to use music as often as possible to communicate with our children.

- Using rhymes and music with preschool children can help to improve their pre-reading skills. This has been demonstrated in the following examples:
    - o Music training, particularly rhythm, can improve the phonological-awareness skills necessary for learning to read. [188]
    - o The ability to tap to a beat is linked to reading ability and can be strengthened by musical training. [189]
    - o Children who are good at spelling are found to be good at tapping out rhythms. [188]
    - o Having an awareness of pitch changes in music is related to improved performance in pre-reading tests. [190] [191]
- Music aids memory.

Babies and young children have been shown to have improved memory when events are linked to a piece of music. [192] We all remember songs from our childhood that were used to help us learn the alphabet, counting, colours, etc. It can be useful to use rhymes and music to help children remember vocabulary, numbers, concepts, etc.

- Music and maths are closely connected.

The link between maths and music has been of interest for hundreds of years, as far back as Pythagoras. The fact that children with musical ability tend to also be good at maths has long been accepted. [193] Considering that musical rhythm is based on mathematical relationships, we can assume that an understanding of music requires some understanding of ratios and repeating patterns. [194] A knowledge of music can help children to understand mathematical principles, such as spatial reasoning, sequencing, predicting patterns, counting and problem-solving. [194] [195] Almost every piece of music has a pattern or sequence built into its melody or lyrics; learning to anticipate patterns and place objects or events in sequence helps to build critical early maths and reading skills.

Sharing music with young children is something parents tend to do naturally, simply because it's fun. In each chapter, I have suggested specific activities involving music that you can do with your child. In the following list, I have made some general suggestions for all ages.

How you can include music in your child's day

- Don't play music all the time! You may think the more music your child hears, the better. In fact, if music is playing constantly throughout the day, it becomes a background noise that your child must try to ignore to focus on what they are doing or what people are saying. Give your child plenty of quiet time throughout the day and include music at specific times when they can give it their total attention.
- Sit quietly and listen to a piece of music together. This may seem overly simple, but having some quiet time with your child while listening to a piece of relaxing music provides a valuable bonding opportunity and will be relaxing for both of you. If you use the same piece of music each time, your child will quickly learn to associate it with being calm and relaxed, and you may find that it can then help at times when they are particularly unsettled.
- Sing to your child. This can be a useful way to calm and settle them before a nap. Children love to hear their own name or the names of familiar people in a song, so make up your own. My four children all loved a song that I used to sing to the tune of 'I Hear Thunder', where I would include the names of everyone in the family and sing: 'Mummy loves you. Daddy loves you. / Yes, we do. Yes, we do,' etc. Before they could say many words, they would 'request' the song by cuing me in with the tune!
- Sing together. Your child won't mind what you sing, whether it's 'Baa, Baa, Black Sheep' or something by Beyonce! We all love a good sing-song, especially

children, and it will benefit them in a variety of ways, as explained previously.

- Provide your child with things that they can use as musical instruments. Toy instruments are good as they tend to be colourful and made for small hands. You can also use things from the kitchen, such as a pan and wooden spoon as a drum, a box of cereal as a shaker, or blowing across the top of a plastic bottle as a wind instrument! You can show your child what you would do, but then let them do their own thing. Try singing along to whatever 'music' they make!

- Dance with your child. Even young babies love to dance. Find a piece of music with a good beat and move your baby in time to it. The benefits of keeping to a beat are listed in the following point, and they may surprise you. Once your child is walking, you can also try marching to the beat of a song.

- Spend some time focusing specifically on keeping to a beat together. You can simply clap or use something that you can bang or shake. If your child is young, you may need to help them at first by holding their hands. Choose a simple piece of music or a nursery rhyme and tap out the beat together.

- Do any fun movement in time to music. As babies, my children loved sitting on my knee at the kitchen table, with me holding their arms and moving them as though they were playing the piano! Bouncing them on your knee in time to music and doing 'Row, Row, Row Your Boat' are other things you can try.

TV/Screen Time

Almost all parents let their preschool children watch TV or play on a tablet/phone, usually in the belief that they will learn something while they are watching. However, studies have demonstrated that not only do some children not benefit from watching TV, but it can have a negative effect on their language development, behaviour and IQ. [196]

As busy parents, we all have times when there is a job that must be done, when we are exhausted and need to sit down, or we are simply bored of reading the same story for the 10th time! TV seems like the ideal solution, and if it isn't overused, it will not do any harm. However, it is important to be aware of the negative impacts of introducing TV too early, allowing your child to watch TV programmes that are not age-appropriate or letting them watch too much TV.

The World Health Organisation's 2019 guidelines suggest that children under two years should not spend any time passively watching screens and that those aged two to five should spend no more than one hour a day doing so. [197] The Royal College of Paediatrics and Child Health states that there is insufficient evidence to provide such guidelines and that parents have to consider what limits are appropriate for their own family. [198]

Whether you agree with the guidelines or not, here's why it is generally recommended that screen time is limited for the under-fives:

- For children under three, watching more than two hours of TV per day is associated with language delay. The more time they spend watching TV, the greater the delay. [199]

   For children under two, watching even one hour of TV a day has a negative impact on their vocabulary development. [200]

   Children under 12 months old who watch TV are at six times the risk of language delay than those who don't. [201]
- Some studies identify a connection between the amount of TV a child watches between the ages of one and three, and their subsequent attention problems at age seven. [202]
- Children under the age of three can't watch something and listen at the same time; i.e. they have single-channelled attention. With TV and other screens, images and sounds are presented at the same time, so until a child is able to connect the two things, they cannot learn from what they are watching. [203] Studies have shown that children under three do not learn new vocabulary from screens. [204] It has also been revealed that they use fewer sounds and words while watching a TV show that has sound than one with just visual images. [205]

At around age three, children start to shift their attention from what they are looking at to whatever they need to listen to, but only with adult help. An adult must attract their attention, make sure they are listening, and then speak to them. This does not happen when a child watches TV or plays on a phone/tablet. They only begin to learn from screens once they have well-developed, flexible attention. Some studies suggest that a child's ability to acquire information from TV appears at age three, when they no longer need adult help to shift their attention from what they can see to what they can hear. [206]

- Children under the age of three learn best from simple activities, pictures and language. TV shows are usually packed with multiple images and sounds, and a young child will struggle to focus on the most important things and ignore the others. There is often a lot going on in the background, with images changing across the whole screen, and music or other sounds playing while characters are talking. It is then impossible for a child to filter out all the background noise and images in order to learn.

- The images and sounds on a TV screen are presented at a rate that is too fast for a young child to process. They can then quickly become over-stimulated because they haven't been given enough time to process one image or sound before another one appears. TV images with strong visual stimuli, such as those in adult programmes, can affect a child's cognitive skills. [207] [208]

When a child is playing and interacting with an adult, natural pauses occur in which the child has the chance to process what they are seeing and hearing, and then make a connection between the two. This is one of the reasons why children learn best through social interaction.

- Having the TV on in a room, even when no one appears to be watching, will reduce the overall number of conversations that go on within a family. Both children and adults will be distracted from time to time. If the programme is adult-focused, then it is likely to be more of a distraction to the adult than the child, but this will still have an impact on interaction. [209]

When a TV is left on, toddlers are much less likely to talk to themselves while they play; this has a negative impact because thinking out loud is an important stage in language development and cognition. [206] [210].

- Although it is better to watch TV with your child than let them watch alone, even when watching together, the quantity and quality of language used by parents decreases. [211] [212]

- All TV watching limits play opportunities and interaction between a child and an adult. [213] [201] Interaction with parents is a vital part of language development: [214] communication occurs when a speaker and listener exchange information through language. With TV, the exchange of information is one-way, so it does not give a child the opportunity to develop their communication skills. [215]

How to make the most of TV/screen time

- Not all TV is bad. Once your child has flexible attention, they will be able to get some benefit from certain TV shows, particularly if they watch them with you. Choose your child's viewing very carefully, especially if you are letting them watch alone. Think about starting with one of these:
    - o Shows that are based on characters from favourite books, e.g. *Kipper, Spot, Winnie the Pooh, Charlie and Lola*.
    - o Shows that have simple imagery, e.g. *Peppa Pig*.
    - o Shows that are based on music and movement or rhymes, e.g. *The Baby Club*.
- When you are watching TV with your child, it is helpful if you can pause it now and again to give them some processing time and the opportunity to talk to you about what they are watching, e.g. to ask the meaning of a word they have never heard before. If you are not with them, the word may be repeated many times without the meaning being made clear, and your child will have missed a valuable learning opportunity.

- Always make sure that the programmes for your child are age-appropriate. This may seem obvious, but it is not always easy to achieve if you have more than one child. It is often the older child who gets their way when choosing what to watch, and although their younger sibling may be entertained by a show made for older children, they will not learn as much from it.

- Between the ages of three and five, children have been found to benefit from watching high-quality, age-appropriate TV programmes. The areas that show improvement include attention, comprehension and vocabulary. A lot of research and planning goes into the production of TV shows for preschool children on channels such as CBeebies. These programmes tend to have a smaller number of visual and auditory stimuli at any one time, a balance between new and familiar words, interesting material for adults to encourage them to watch with their child, and opportunities for interaction and participation through the use of songs and questions.

- Don't leave the TV on in the background as 'company' for your child while you get on with your jobs. You are simply creating background noise that they may be unable to filter out.

- Try to have a set time for TV, so that your child doesn't expect to be able to watch it at any time during the day. Also, try to have a time limit or allow them to watch a set number of programmes before you turn it off.

- If your child becomes overstimulated by fast-paced TV shows, it may then take a while for their brain to return to normal. You cannot expect them to watch an exciting TV show and then immediately settle down to a quiet learning activity. It will help to give them an opportunity to do some sort of physical activity, outside if possible, and be noisy for a while.

  This is why it is never a good idea for a young child to watch TV just before they go to bed. Ideally, they should have an hour to wind down after watching TV or playing on a screen before you can expect them to be ready for bed. Bath time can be a useful time for them to move around, splash and be noisy, and then calm down gradually with a bedtime story.

Parents should never feel guilty about using the TV, a tablet or a phone as a short-term babysitter. We all look to CBeebies to help us out occasionally! We simply need to weigh up the benefits and risks of screen time, according to our child's age, and then decide what we allow them to watch, when and for how long.

Reading

We all know that reading books with young children is a good idea, but may not fully appreciate what the benefits are.

- Babies respond to being read to even before they are born; they do this by moving and kicking. After they are born, babies will respond by sucking more when they hear familiar stories read to them often during pregnancy. [87] [88] So, you can start your child's reading journey even before they are born!
- Reading with young children is strongly associated with them developing better language skills, as well as better literacy and maths skills. [216] [217] [218]
- Shared reading includes opportunities for joint attention, which is known to be a vital skill for all learning. [219] [220] It is one of the best ways to encourage a child to sustain their attention for longer. [221]
- Frequent shared reading is associated with increased vocabulary. [220] [222] Books contain a wider variety of words than a child would normally hear in their home, [223] and when commenting on the content of books, parents use a wider range of vocabulary and more complex grammar than they do during other activities. [224] [225]
- Parents often naturally keep their language simple when talking to young children. However, it is useful for children to be exposed to more

complex language from time to time. [226] The text in picture books can be an important source of complex sentences. [227] [228] The more often children hear complex sentences, the faster they learn to understand and use them.

- The ability of children to be able to understand and tell stories or to describe events (narrative skills) is important, especially once they start school. These skills are more well developed in children who have regularly shared books with their parents. [229]
- Learning the meaning of new vocabulary requires hearing the words multiple times. [230] Reading favourite stories over and over provides an ideal opportunity to hear words repeated and, subsequently, to learn to understand and use them. [231] [232]
- Dialogic reading is a way of sharing books with children that is proven to boost their vocabulary skills. [233] [234] It involves having a conversation or dialogue with the child about the book that is being read to them. It includes asking open-ended questions about the story, asking them to summarise the story from time to time, leaving gaps for them to fill in, and relating the story to the child's experiences.
- Although sharing books at bedtime may mean that a child is too tired to join in much by answering questions, etc. it is a valuable opportunity to read and reinforce stories that you have read with your child during the day. Sleep has been shown to consolidate a child's memory of words they have learned in stories read to them shortly before going to sleep. [235]
- Sharing books from an early age helps a child to understand that printed letters code the sounds of language and that print conveys meaning. [236] This is one of the skills necessary for the later development of word recognition and reading comprehension.

Pre-reading skills

There are several pre-reading skills that you can help your child to develop before they start school, which will make it much easier for them to learn to read and will make them a more successful reader. These include the following:

- Language skills, including vocabulary and the ability to understand and tell stories.
- Print awareness, i.e. the knowledge that written words have meaning related to spoken words.

- Phonological awareness, which is a child's ability to pay attention to, identify and manipulate sounds in words, including the following elements:
  o Rhymes (e.g. 'cat', 'hat', 'mat' and 'sat')
  o Stress patterns in words (e.g. the stress is on the first syllable of 'water' and on the second syllable of 'begin')
  o Syllables or 'beats' (e.g. 'elephant' has three syllables: 'el-e-phant')
  o How words can be broken down or segmented into individual sounds (e.g. 'dog' ['d-o-g'] is not the same word as 'dot' ['d-o-t'])
  o How individual sounds can be put together or 'blended' to make words (e.g. d + o + g = dog, a four-legged canine.)
- Motivation to read, which is when your child enjoys sharing books, is eager to read and will often choose to read with you rather than doing other activities.

When working on these pre-reading skills, the goal should not be to teach your child to read. If your child is keen to carry on, you can progress to phonics and reading. When introducing phonics (letters and their corresponding sounds) to your child, remember to check that they are developmentally ready to produce those sounds before you expect them to recognise and read them (see the *Sound Wheel* on page 223). I have included some simple phonics activities in the *Chatterbox time* section at the end of Chapters 6 and 7 (pages 169 and 189).

Don't worry if your child shows little interest beyond the skills in the previous list. All children are different. Only one of my four children showed much interest in reading before school, which was partly because she was the youngest and wanted to join in homework sessions with her brothers. Starting school as a fluent reader does have some disadvantages, and it is never worth pushing your child to learn if they are not interested. Sending them to school with strong pre-reading skills will be enough to give them a head start in literacy.

When reading with your child, do the following:

- Always read *with* your child, not *to* them. Reading should be a shared experience. There will be times when your child simply wants to listen (such as when they are tired), but at other times, they may want to do most of the talking, and this should be encouraged. Think of books as a way to encourage a conversation: make a comment or read some text then look at your child and pause; they will let you know if they want to comment in some way or if they just want you to read more.
- Don't stick to just the text, especially when your child is young. Talk about the pictures, particularly if your child points to them or shows obvious interest.

- Keep the books short to begin with. You will both feel a sense of achievement if you get to the end of a book, so try to make sure the books are age-appropriate.
- Treat books like toys when your child is young. To encourage a love of reading, it is important that your child has access to books, even if they just want to handle them and have a little chew! If you wait until they are careful enough to turn the pages one by one without damaging them, you will have missed a huge opportunity. It is so satisfying to see your child picking up a book and pretending to read to themselves or one of their toys.
- Choose books that reflect your child's daily life and routines. Books are an ideal way to reinforce new vocabulary, and your child will love reading stories about events that they recognise.
- Pause at the end of each page to give your child the opportunity to comment or react, even if it's only to say, 'Turn over!'
- Have toys or objects available that appear in a book. This will make the experience more interactive for your child: they can look out for the items in the story, they can act out the story as you read, and they can retell the story with the toys and objects afterwards.
- Include some non-fiction books. Children who don't seem to enjoy listening to stories can often be persuaded to look at a book about a favourite topic, e.g. dinosaurs.
- If your child wants to read the same book several times, then do it. They will learn more from doing that than moving reluctantly through several different books. You can add some new vocabulary each time, but this isn't necessary, as it is the repetition and predictability that children like and learn from.
- Use books that prompt a reaction or use the books that you already have in a different way, such as making obvious mistakes. For example, when you are naming objects, you could deliberately get one wrong, e.g. if there is a picture of a brick, say, 'This is a ball.' Children love correcting adults' mistakes, and this will often prompt a child to talk who is normally reluctant to do so.
- Once your child is using sentences, offer your thoughts or opinions, and give them the chance to do the same, e.g. saying, 'I think the boy is sad,' or, 'I wonder where the dog will go?'
- Once your child understands question words, ask some open questions, such as 'What do you think will happen next?' or 'Why do you think he did that?' This will encourage them to think more deeply about the story, and to use their sequencing and narrative skills to respond.
- From the beginning, draw your child's attention to the printed words as well as the pictures. It is important that children recognise the relationship

between the written word and the spoken word, and the sooner you start, the better. Point to the picture and say the name, then point to the word and explain, 'This says...'

- Help your child to make connections between the stories you read and their own life by making comments such as 'Do you remember when we went to the seaside?' or 'If you were having a party, what food would you have?'

Developmental Language Disorder (DLD)

Although I have chosen not to list the many and varied speech and language disorders that can occur in childhood, I do feel that DLD deserves a mention. It is, as Professor Dorothy Bishop of the University of Oxford describes, 'the most common condition you've never heard of'. It is more common than autism or dyslexia, conditions we are all familiar with, and it affects approximately two children in every class.

DLD is a type of speech, language and communication need that affects the way children understand and use language. With DLD, these difficulties create barriers to social interaction and learning; they are long term, often persisting to adolescence and beyond; and they are not associated with a known biomedical condition such as autism spectrum disorder, cerebral palsy, Down's syndrome or sensorineural hearing loss.

DLD is usually diagnosed after 5 years of age, but can be diagnosed in younger children if there are clear indicators. It does not resolve on its own and children with DLD will need speech and language therapy and other targeted support to help them develop their language skills. As well as targeting specific areas of speech and language, the speech and language therapist will help the child and those around them to develop strategies to reduce the impact of their difficulties on communication and improve their access to education and social activities. Children with DLD can become withdrawn as a result of their difficulties or frustrated, leading to poor behaviour in class and in the playground.

Children with DLD will typically have been late with all their language milestones such as babbling, first words and putting words together in sentences, and they will continue to show some of the following signs:

- Limited use of gestures to try and communicate.
- Poor vocabulary.

- Difficulty finding the right word so will often use general terms such as 'that one', 'there'.
- Limited use of verbs/action words.
- Speech that is difficult to understand due to difficulties using specific sounds.
- Difficulty following instructions.
- Difficulty understanding or remembering what is said to them.
- Their language may sound immature for their age.
- Difficulty using grammatical markers such as verb tenses, plurals, pronouns.
- Difficulty using language appropriate to the context. A child may not understand humour or sarcasm, they may be over-familiar with a teacher, they may interrupt a lot or go off on a tangent during conversations.
- Taking extra time to process and respond to what is said to them.
- Because of their difficulties expressing themselves, they may talk less than their peers and become frustrated.

Once they start school, more difficulties will become noticeable, including the following:

- Paying attention in class.
- Making and keeping friends.
- Following rules of playground games.
- Difficulties with literacy: reading, writing and spelling.
- Using language appropriate for different social situations.
- Expressing and managing emotions.
- Staying on topic, so they may interrupt and often change the subject.
- Taking language literally so failing to understand jokes, sarcasm etc.
- Sequencing thoughts to create narratives e.g. telling parents what they have done at school.
- Behaviour problems.

As with all SLCNs, the best prognosis for DLD is as a result of early diagnosis and intervention. In addition to targeted work following a detailed assessment of a child's speech and language skills, there are general ways that you can support a child with DLD, including the following:

- Make sure you have their full attention before you ask them a question or give them an instruction. Say their name and establish eye contact so that you know they are listening.

- Keep background noise to a minimum if possible or move to a quiet area.
- Use simple language, including familiar vocabulary.
- If you are unsure whether they have understood, ask them to repeat the question or instruction back to you.
- Give them extra time to process what you have said, think, find the right words and formulate their response.
- Use visual prompts such as gestures, objects or pictures to help them understand and remember information.
- Support their confidence in speaking by praising their attempts and acknowledging what they have to say.
- Encourage them to communicate in whatever way they can and accept their attempts to respond with words, gestures or facial expressions.

From an early age, children with DLD are likely to show many of the problems listed under the red flags in each chapter, alerting you to the need to seek professional advice.

Bilingualism

Many children are raised in families that speak more than one language and being bilingual is a great life skill to have. Between birth and three years old is a critical time for learning language, so children will find it easier if they are exposed to both languages from birth. By the time they are born, babies show a preference for both languages over others and have already started to tell the difference between them. [237]

There are distinct advantages to being bilingual:

- The constant need to shift attention between languages leads to improved 'executive functioning' of the brain; i.e. bilingual children are able to shift their attention between tasks, multitask and solve problems more easily. [238]
- Bilingual children have been found to have increased metalinguistic skills, which is the ability to understand how language works. [239]
- Being bilingual can make learning a third language easier, as the brains of bilingual children seem to stay open to perceiving the differences between the sounds of other languages longer than children who only speak a single language. [240]

Common parental concerns about bringing children up bilingual include:

- **If a child learns two languages, they are more likely to be language delayed.** Bilingual children develop language skills just as other children do and are no more or less likely to have a language delay. They may have fewer words in each language, but if you add their vocabulary in each language together, it will equal or be even greater than the vocabulary of any other child.

- **Children get confused when they hear two languages spoken around them.** This simply doesn't appear to be the case, and children find it completely natural to hear two different languages, particularly if they have both been used since birth.

- **Bilingual children will start to mix the two languages.** This is actually true, but it seems to be a deliberate process based on learning the rules of each language rather than being due to making mistakes. Mixing the grammatical rules as well as individual words is a normal part of becoming bilingual. Bilingual adults continue to do it and have words in one language that they prefer to use, no matter which language they are speaking. There is an obvious advantage to this in that if a child doesn't know a word in one language, they can borrow a word from their second language.

How to help a child become bilingual

There is no one way that works best for all families. There are several different approaches, including the following:

- **One person, one language** This is when each parent only uses one language, and it is often used where each parent has a different first language, so that they each speak the language that they find most natural. However, it can be difficult to achieve a balanced exposure to both languages if one parent is at home with the child while the other is at work.

- **One language at home, and the other language at school or nursery** This can mean that a child has less exposure to the second language in their early years and will take longer to become fluent. Once they are at school, that will be the language that then becomes dominant for them as they will spend more time hearing and using it.

- **Time-and-place method**

  This is where one language is spoken at a particular time of day or on certain days of the week, and during that time, the child is immersed in only one language. This method is commonly used in bilingual schools.

- **Mixed language policy**

  This is where parents use the language that seems most appropriate to each situation, e.g. one language may be used at mealtimes while another is used to talk about school topics.

  The most important thing is that a child is exposed to both languages as much as possible, including during the activities that I have suggested in each chapter: listening to and playing with speech sounds; sharing music, songs and rhymes, books and games. Children should be given the opportunity to use both languages to make their needs and wishes known, so that they don't feel one language is more useful than the other.

Autism

For many of the parents I have worked with whose children have been slow to develop their communication skills, the possibility of autism has been one of their earliest concerns. Whether a child is subsequently diagnosed as autistic or not, the best way of helping that child and their parents is with accurate information.

Although more is now commonly known about autism, there is still a lot of misinformation, and one notable example is regarding eye contact. Some parents still worry that poor eye contact means that their child is probably autistic, and parents of autistic children often feel that improving their child's eye contact should be one of their primary goals. Neither of these things are necessarily true.

While avoiding eye contact is one of the many features of autism, there are a number of other reasons why a child may go through a phase of not wanting to socialise or engage with other people, and not looking at someone is the best way to avoid interaction with them. This may result from one of the following:

- The child is nervous of or dislikes the person who is trying to make eye contact with them.
- They have a hearing problem and are unaware that they should look at someone.

- They are generally very shy or socially anxious.
- They come from a culture that sees direct eye contact as a sign of disrespect.

It doesn't mean that you should discount autism altogether, but that you should watch your child carefully in different social situations for a period of time before becoming overly concerned.

Children with autism generally seem to avoid eye contact for different reasons, such as these:

- They lack the social motivation to make eye contact.
- They find it difficult to focus both on spoken language and on another person's eyes at the same time.
- They do not understand that watching another person's eyes is more revealing than, for example, watching that person's mouth or hands.
- They find eye contact to be an intense and potentially overwhelming sensory experience.

Instead of persisting with eye contact as a primary goal, you can encourage it while teaching other strategies for a child to show that they are listening and interested:

- Encourage them to stay within a certain distance rather than walking away.
- Help them to show their interest verbally, by simply saying, 'I'm listening,' or non-verbally by nodding occasionally.
- Praise even fleeting eye contact.
- Encourage eye contact by talking about one of a child's special interests.

Poor eye contact is just one example of behaviour that may be a symptom of autism or of something else; even if it is part of an autistic child's communication profile, it doesn't mean that we should view it as something to be fixed. Just like children with other communication disorders, every autistic child is unique, and there is no one-size-fits-all approach. They will each have different strengths and weaknesses to other autistic children, and the aim of speech and language therapy is to identify both of these so that we can use the strengths to build on the weaknesses. The aim is never to try to make autistic children communicate like a typically developing child, but to give them the skills to optimise their communication.

What autism is

Autism is a lifelong developmental disability that affects how people communicate and interact with the world.

According to the National Autistic Society, one in 100 people are on the autism spectrum, and there are around 700,000 autistic children and adults in the UK. It is three times more common in boys than in girls. There is strong evidence to suggest that autism is caused by a variety of factors affecting brain development, and that there is a genetic component.

Autism is a spectrum condition with all autistic people sharing certain difficulties but also having a lot of individual differences. Asperger syndrome is a diagnosis that was previously given to certain autistic individuals, but now autism spectrum disorder is the most commonly given diagnosis. People with Asperger syndrome don't have the learning disabilities that many autistic people have, but they may have specific learning difficulties. They may have fewer problems with speech but may have difficulties understanding and processing language. They may also have mental health issues, which means that they will need different support. Some people with a diagnosis of Asperger syndrome prefer to use that term while others would rather refer to themselves as being on the autistic spectrum.

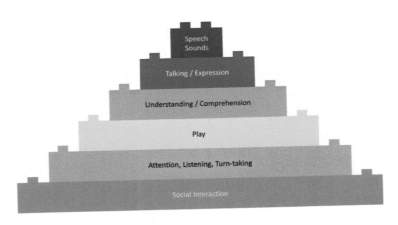

If we consider the communication pyramid again, we can see that many of the primary difficulties that autistic children present with are right at the bottom, in social interaction. While they will gradually move up the pyramid, persistent gaps near the bottom will mean that their progress may be slow, and they will continue to need support at all levels.

How autism is diagnosed

As the parents of any child diagnosed with autism will tell you, it can be a very long and drawn-out process with a whole team of professionals involved, including (among others) a paediatrician, a clinical or educational psychologist, a speech and language therapist, and an occupational therapist.

The main two diagnostic features of autism are these:

1. **Persistent difficulties with social communication and social interaction**
   Autistic children have difficulty understanding both verbal and non-verbal communication, which can mean that they need more time to process language and respond to questions. Echolalia is common, where a child repeats back what is said to them. Some have speech difficulties, while others have good language skills but have problems understanding concepts such as sarcasm or humour, so they can take things literally.

   Autistic children have difficulty understanding and expressing emotions. They can find it difficult to form friendships and may prefer to spend time alone. They can come across as insensitive and may behave in ways that come across as inappropriate.

2. **Restricted and repetitive patterns of behaviours, activities or interests**
   When children can predict what is going to happen next, it makes them feel safe. Autistic children need this predictability even more, and they prefer to have a strict routine to follow. Any change to their routine can be distressing and make them feel very anxious. Using repetitive actions such as hand flapping, rocking, or opening and closing a door can feel enjoyable and reassuring and can make them feel safe in an anxious situation.

   Parents often notice that their autistic child displays repetitive play routines, such as lining up toys and spinning wheels, and they may persist with the same behaviour for long periods of time. Many autistic children also find comfort lying down on the floor to play.

Other typical features include the following:

- **Over- or under-sensitivity to sounds, touch, tastes, smells, light, colours, temperatures or pain**
  Everyday situations in school, work, shops, etc. can be particularly overwhelming and cause sensory overload.

- **Intense and highly focused interests**

  These often occur from a very early age, so that they develop a huge wealth of knowledge in that area. This means that many autistic people do well academically and at work but focusing on one particular aspect of their lives may mean that other areas are neglected.

- **Anxiety**

  Over one-third of autistic people have serious mental health issues and need help with strategies to deal with their anxiety.

- **Meltdowns and shutdowns**

  A meltdown occurs when a child becomes overwhelmed by a situation and loses behavioural control. Because this may include screaming and shouting, or physically lashing out, it can be mistaken for a temper tantrum by those who don't know the child.

  A shutdown is the opposite reaction to being overwhelmed, where a child seems to switch off. This may seem easier to handle, but it can be just as much of a problem.

If you are concerned that your child is displaying the primary features of autism, you should talk to your GP or health visitor. For a preschool child, they may carry out a screening interview, such as the Modified Checklist for Autism in Toddlers, to help them decide whether a referral is appropriate.

A diagnosis can be a positive thing as it can help you to better understand your child's needs and how best to meet them, and it can mean that additional support may be made available to your child at school or nursery. Even if you are unsure whether you want to go ahead with an assessment, it is worth asking for a referral while you make your decision, as it can take many months to get an initial appointment.

You can also ask for your child to be referred for support services, such as speech and language therapy and occupational therapy. Again, waiting times can potentially be several months, so using the strategies I have suggested throughout this book can be helpful in the meantime. Remember to work from the level where your child is functioning, rather than just their chronological age and work on skills from the bottom of the communication pyramid upwards.

The National Autistic Society is an excellent source of information.

APPENDICES

Ages and Stages Charts

Understanding	
Age	**Progress Summary**
0–6 months	• Turns towards sounds. • Is startled by loud noises. • Quietens when spoken to. • Watches your face when you talk to them. • Recognises your voice and other familiar voices. • When upset, is calmed by your voice. • Gets excited when they hear you approaching.
6–12 months	• Pays attention to familiar voices. • Pays attention to sounds around them, e.g. a dog barking or a phone ringing. • Works out where a voice is coming from and turns towards it. • Looks at your face when you start talking to them. • Looks at familiar people and objects when their name is mentioned. • Looks at things you point at when you say, 'Look.' • Recognises their own name and looks up when they hear it. • Understands familiar small phrases in context, e.g. 'Up you come' and 'Come here', especially if a gesture is used as well. • Smiles at lot, often before someone smiles at them. • Enjoys songs and rhymes, especially those with actions, and shows excitement when they hear them.
12–18 months	• Understands the names of many familiar objects, toys and people. • When asked, they can point to parts of their body, such as eyes, nose, ears and toes. • Follows simple instructions such as 'Go and get your shoes.' • Enjoys sharing picture books and can point to a few familiar pictures on request. • Enjoys simple songs and rhymes and joins in with the actions. • Moves or 'dances' in time to music. • Begins to pretend in play, e.g. talking on the phone.
18–24 months	• Understands 200–500 words, including all the words (objects and actions) involved in their daily life. • Finds objects when they are named, without being given extra clues such as gestures. • Can follow two-part instructions, e.g. 'Get your coat and give it to Daddy.' • Understands two words together, e.g. 'Where are *Mummy's shoes*?' • Remembers a sequence involving two words, e.g. 'Give me the *cup* and the *spoon*.' • Understands the different ways that language is used, so they use a greeting when visitors arrive, answer a question or follow an instruction when asked.

2–3 years	• Follows more complex instructions, e.g. 'Get the ball from the box and give it to Daddy.' • Recognises some colours and shapes. • Understands some basic concepts, such as 'big'/'little', 'in'/'out' and 'up'/'down'. • Responds correctly to 'what', 'where' and 'who' questions. • Understands the functions of objects, e.g. being able to answer when asked, 'What do we sleep in?' • Understands and remembers simple stories. • Understands the concept of quantity, e.g. 'more', 'a bit' and 'a lot'.
3–4 years	• Responds to an instruction without stopping what they are doing. • Understands position concepts, such as 'in front', 'behind', 'next to' and 'between'. • Understands most colour and shape names. • Understands the concept of 'same'/'different'. • Listens to a story and answers questions about characters and events. • Predicts what might happen next in a story. • Follows more complex instructions that include words such as 'and' and 'then'. • Understands the time concepts of 'past', 'present' and 'future', and can respond to questions about 'yesterday', 'today' and 'tomorrow'. • Responds correctly to 'why' questions.
4–5 years	• Follows simple stories without pictures. • Understands nearly everything that is said to them at home. • Understands a sequence of instructions, e.g. 'First… Next… And then…' • Understands more concepts, such as 'first'/'last', 'above'/'below', 'light'/'heavy', 'front'/'back', 'near'/'far', and 'first', 'second', and 'third'. • Understands comparative and superlative, e.g. 'big', 'bigger' and 'biggest'; and 'tall', 'taller' and 'tallest'. • Asks when they don't understand what a word means.

Expressive Language	
Age	**Progress Summary**
0–6 months	• Uses different cries to express different needs. • Shows excitement by waving their arms and legs. • Responds with a smile or laugh to other people smiling and laughing. • Coos or squeals to get your attention. • Makes noises when spoken to.
6–12 months	• Takes turns in little 'conversations' where you talk, and they babble back. • Uses gestures, such as waving and pointing. • May have a few single words. • Initiates favourite games (such as peekaboo) with adults, using gestures, sounds or words.

12–18 months	• Uses gestures to make their needs known, e.g. puts their arms up when wants to be picked up. • Copies adult actions such as waving. • Imitates a few animal sounds. • Uses about 20 recognisable words. • Imitates a few phrases, e.g. 'All gone milk' and 'Bye-bye, Daddy.' • Still uses long strings of babble and nonsense words, but with features of real speech, e.g. taking turns or using the intonation of a question.
18–24 months	• Uses at least 50 single words. • Uses some word types other than just nouns, e.g. verbs, adjectives and question words. • Is starting to put two words together in short sentences, e.g. 'Teddy gone' or 'Mummy up.' • Names pictures in books. • Uses their own name, often instead of 'me' or 'I', e.g. 'Harry do it.' • Joins in with nursery rhymes. • Makes lots of animal sounds. • Asks questions such as 'What's that?' and 'Where we going?' • Attempts some simple past tense verbs, but often with errors, e.g. 'Mummy goed.'
2–3 years	• Has around 200–300 words, including lots of action words (verbs). • Uses sentences with three main parts, e.g. 'Daddy kicked the ball.' • Uses lots of phrases with words such as prepositions, e.g. 'in', 'on' and 'under', adjectives, e.g. 'hot'/'cold', 'happy'/'sad' and 'big'/'small'. • Uses pronouns such as 'him', 'her' and 'it', and refers to themselves with 'I' or 'me' rather than their name. • Asks lots of questions using question words such as 'what' and 'where'. • Gives instructions during play, e.g. saying, 'Put that brick on the floor,' or 'Give me the car.' • Starts using word endings for things such as plurals and verb tenses. • Enjoys having a chat but may often change the subject.
3–4 years	• Uses full sentences with only occasional grammatical errors, such as plurals or past tense errors. • Links sentences together with words such as 'and', 'then', 'but' and 'because'. • Uses past, present and future tenses. • Uses pronouns correctly, e.g. 'I', 'you', 'we' and 'they'. • Can use thousands of words. • Asks lots of questions, including those starting with 'who', 'where', 'what' or 'why'. • Often starts conversations with others. • Makes up long stories, sometimes confusing fact and fiction, but often not as deliberate lies. • Uses language to problem-solve, e.g. can work out a response to the question 'What shall we do if it starts to rain?' • Tells simple jokes and enjoys the attention they bring. • Understands the social aspects of communication, e.g. will whisper secrets, will be more polite with strangers, and will use baby talk with younger children.

 4–5 years	• Uses long, complex and complete sentences with only occasional grammatical errors. • Uses lots of descriptive words, e.g. 'wet'/'dry' and 'hard'/'soft'. • Tells stories with the events in the correct sequence. • Tells stories using the past, present and future tenses. • Uses language to solve problems, thinking them through out loud. • Uses language to negotiate and agree rules of games. • Is skilled at taking turns in long, complicated conversations. Is less likely to interrupt or change the subject when someone else is talking. • Can share their feelings and opinions. • Can make up stories from their imagination.

Speech Sounds	
Age	**Progress Summary**
0–6 months	• Plays with sounds, making lots of different consonants and vowels, with no real meaning attached, which is known as 'cooing' or 'gurgling'.
6–12 months	• Uses long strings of babble, often using more than one consonant, e.g. 'badabada'. • Uses the rhythm and intonation of adult speech, so their babble sounds like they are talking.
12–18 months	• Uses the sounds 'p', 'b' and 'm' in words and babble, and may also use 't', 'd', 'n' and 'w'. • Still babbles when playing. • They are understood around 25% of the time.
18–24 months	• Speech sounds are immature, but they are understood at least half of the time. • Uses the sounds 'p', 'b', 'm', 't', 'd', 'n' and 'w' in words. • Misses sounds off the beginning and/or end of words.

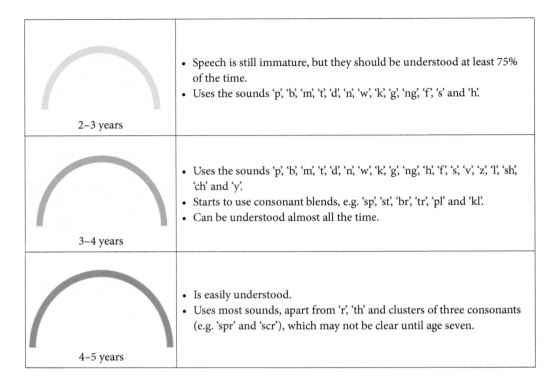

2–3 years	• Speech is still immature, but they should be understood at least 75% of the time. • Uses the sounds 'p', 'b', 'm', 't', 'd', 'n', 'w', 'k', 'g', 'ng', 'f', 's' and 'h'.
3–4 years	• Uses the sounds 'p', 'b', 'm', 't', 'd', 'n', 'w', 'k', 'g', 'ng', 'h', 'f', 's', 'v', 'z', 'l', 'sh', 'ch' and 'y'. • Starts to use consonant blends, e.g. 'sp', 'st', 'br', 'tr', 'pl' and 'kl'. • Can be understood almost all the time.
4–5 years	• Is easily understood. • Uses most sounds, apart from 'r', 'th' and clusters of three consonants (e.g. 'spr' and 'scr'), which may not be clear until age seven.

Red Flags	
Age	**Concern**
0–6 months	• Has any difficulty with eating or drinking. • Is not startled by loud sounds. • Does not look at you when you speak. • Is not responding to speech (especially familiar voices) or other sounds by turning or quietening. • Is not interacting socially, with eye contact and smiles. • Is not starting to make a variety of different sounds.
6–12 months	• Does not turn to look when you speak to them, especially when their name is called. • Does not respond to and enjoy social games and rhymes such as peekaboo and 'Pat-a-cake, Pat-a-cake'. • Does not babble using a variety of consonant and vowel sounds. • Does not look for familiar objects when you talk about them. • Does not look at things you point to. • Does not use simple gestures to communicate, e.g. waving bye-bye or putting their arms up to be lifted. • Does not try to point.

12–18 months	• Does not respond to simple instructions such as 'Where is your cup?' • Cannot point to a few body parts when asked. • Does not enjoy simple songs, rhymes and stories. • Does not take turns with you in making sounds to each other. • Does not use one or two simple words, e.g. 'mama' and 'dada'. • Does not use lots of babble that has the rhythm and intonation of real speech.
18–24 months	• Does not understand the names of lots of everyday objects, such as toys, food and clothes. • Cannot concentrate on an activity of their own choosing for more than a couple of minutes. • Cannot follow instructions such as 'Go and get your shoes and bring them to Mummy.' • Does not have at least 25 words. • Does not use a few simple phrases, such as 'More juice' and 'Where Daddy?' • Does not copy your actions and want to join in, e.g. reading, cleaning and brushing your hair. • Their speech is not understood by familiar adults.
2–3 years	• Moves quickly from one activity to another and cannot concentrate on one for 5–10 minutes. • Does not enjoy listening to longer stories. • Does not engage in pretend or imaginary play a lot of the time, such as feeding a teddy or putting it to bed. • Does not show interest in playing with other children. • Does not like you joining in their play. • Has difficulty understanding what you say or just repeats what you have said. • Is not using smaller grammatical markers, such as plurals ending in 's' and pronouns, e.g. 'me' and 'mine'. • Does not ask lots of questions. • A lot of their speech is difficult to understand. • Cannot follow two-step instructions, e.g. 'Get the ball and put it in the box.' • Is not learning lots of new words every week. • Does not use lots of phrases e.g. 'go shops', 'where teddy?' and some longer sentences e.g. 'Let's go to the park.'
3–4 years	• Doesn't understand the things you ask them to do. • Doesn't want to play with other children very often. • Doesn't respond to 'who', 'what' or 'where' questions. • Still shows poor concentration. • Doesn't ask lots of questions. • Can't tell you about the things that they have done. • Doesn't use lots of grammatical markers, such as plurals, verb endings, tenses and pronouns. • Is not starting to use more complex sentences, e.g. 'I got up *and* I went to nursery.' • Still has unclear speech. • Is very non-fluent and struggles to get their words out.

 4–5 years	• Cannot follow an instruction or answer a question while focusing on an activity. • Cannot follow a sequence of instructions in the right order. • Cannot answer questions about a story they have heard. • Makes lots of grammatical mistakes. • Cannot organise their thoughts to retell a story or recount an event. • Is non-fluent and struggles to get their words out. • Makes mistakes with particular sounds. • Can be difficult to understand at times.

Sound Wheel

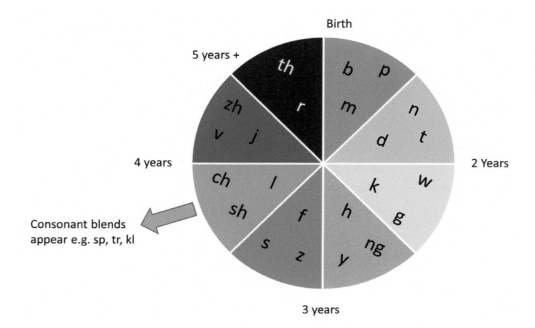

This wheel shows the average age that a child develops their sounds. [241] [242] Some children will learn to say the sounds before the ages on the wheel, and others will be a little later.

Some sounds are more difficult to say than others due to finer muscle coordination being needed to produce them, so don't expect the sounds at the end of the wheel to appear until after the earlier ones.

Regardless of the sounds that they have, you should be able to understand what your child says to the following degrees: [122]

- 18 months   →   At least 25% of the time
- 2 years   →   At least 50% of the time
- 3 years   →   At least 75% of the time
- 4 years   →   Almost all the time

Table of Phonological Processes

Process	Definition	Examples	Approximate Age of Elimination
Reduplication	When a syllable is repeated	daddy → dada biscuit → bibi	3 years
Assimilation/ consonant harmony	When a consonant is repeated	dog → gog bus → bub	3 years, 9 months
Weak syllable deletion	When a weak or unstressed syllable is deleted	banana → nana spaghetti → getti potato → tato	4 years
Prevocalic voicing	When a voiceless consonant, e.g. 'p', 't', 'k', at the beginning of a word becomes voiced, e.g. 'b', 'd', 'g'	pig → big toe → doe car → gar	3 years
Final consonant de-voicing	When a voiced consonant at the end of a word is substituted with a voiceless consonant	pig → pick head → het	3 years
Final consonant deletion	When the final consonant in a word is missed off	cat → ca up → u	3 years, 3 months
Fronting	When a sound made with the back of the tongue, such as 'k' or 'g', is replaced by one made with the front, such as 't' or 'd'	car → tar cake → tate key → tea	3 years, 6 months
Stopping	When a fricative or affricate consonant, e.g. 'f', 's', 'sh', 'ch', is replaced by a stop consonant, e.g. 'p', 'b', 't', 'd'	sun → dun four → door very → bery shop → dop jump → dump	3 years for 'f' and 's' 3 years, 6 months for 'v' and 'z' 4 years, 6 months for 'sh', 'ch' and 'j' 5 years for 'th'

Cluster reduction	When a consonant cluster, such as 'sp', bl', 'gr'. is reduced to a single consonant	spoon → poon blue → bue green → geen	4 years
Gliding	When liquid consonants such as 'l' and 'r' are replaced with glides such as 'y' and 'w'	leg → yeg rabbit → wabbit yellow → yeyow	5 years

Development of Play

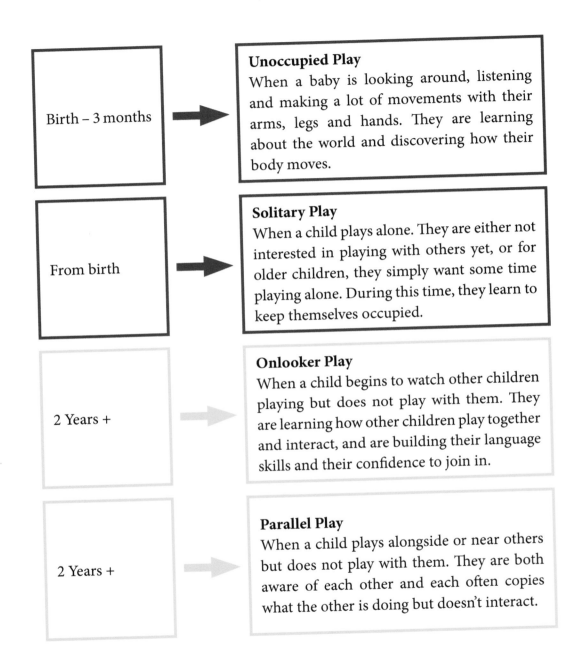

Birth – 3 months →

Unoccupied Play
When a baby is looking around, listening and making a lot of movements with their arms, legs and hands. They are learning about the world and discovering how their body moves.

From birth →

Solitary Play
When a child plays alone. They are either not interested in playing with others yet, or for older children, they simply want some time playing alone. During this time, they learn to keep themselves occupied.

2 Years + →

Onlooker Play
When a child begins to watch other children playing but does not play with them. They are learning how other children play together and interact, and are building their language skills and their confidence to join in.

2 Years + →

Parallel Play
When a child plays alongside or near others but does not play with them. They are both aware of each other and each often copies what the other is doing but doesn't interact.

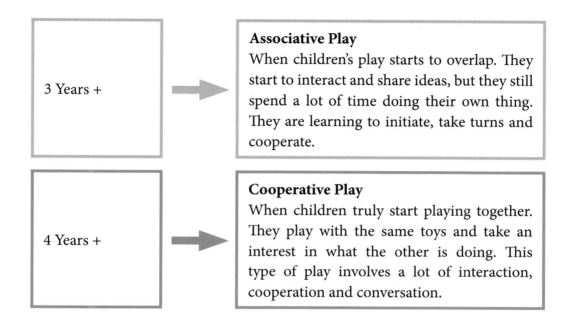

| 3 Years + | **Associative Play**
When children's play starts to overlap. They start to interact and share ideas, but they still spend a lot of time doing their own thing. They are learning to initiate, take turns and cooperate. |
| 4 Years + | **Cooperative Play**
When children truly start playing together. They play with the same toys and take an interest in what the other is doing. This type of play involves a lot of interaction, cooperation and conversation. |

Play Skills

Child's Age	Type of Play	What Children Learn	Best Toys
From birth	People play: Interacting with others physically and socially, and watching and listening to people.	People are fun! Attention and listening skills. Social skills and turn-taking. Understanding non-verbal communication, such as facial expressions and body language.	Other people!
From birth	Sensory/ exploratory play: Using their whole bodies and all their senses to explore their world.	By touching, mouthing and banging objects, children learn about the texture, taste and function of things in their environment. Cause and effect. Gross and fine motor skills.	Their own hands and feet. Other people, especially their faces and hair! Bubbles, baby gym, musical instruments and activity boards. Food! PlayDoh, paint, sand and water.
From birth	Physical play	Gross motor skills, including control for balance, speed and accuracy. How to be gentle with others.	Other people, including cuddling, rough and tumble, and dancing together. Outdoor play, including running, climbing and jumping.
1 year+	Construction play	Manipulation, building and fitting things together. Problem-solving skills, as children work out which things work best together and what to do if things go wrong.	Household items, including boxes, tubs and bubble wrap. Wooden bricks, train sets, Duplo, Lego, etc.
1 year +	Creative play	Fine motor skills, including manipulating different materials. Imagination and self-expression.	Household/garden items, including pasta, buttons, leaves and flowers. Glue, glitter, paint and crayons.

18 months+	Pretend play	Understanding of symbols, including using one thing to represent something else, e.g. a box as a house, car or boat. To use their imagination; i.e. children pretend to be someone else and act out different situations. Language skills. How to cooperate. To understand others' feelings and develop empathy.	Dressing-up clothes. Dolls and teddies. Tea sets, toy kitchen equipment, toy food, shopping basket, etc. Toy farm, doll's house, garage, etc. Doctor's kit. Blankets to make dens. Large boxes or bricks to make a house. Writing materials to play 'schools' or 'post office'.
Age 4+	Games with rules: Children follow set rules or create their own to reach a shared goal in a game.	Language skills for sharing information, asking questions and negotiating. That turn-taking is important. How to cooperate. How to deal with losing.	Card games such as snap, lotto, etc. Board games such as snakes and ladders, Pop-Up Pirate, etc. Group sports. Made-up games.

First-Words Checklist

Word	Understands	Says
Mummy		
Daddy		
Family names		
Hello/hiya		
Bye-bye		
More		
(All) gone		
Yes		
No		
Milk		
Juice		
Ball		
Biscuit		
Banana		
Car		
Dog		
Cat		
Nose		
Eyes		
Bath		
Book		
Shoes		
Hot		
Thank you		
Baby		
Hat		
Nappy		

Other Early Words

	Word	Understands	Says
Social	Please		
	Sorry		
	Uh-oh		
	Ouch		
Names	Apple		
	Water		
	Cheese		
	Yoghurt		
	Chocolate		
	Hands		
	Feet		
	Arms		
	Legs		
	Mouth		
	Ears		
	Fingers		
	Toes		
	Tummy		
	Teeth		
	Hair		
	Socks		
	Trousers		
	Hat		
	Gloves		
	Coat		
	Cup		
	Bottle		
	Spoon		
	Bowl		
	Plate		

	Word	Understands	Says
Names	Buggy/pushchair		
	Bag		
	Teddy		
	Bricks		
	TV/telly		
	Phone		
	Table		
	Chair		
	Bed		
	Door		
	Window		
	Potty/toilet		
	Brush		
	Towel		
	Light		
	House		
	Tree		
	Flower		
	Swing		
	Slide		
	Star		
	Bird		
	Duck		
	Cow		
	Horse		
	Chicken		
	Monkey		
	Lion		
	Elephant		
	Snake		
	Crocodile		
	Pig		
	Rabbit		

	Word	Understands	Says
Names	Fish		
	Frog		
	Butterfly		
	Bear		
	Plane		
	Train		
	Bike		
	Boat		
	Rain		
	Sun		
Actions	Eat		
	Drink		
	Sleep		
	Look		
	Listen		
	Play		
	Read		
	Give		
	Walk		
	Dance		
	Jump		
	Sit		
	Run		
	Stand		
	Help		
	See		
	Watch		
	Fall		
	Stop		
	Go		
	Wash		
	Open		
	Close		

	Word	Understands	Says
Actions	Throw		
	Catch		
	Tickle		
	Come		
	Hug		
	Love		
	Kiss		
	Hurt		
	Cry		
	Want		
	Climb		
	Shake		
	Push		
	Pull		
	Fix		
Descriptive Words	Big		
	Little		
	Cold		
	Clean		
	Dirty		
	Wet		
	Dry		
	Loud		
	Quiet		
	More		
	Yucky		
	Silly		
	All		
	Some		
	Funny		
	Up		
	Down		
	In		

	Word	Understands	Says
Descriptive Words	Out		
	On		
	Off		
	Here		
	There		
Pronouns	Me		
	You		
	It		
	My		
	Mine		

References

[1]   M. D. S. Ainsworth and S. M. Bell, "Infant Crying and Maternal Responsiveness," *Journal of Child Development,* 1972.

[2]   Roulstone et al, "Investigating the Role of Language in Children's Early Educational Outcomes," 2011.

[3]   S. Yoleri, "Teacher-child Relationships in Preschool Period: The Roles of Child Temperament and Language Skills," *International Electronic Journal of Elementary Education,* vol. 9, no. 1, pp. 210–224, 2016.

[4]   Feinstein and Duckworth, "The Communication Trust: Talking About a Generation," 2017.

[5]   M. L. Rice, M. A. Sell and P. A. Hadley, "Social Interactions of Speech and Language Impaired Children," *Journal of Speech & Hearing Research,* pp. 34–36, 1991.

[6]   Public Health England, "The Mental Health of Children and Young People in England," 2016.

[7]   E. Knox and G. Conti-Ramsdem, "Bullying Risks of 11 Year Old Children with Specific Language Impairment: Does School Placement Matter?," *Journal of Language & Communication Disorders,* vol. 38, 203.

[8]   G. Blood, Bullying in Children Who Stutter: Speech-Language Pathologists' Perceptions and Intervention Strategies, 2010.

[9]   Hirsch, "The Effects of Weaknesses in Oral language on Reading Comprehension Growth," 1996.

[10]   Ripley and Yuill, "Patterns of Language Impairment and Behaviour in Boys Excluded from School," *British Journal of Educational Psychology,* 2005.

[11]   Clegg et al, "Language Abilities of Secondary Age Pupils at Risk of School Exclusion: A Preliminary Report," *Child Lanugage, Teaching & Therapy,* vol. 25, pp. 123–139, 2009.

[12]   Clegg et al, "Language Abilities of Secondary Age Pupils – A Follow Up in Later Adult Life: Cognitive, Language & Psychosocial Outcomes," *Journal of Child Psychology and Psychiatry,* vol. 46, no. 2, pp. 128–149, 2015.

[13]   Bryan et al, "Language and Communication Difficulties in Juvenile Offenders," *International Journal of Language and Communication Disorders,* vol. 42, 2007.

[14]   Bryan et al, "Language Difficulties and Criminal Justice: the Need for Earlier Identification," *International Journal of Language and Communication Disorders,* 2005.

[15]   N. Elliott, "An Investigation into the Communication Skills of Long-Term Unemployed Young Men," 2009.

[16]   R. Ruben, "Redefining the Survival of the Fittest: Communication Disorders in the 21st Century," 2000.

[17]   Department for Education,, "National Statistics: Information from the School Census on Pupils with Special Educational Needs," 2017.

[18]   F. Mensah et al, "Health-Related Quality of Life of Children With Low Language From Early Childhood to Adolescence: Results From an Australian Longitudinal Population-Based Study.," *Journal of Child Psychology and Psychiatry,* 2020.

[19]   Bercow, "Ten Years On," 2018.

[20]   E. Locke, J. Ginsborg and I. Peers, "Development and Disadvantage: Implications for Early Years," *International Journal of language & Communication Disorders,* 2002.

[21]   J. Law, K. McBean and R. Rush, "Communication Skills in a Population of Primary School Aged Children Raised in an Area of Pronounced Social Disadvantage," *International Journal of Language & Communication Disorders,* vol. 10.

[22]   G. Lindsay, J. Dockrell, C. Mackie and B. Letchford, " Educational Provision for Children with Specific Speech and Language Difficulties in England and Wales," 2002.

[23]   Norbury et al, "The Impact of Nonverbal Ability on Prevalence & Clinical Presentation of Language Disorder," *Journal of Child Psychology & Psychiatry,* vol. 57, pp. 1247–1257, 2016.

[24]   Lindsay et al, "Effective and Efficient Use of Resources in Services for Children and Young People with Speech, Language and Communication Needs," 2008.

[25]   J. P. Shonkoff and D. A. Phillips, From Neurons to Neighbourhoods: The Science of Early Childhood Development, 2000.

[26]   J. P. Dr Shonkoff,, "Rethinking the Definition of Evidence-Based Interventions to Promote Early Childhood Development," 2017.

[27]   B. Gallagher, Reach Out and Read Program, 2011.

[28]   B. Hart and T. R. Risley, The Early Catastrophe: The 30 Million Word Gap by Age 3, 2003.

[29]   R. Shore, Rethinking the Brain: New Insights into Early Development, 1997.

[30]   R. e. al, "Beyond the 30-Million-Word Gap: Children's Conversational Exposure is Associated with Language-Related Brain Function," *Psychological Science,* vol. 29, no. 5, pp. 700–710, 2018.

[31]   American Academy of Pediatrics, "Year 2007 Position Statement: Principles and Guidelines for Early Hearing Detection and Intervention Programs," American Academy of Pediatrics, 2007.

[32]   C. Zhoo, "Mothers's Behavioral Connections Tone Infant's Brain to Angry Tone," *PLOS,* 2019.

[33]   A. Graham et al, "Arguments in the Home Linked with Babies Brain Functioning," *Science Daily,* 2013.

[34]   National Literacy Trust, "Face to Face Buggy Research Project 2008-2010," 1 October 2010. [Online]. Available: https://literacytrust.org.uk/research-services/research-reports/face-face-buggy-research-project-2008-2010.

[35]   S. Zeedyck, "Whats Life in a Buggy Like?," 21 November 2008. [Online]. Available: https://cdn.literacytrust.org.uk/media/documents/2008_01_01_free_research_-_whats_life_in_a_buggy_like_2008_iHvVXnx.pdf.

[36]   Albert Einstein College of Medicine, "Developmental Milestones: Baby Talk from First Sounds to First Words," 2015.

[37]   R. Knox, 1937.

[38]   H. C. Stuart and S. S. Stevenson, Physical Growth and Development, Philadelphia: Nelson, 1950.

[39]   WHO, UNICEF & World Bank Group, "Nuturing Care for Early Child Development: A Framework for Helping Children Survive and Thrive to Transform Health and Human Potential," Geneva, 2018.

[40]   G. E. Walton, N. J. Bower and T. G. Bower, "Recognition of Familiar Faces by Newborns," *Infant Behavior and Development,* vol. 15, pp. 265–269, 1992.

[41]   I. W. Bushnell, F. Sai and J. T. Mullin, "Neonatal Recognition of the Mother's Face," *British Journal of Developmental Psychology,* vol. 7, pp. 3-15.

[42]   M. Whitehead, The Development of Language and Literacy, London: Hodder and Stoughton, 1996.

[43]   K. Begus, T. Glega and V. Southgate, "Infants' Preferences for Native Speakers are Associated with an Expectation of Information," *Journal of Psychological and Cognitive Sciences,* 2016.

[44]   F. Ramirez, N. N. Ramirez, M. Clarke, S. Taulu and P. K. Kuhl, "Speech Discrimination in 11 month-old Bilingual and Monolingual Infants: A Magnetoencephalography Study," *Developmental Science,* vol. 20, no. 1, 2017.

[45]   X. Mai, L. Xu, M. Li, J. Shao, Z. Zhao, R. A. de Regnier, C. Nelson and B. Lozoff, "Auditory Recognition Memory in 2 Month Old Infants as Assessed by Event-Related Potentials," *Journal of Developmental Neuropsychology,* 2012.

[46]   G. Y. Lee and B. S. Kisilevsky, "Foetus's Respond to Father's Voice but Prefer Mother's Voice After Birth," *Journal of Developmental Psychobiology,* 2014.

[47]   E. E. Hilbrink et al, "Early Developmental Changes in the Timing of Turn-taking: a Longitudinal Study of Mother – Infant Interaction," *Frontiers in Psychology,* vol. 6, 2015.

[48]   J. Dunn and C. Kendrick, "The Speech of Two- and Three-Year-Olds to Infant Siblings: 'Baby Talk' and the Context of Communication," *Journal of Child Language,* vol. 9, 1982.

[49]   D. Falk, "Prelinguistic Evolution in Early Hominins: Whence Motherese?," *Behavioural Brain Science,* vol. 27, 2004.

[50]   D. L. Grieser and P. K. Kuhl, "Maternal Speech to Infants in a Tonal Language: Support for Universal Prosodic Features in Motherese," *Developmental Psychology,* vol. 24, 1988.

[51]   R. P. Cooper, J. Abraham, S. Berman and M. Staska, "The Development of Infants' Preference for Motherese," *Infant Behavioural Development,* vol. 20, 1997.

[52]   A. Fernald, "Four-Month-Old Infants Prefer to Listen to Motherese," *Infant Behavioural Development,* vol. 8, 1985.

[53]   L. Singh, J. L. Morgan and C. T. Best, "Infants' Listening Preferences: Baby Talk or Happy Talk?," *Journal of Infancy,* vol. 3, 2002.

[54]   C. Kitamura and D. Burnham, "The Infant's Response to Maternal Vocal Affect," *Advances in Infancy Research,* vol. 12, 1998.

[55]   R. P. Cooper and R. N. Aslin, "Preference for Infant-Directed Speech in the First Month After Birth," *Child Development,* vol. 61, 1990.

[56]   J. Yung Song, "Effects of the Acoustic Properties of Infant-Directed Speech on Infant Word Recognition," *Journal of the Acoustical Society of America,* vol. 128, 2010.

[57]   R. Zangl, L. Klarman, D. Thal, A. Fernald and E. Bates, "Dynamics of Word Comprehension in Infancy: Developments in Timing, Accuracy, and Resistance to Acoustic Degradation," *Journal of Cognitive Development,* vol. 6, 2005.

[58]   D. D. Albin and C. H. Echols, "Stressed and Word-Final Syllables in Infant-Directed Speech," *Infant and Behaviour Development,* vol. 19, no. 4, pp. 401–418, 1996.

[59]   C. H. Echols and E. L. Newport, "The Role of Stress and Position in Determining First Words," *Language Acquisition,* vol. 2, no. 3, pp. 189–220, 1992.

[60]   C. Floccia et al, "British English Infants Segment Word only with Exaggerated Infant-Directed Speech Stimuli," *Cognition,* vol. 148, 2016.

[61]   A. Fernald, T. Taeschner, J. Dunn, M. Papousek, B. De Boysson-Bardies and I. Fukui, "A Cross-Language Study of Prosodic Modifications in Mothers' and Fathers' Speech to Preverbal Infants," *Journal of Child Language,* vol. 16, 1989.

[62]   D. N. Stern, S. Spieker, R. K. Barnett and K. MacKain, "The Prosody of Maternal Speech: Infant Age and Context Related Changes," *Journal of Child Language,* vol. 10, 1983.

[63]   B. Ambridge et al, "The Ubiquity of Frequency Effects in First Language Acquisition," *Journal of Child Language,* vol. 42, 2015.

[64]   M. R. Brent and J. M. Siskind, "The Role of Exposure to Isolated Words in Early Vocabulary Development," *Cognition,* vol. 81, 2001.

[65]   M. Ota and B. Skarabela, "Reduplicated Words are Easier to Learn," *Language Learning and Development,* vol. 1, no. 10, 2016.

[66]   D. G. Kemler Nelson, K. Hirsh-Pasek, P. W. Jusczyk and K. W. Cassidy, "How the Prosodic Cues in Motherese Might Assist Language Learning," *Journal of Child Language,* vol. 16, 1989.

[67]   D. Formby, "Maternal Recognition of Infant's Cry," *Developmental Medicine & Child Neurology,* vol. 9, 1967.

[68]   G. Morsbach and C. Bunting, "Maternal Recognition of their Neonates' Cries," *Developmental Medicine & Child Neurology,* vol. 21, 1979.

[69]   J. A. Green and G. E. Gustafson, "Individual Recognition of Human Infants on the Basis of Cries Alone," *Journal of Developmental Psychobiology,* vol. 16, 1983.

[70]   E. Gustafsson, F. Levrero, D. Reby and N. Mathevon, "Fathers are Just as Good as Mothers at Recognising the Cries of Their Baby," *Journal of Nature Communications,* vol. 4, 2013.

[71]   Bornstein et al, "Neurobiology of Culturally Common Maternal Responses to Infant Cry," *Psychological and Cognitive Sciences,* 2017.

[72]   R. Golinkoff and K. Hirsch-Pasek, *How Babies Talk,* New York: Penguin, 2000.

[73]   P. J. Fleming et al, "Pacifier Use and Sudden Infant Death Syndrome: Results from the CESDI/SUDI Case Control Study," *Arch. Dis. Child,* vol. 81, no. 2, pp. 112–116, 1999.

[74]   J. Niemela, M. Uharim and M. Mottonen, "A Pacifier Increases the Risk of Recurrent Acute Otitis Media in Children in Day Care Centres," *Pediatrics,* vol. 96, no. 5 Pt 1, pp. 884–888, 1995.

[75] S. Hanafin and P. Griffiths, "Does Pacifier Use Cause Ear Infections in Young Children?," *British Journal of Community Nursing,* vol. 7, no. 4, pp. 208–211, 2002.

[76] M. M Rovers et al, "Is Pacifier Use a Risk Factor for Otitis Media? A Dynamic Cohort Study," *Fam Pract,* vol. 25, no. 4, pp. 233–236, 2008.

[77] E. Baker, "The Pros and Cons of Dummies: What a Speech Pathologist Should Know," *Acquiring Knowledge in Speech, Language and Hearing,* vol. 4, no. 3, pp. 134–136, 2002.

[78] L. Dimberg et al, "Prevalence of Malocclusion Traits and Sucking Habits Among 3 Year Old Children," *Swed. Dent.,* vol. 34, no. 1, pp. 35–42, 2010.

[79] K. M. Schmidt et al, "The Effect of Pacifier Sucking on Orofacial Structure: a Systematic Literature Review," *Prog. Orthodontics,* vol. 19, no. 8, 2018.

[80] Verrestro et al, "Occlusal and Orofacial Myofunctional Evaluation in Children with Primary Dentition, Open Biteand Pacifier Sucking Habit.," *International Journal of Orofacial Myology,* vol. 32, no. 7, pp. 7–21, 2006.

[81] "Pacifiers (soothers): A User's Guide for Parents," *Journal of Child Health,* vol. 8, no. 8, pp. 520-521, 2003.

[82] L. Shotts et al, "The Impact of Prolonged Pacifier Use on Speech Articulation : A Preliminary Investigation," *Contemporary Issues in Communication Science and Disorders,* vol. 35, pp. 72–75, 2008.

[83] M. Maclean, P. Bryant and L. Bradley, "Nursery Rhymes and Reading in Early Childhood," *Merrill-Palmer Quarterly,* vol. Vol. 33 No. 3, pp. 255–281, 1987.

[84] Bryant et al, "Nursery Rhymes, Phonological Awareness and Reading," *Journal of Child Language,* vol. 16, no. 2, pp. 407–428, 1989.

[85] C. H. Echols and E. L. Newport, "Repetition a Key Factor in Language Learning," *Language Acquistion,* vol. 2, no. 3, pp. 189–220, 1992.

[86] University of Helsinki, "Repetition a Key Factor in Language Learning," *Science Daily,* vol. 2, 2017.

[87] G. B. Kolata, "Studying Learning in the Womb," *Science,* vol. 225, 1984.

[88] A. J. De Casper and W. P. Fifer, "Of Human Bonding: Newborns Prefer their Mothers' Voices," *Science,* vol. 208, 1980.

[89] S. N. Iyer and D. K. Oller, "Prelinguistic Development in Infants with Typical Hearing and Infants with Severe-to-Profound Hearing Loss," *Volta Rev,* 2008.

[90] E. Hoff, "The Specificity of Environmental Influence: Socioeconomic Status Affects Early Vocabulary Development via Maternal Speech," *Child Development,* vol. 74, 2003.

[91] D. V. Bishop, "Genetic and Environmental Risks for Specific Language Impairment in Children," *International Journal of Pediatric Otorhinolaryngology,* vol. 67.

[92] M. A. Novack, S. Goldin-Meadow and A. L. Woodward, "Learning from Gesture: How Early Does it Happen?," *Cognition,* vol. 142, pp. 138–147, 2015.

[93] M. L. Rowe, "Pointing and Talk by Low-Income Mothers and Their 14 Month-Old Children," *First Langauge ,* vol. 20, pp. 305–330, 2000.

[94] Rowe et al, "Learning Words by Hand: Gesture's Role in Predicting Vocabulary Development," *First Language,* vol. 28, no. 2, pp. 182–199, 2008.

[95] Pan et al, "Maternal Correlates of Growth in Toddler Vocabulary Production in Low-Income Families," *Child Development,* vol. 76, no. 4, pp. 763–782, 2005.

[96] J. M. Iverson and S. Goldin-Meadow, "Gesture Paves the Way for Language Development," *Psychological Science,* vol. 16, no. 5, pp. 367–371, 2005.

[97] P. Zukow-Golring, "Sensitive Caregiving Fosters the Comprehension of Speech: When

Gestures Speak Louder than Words.," *Early Development and Parenting,* vol. 5, no. 4, pp. 195–211, 1996.

[98] J. Xu et al, "Symbolic Gestures and Spoken Language are Processed by a Common Neural System.," *PNAS,* vol. 106, no. 49, pp. 20664–20669, 2009.

[99] L. P. Acreddo and S. Goodwin, "Symbolic Gesturing in Normal Infants," *Child Development,* vol. 59, pp. 450–466, 1988.

[100] J. M. Iverson et al, "Gesturing in Mother-Child Interactions," *Cognitive Development,* vol. 14, pp. 57–75, 1999.

[101] L. L. Namy et al, "Verbal Labels and Gestural Routines in Parental Communication with Young Children," *Journal of Nonverbal Behaviour,* vol. 24, pp. 63–79, 2000.

[102] S. W. Goodwyn et al, "The Impact of Symbolic Gesturing on Early Language Developmet," *Journal of Nonverbal Behaviour,* vol. 24, pp. 81–103, 2000.

[103] S. Ozcaliskan and S. Goldin-Meadow, "Sex Differences in Language First Appear in Gesture," *Dev. Sci.,* vol. 13, no. 5, pp. 752–760, 2010.

[104] McGregor et al, "Gesture as a Support for Word Learning: The Case of 'Under'.," *Journal of Child Language,* vol. 36, no. 4, pp. 807–828, 2009.

[105] O. E. Demir et al, "A Tale of Two Hands: Children's Early Gesture Use in Narrative Production Predicts Later Narrative Structure in Speech," *Journal of Child Language,* vol. 42, no. 3, pp. 662–681, 2015.

[106] S. Goldin Meadow et al, "Explaining Math: Gesturing Lightens the Load," *Psychological Science,* vol. 12, no. 6, pp. 516–522, 2001.

[107] Cook et al, "Hand Gesture and Mathematics Learning: Lessons from an Avatar," *Cognitive Science,* vol. 41, pp. 518–535, 2017.

[108] Oller et al, "Precursors to Speech in Infancy: The Prediction of Speech and Language Disorders," *J of Communication Disorders,* vol. 32, no. 4, pp. 223–245, 1999.

[109] UK Government and Scientific Advisory Committee on Nutrition, "Feeding in the First Year of Life," 17 July 2018. [Online]. Available: https://www.gov.uk/government/publications/feeding-in-the-first-year-of-life-sacn-report.

[110] A. Lennox, J. Sommerville, K. Ong, H. Henderson and R. Allen, "Diet and Nutrition Survey of Infants and Young Children," 2011.

[111] Ahern et al, "Learning to Like Vegetables: the Importance of Exposure in the Food Preference Development of Preschool Children," The University of Leeds Institute of Psychological Sciences, 2013.

[112] Coulthard et al, "Delayed Inroduction of Lumpy Foods to Children During the Complimentary Feeding Period Affects Child's Food Acceptance and Feeding at 7 Years of Age," *Maternal Child Nutrition,* vol. 5, no. 1, pp. 75–85, 2009.

[113] M. Tomasello and M. J. Farrar, "Joint Attention and Early Language," *J of Child Development,* vol. 57, no. 6, pp. 1454–1463, 1986.

[114] National Research Council, Preventing Reading Diffculties in Young Children, National Academies Press, 1998.

[115] J. R. Paratore, C. M. Cassano and J. A. Schickedanz, "Supporting Early (and Later) Literacy Development at Home and at School," *Handbook of Reading Research,* vol. 4, pp. 107–135, 2011.

[116] E. Orr and R. Geva, "Symbolic Play and Language Development," *Joutnal of Infant Behaviour and Development,* vol. 38C, pp. 147–161, 2015.

[117] M. A. Moreno and G. C. van Orden, "Cognitive Psychology of Word Recognition," in

International Encyclopaedia of the Social and Behavioural Sciences., Amsterdam, Elsevier, 2001, pp. 16556–16561.

[118]   B. Davis and S. Van Der Fest, "Speech Sound Characteristics of Early Words: Influence of Phonological Factors Across Vocabulary Development," *Journal of Child Language,* vol. 45, no. 3, pp. 1–30, 2017.

[119]   M. Braginsky et al, "Consistency and Variabliity in Children's Word Learning Across Lanuages," *Open Mind,* vol. 3, 2019.

[120]   L. Rescorla, "The Language Development Survey: A Screening Tool for Delayed Language in Toddlers.," *Journal of Speech and Hearing Disorders,* vol. 54, no. 4, 1989.

[121]   B. M. Prizant and A. M. Wetherby, "Communicative Temptations, International Communicative Behaviour of Children with Autism: Theoretical and Practical Issues.," *Australian Journal of Human Communicative Disorders,* vol. 13, no. 2, pp. 42–43, 1985.

[122]   Lynch et al, 1980. [Online]. Available: http://www.speech-language-therapy.com/. [Accessed 10 June 2020].

[123]   L. E. Bahrick and L. Moss, "Development of Visual Self-Recognition in Infancy," *Ecological Psychology,* vol. 8, no. 3, pp. 189–208, 1996.

[124]   JoVE Science Education Database – Developmental Psychology, "The Rouge Test: Searching for a Sense of Self," JoVE.

[125]   B. Amsterdam, "Mirror Self-Image Reactions Before Age Two," *Developmental Psychobiology,* vol. 5, pp. 297–305, 1972.

[126]   J. M. Rudolph and L. B. Leonard, "Early Language Milestones and Specific Language Impairment," *Journal of Early Intervention,* vol. 38, no. 1, pp. 41–58, 2016.

[127]   J. Berko, "The Child's Learning of English Morphology," *Word,* vol. 14, pp. 150–177, 1958.

[128]   S. M. Kahlenberg and R. W. Wrangham, "Sex Differences in Chimpanzees' Use of Sticks as Play Objects Resemble Those of Children," *Journal of Current Biology,* vol. 20, no. 24, pp. 1067–1068, 2010.

[129]   S. E. Gathercole, L. Brown and S. J. Pickering, "Working Memory Assessments at School Entry as Longitudinal Predictors of National Curriculum Attainment Levels," *Educational and Child Psychology,* vol. 20, no. 3, 2003.

[130]   T. P. Alloway and R. G. Alloway, "Investigating the Predictive Roles of Working Memory and IQ in Academic Attainment," *Journal of Experimental Child Psychology,* vol. 106, pp. 20–29, 2010.

[131]   Ellenbogen et al, "The Sleeping Brain's influence on Verbal Memory: Boosting Resistance to Interference," *PLOS ONE,* 2009.

[132]   E. Yairi and N. Ambrose, "Epidemiology of Stuttering: 21st Century Advances," *Journal of Fluency Disorders,* vol. 38, no. 2, pp. 66–87, 2013.

[133]   V. Tumanova, E. G. Conture, E. W. Lambert and T. A. Walden, "Speech Disfluencies of Preschool-Age Children Who do and do not Stutter," *Journal of communication disorders,* vol. 49, pp. 25–41, 2014.

[134]   R. W. Sander and C. A. Osbourne, "Stuttering: Understanding and Treating a Common Disability," *American Family Physician,* vol. 100, no. 9, pp. 556–560, 2019.

[135]   S. Reilly, M. Onslow, A. Packman, E. Cini, L. Conway, C. Obioha and M. Wake, "Natural History of Stuttering to 4 Years of Age: A Prospective Community-Based Study," *Pediatrics,* vol. 132, pp. 460–467, 2013.

[136]   N. Gordon, "Stuttering: Incidence and Causes," *Developmental Medicine & Child Neurology,* vol. 44, no. 4, pp. 278–281, 2002.

[137] B. Guitar, Stuttering: An Integrated Approach to Its Nature and Treatment, 2005.

[138] D. Ward, Stuttering and Cluttering: Frameworks for Understanding Treatment, Hove and New York City: Psychology Press, 2005.

[139] D. Choi et al, "Young Children's Family History of Stuttering and Their Articulation, Language and Attentional Abilities: An Exploratory Study," *Journal of Communication Disorders,* vol. 71, pp. 22–36, 2018.

[140] S. E. Chang, K. I. Erickson, N. G. Ambrose, M. A. Hasegawa-Johnson and C. L. Ludlow, "Brain anatomy differences in childhood stuttering," *Neuroimage,* vol. 39, no. 3, pp. 1333–1344, 2008.

[141] P. University, "Stuttering More Than Talk – Research Shows Brain's Role In Disorder," *Science Daily,* 2004.

[142] E. Yairi and N. G. Ambrose, "Early Childhood Stuttering I: Persistency and Recovery Rates," *Journal of Speech, Language,* vol. 42, no. 5, pp. 1097–1112, 1999.

[143] A. Craig, K. Hancock, Y. Tran, M. Craig and K. Peters, "Epidemiology of Stuttering in the Community Across the Entire Life Span," *Journal of Speech, Language, and Hearing Research,* vol. 45, pp. 1097–1105, 2002.

[144] K. Ntourou, E. G. Conture and M. W. Lipsey, "Language Abilities of Children Who Stutter: A Meta-Analytical Review," *American Journal of Speech-Language Pathology,* vol. 20, no. 3, pp. 163–179, 2011.

[145] P. E. McGhee, Humor, Health and Happiness: How to Get the FUNtastic Benefits of Humor into Your Life., Singapore: Mind Edge, 2011.

[146] L. A. James and C. L. Fox, "Children's Understanding of Self-Focused Humor Styles," *European Journal of Psychology,* vol. 12, no. 3, pp. 420–433, 2016.

[147] V. Biasi et al, "Relation Between Stress Conditions, Uncertainty and Incongruity Intolerance, Rigidity and Mental Health: Experimental Demonstrations," *Health,* vol. 7, no. 1, 2015.

[148] M. Bennet et al, "The Effect of Mirthful Laughter on Stress and Natural Killer Cell Activity," *Alternative Therapeutic Health Medecine,* vol. 9, no. 2, pp. 38–45, 2003.

[149] P. McGhee, Humor: The Lighter Path to Resilience and Health, AuthorHouse, 2010.

[150] C. A. Stifter and N. A. Fox, "Preschool Children's Ability to Identify and Label Emotions," *Journal of Nonverbal Behaviour,* vol. 11, pp. 43–54, 1987.

[151] A. Kujawa et al, "Emotion Recognition in Preschool Children: Associations with Maternal Depression and Early Parenting," *Developmental Psychopathology,* vol. 26, no. 1, pp. 159–170, 2014.

[152] C. Izard, S. Fine, D. Schultz, A. Mostow, B. Ackerman and E. Youngstrom, "Emotion Knowledge as a Predictor of Social Behaviour and Academic Competence in Children at Risk," *Psychological Science,* vol. 12, no. 1, pp. 18–23, 2001.

[153] C. Schaefer and H. Millman, "How to Help Children with Common Problems," Northvale, NJ, Jason Aronson Inc., 1994, p. 18.

[154] H. A. Ruff and K. R. Lawson, "Development of Sustained, Focused Attention in Young Children During Free Play," *Developmental Psychology,* vol. 26, no. 1, pp. 85–93, 1990.

[155] E. M. Mahone and H. E. Schneider, *Neuropsychology Review,* vol. 22, no. 4, pp. 361–383, 2012.

[156] J. S. Palfrey, M. D. Levine, D. K. Walker and M. Sullivan, "The Emergence of Attention Deficits in Early Childhood: A Prospective Study," *Journal of Developmental and Behavioral Pediatrics,* vol. 6, pp. 339–348, 1985.

[157] D. A. Christakis, F. J. Zimmerman, D. L. DiGiuseppe and C. A. McCarty, "Early Television Exposure and Subsequent Attentional Problems in Children," *Pediatrics,* vol. 113, pp. 708–713, 2004.

[158] A. S. Lillard and J. Peterson, "The Immediate Impact of Different Types of Television on Young Children's Executive Function," *Pediatrics,* vol. 128, pp. 644–649, 2011.

[159] S. Palmer, "Upstart: The Case for Raising the School Starting Age and Providing What the Under-Sevens Really Need," 2016.

[160] Fekonja et al, "Free Play and Other Daily Preschool Activities as a Context for Child's Language Development," *Studia Psychologica,* vol. 47, no. 2, pp. 103–117, 2005.

[161] Kendeou et al, "Children's Inference Generation Across Different Media," *Journal of Research in Reading,* vol. 31, no. 3, pp. 259–272, 2008.

[162] Paris and Paris, "Assessing Narrative Comprehension in Young Children," *Reading Research Quarterly,* vol. 38, pp. 36–76, 2003.

[163] V. Tomkins et al, "Inference Generation, Story Comprehension and Language in the Preschool Years," *Reading and Writing,* vol. 26, no. 3, pp. 403–429, 2013.

[164] Griffin et al, "Oral Discourse in the Preschool Years and Later Literacy Skills," *First Language,* vol. 24, pp. 123–147, 2004.

[165] K. Cain et al, "Children's Reading Comprehension Ability: Concurrent Prediction by Working Memory, Verbal Ability, and Component Skills," *Journal of Educational Psychology,* vol. 96, pp. 31–42, 2004.

[166] L. Yore, "Examining the Literacy Component of Science Literacy: 25 Years of Language, Arts and Science Research," *International Journal of Science Education,* vol. 26, no. 6, pp. 689–725, 2003.

[167] W. Harlen, The Teaching of Science in Primary Schools 3rd Edition, London: David Fulton, 2000.

[168] J. Johnston, "What Does the Skill of Observation Look Like in Young Children?," in *British Educational Association Annual Conference,* Edinburgh, 2008.

[169] G. Grambo, *The Art and Science of Observation,* vol. 17, 1994, pp. 32–33.

[170] B. Keogh and S. Naylor, "'Do do as I do'; Being a Role Model in the Early Years," *Primary Science Review,* vol. 78, pp. 7–9, 2003.

[171] L. Vygotsky, Thought and Language, Cambridge: MIT Press, 1962.

[172] R. Driver, *The Pupil as a Scientist,* Milton Keynes: Open University Press, 1983.

[173] L. Xiang, The Xunzi, Appox 818 AD.

[174] M Corbeil et al, "Singing Delays the Onset of Infant Distress," *Infancy,* vol. 10, 2015.

[175] S. E. Trehub, "Musical Predispositions in Infancy," *Annals of the New York Academy of Sciences,* vol. 930, pp. 1–16, 2001.

[176] M. Zentner and T. Eerla , "Rhythmic Engagement with Music in Infancy," *Proceedings of the National Academy of Sciences,* vol. 10, 2010.

[177] N. Kraus and B. Chandrasekaran, "Music Training for the Development of Auditory Skills," *Nat. Rev. Neuroscience,* vol. 11, pp. 599–605, 2010.

[178] M. Besson, J. Chobert and C. Marie, "Transfer of Training Between Music and Speech – Common Processing, Attention, and Memory," *Frontiers in Psychology,* vol. 2, p. 94, 2011.

[179] A. Tierney and N. Kraus, "The Ability to Tap to a Beat Relates to Cognitive, Linguistic and Perceptual Skills," *Brain and Language,* vol. 124, pp. 225–231, 2013.

[180] K. H. Corriveau and U. Goswami, "Rhythmic Motor Entrainment in Children with

Speech and Language Impairments: Tapping to the Beat," *Cortex,* vol. 45, pp. 119–130, 2009.

[181]   A. Tierney and N. Kraus , "The Ability to Move to a Beat Is Linked to the Consistency of Neural Responses to Sound," *Journal of Neuroscience,* vol. 33, pp. 14981–14988, 2013.

[182]   A. D. Patel, "Why Would Musical Training Benefit the Neural Encoding of Speech? The OPERA Hypothesis," *Frontiers in Psychology,* vol. 2, p. 142, 2011.

[183]   E. B. Carlton, "Learning Through Music: The Support of Brain Research," *Child Care Exchange,* vol. 133, pp. 53–56, 200.

[184]   K. J. Gerhardt and R. M. Abrams, "Fetal Exposures to Sound and Vibroacoustic Stimulation," *Journal of Perinatal,* vol. 8, pp. 21–30, 2000.

[185]   D. K. James et al, "Fetal Learning: a Prospective Randomized Controlled Study," *Ultrasound Obstet Gynecol,* vol. 20, pp. 431–438, 2002.

[186]   P. G. Hepper, "Foetal Soap Addiction," *Lancet,* vol. 11, pp. 1347–1348, 1988.

[187]   P. Newham, "Making a Song and Dance: the Musical Voice of Language," *Journal. Imag. Lang. Learn. Teaching,* vol. 111, pp. 1–10, 1995–1996.

[188]   K. Overy, "Dyslexia and Music: From Timing Deficits to Musical Intervention," *Annals of the New York Academy of Sciences,* vol. 999, pp. 497–505, 2003.

[189]   J. Slater et al, "At-Risk Elementary School Children with One Year of Classroom Music Instruction are Better at Keeping a Beat," *PLoS ONE,* vol. 8.

[190]   S. J. Lamb and A. H. Gregory, "The Relationship between Music and Reading in Beginning Readers," *Educational Psychology,* vol. 13, no. 1, pp. 19–27, 1993.

[191]   J. Bolduc and I. Montésinos-Gelet, "Pitch Processing and Phonological Awareness," *Psychomusicology,* vol. 19, no. 1, pp. 3–14, 2005.

[192]   B. Ilari and L. Polka, "Music Cognition in Early Infancy: Infants' Preferences and Long-Term Memory for Ravel," *International Journal of Music Education,* vol. 24, no. 1, pp. 7–20, 2006.

[193]   S. Hallam, "The Power of Music: Its Impact on the Intellectual, Social and Personal Development of Children and Young People," *International Journal of Music Education,* vol. 28, no. 3, pp. 269–289, 2010.

[194]   K. Geist, E. A. Geist and K. Kuznik, "The Patterns of Music: Young Children Learning Mathematics Through Beat, Rhythm, and Melody," *Young Children,* vol. 67, no. 1, pp. 74–79, 2012.

[195]   W. Gruhn and F. Rauscher, "The Neurobiology of Music Cognition and Learning.," *The New Handbook of Research on Music Teaching and Learning,* pp. 445–460, 2002.

[196]   J. Law et al, "Early Home Activities and Oral Language Skills in Middle Childhood: A Quantile Analysis," *Journal of Child Development,* vol. 89, no. 1, pp. 295–309, 2018.

[197]   World Health Organisation, "To Grow Up Healthy, Children Need To Sit Less and Play More," 24 April 2019. [Online]. Available: https://www.who.int/news-room/detail/24-04-2019-to-grow-up-healthy-children-need-to-sit-less-and-play-more. [Accessed 13 June 2020].

[198]   R. Viner, M. Davie and A. Firth, "The Health Impacts of Screen Time: A Guide for Clinicians and Parents," Royal College of Paediatrics and Child Health, 2019.

[199]   H. Byeon and S. Hong, "Relationship Between Television Viewing and Language Delay in Toddlers: Evidence from a Korea National Cross-Sectional Survey," *PLoS ONE,* vol. 10, no. 3, 2015.

[200]   F. J. Zimmerman et al, "Associations Between Media Viewing and Language Development in Children Under 2," *Journal of Paediatrics,* vol. 151, pp. 364–268, 2007.

[201] W. Chonchaiya and C. Pruksananonda, "Television Viewing Associated with Delayed language Development," *Acta Paediatrica,* vol. 97, pp. 977–982, 2008.

[202] D. A. Christakis et al, "Early Television Exposure and Subsequent Attention Problems in Children," *Journal of Child Care, Health and Development,* vol. 30, no. 5, 2004.

[203] D. R. Anderson and T. A. Pempek, "Television & Very Young Children," *Journal of American Behavioural Science,* vol. 48, no. 5, pp. 505–522, 2005.

[204] R. Barr and H. Hayne, "Developmental Changes in Imitation from Television During Infancy," *Child Development,* vol. 70, pp. 1067–1081, 1999.

[205] M. Krcmar et al, "Can Toddlers Learn Vocabulary from Television? An Experimental Approach," *Journal of Media Psychology,* vol. 10, no. 1, pp. 41–63, 2007.

[206] A. Hollenbeck and R. Slaby, "Infant Visual and Vocal Responses to Television," *Child Development,* vol. 50, pp. 41–45, 1979.

[207] D. R. Anderson and M. K. Evans, "Peril and Potential of Media for Infants and Toddlers," *Zero to Three: National Center for Infants, Toddlers and Families,* vol. 22, pp. 10–16, 2001.

[208] D. L. Linebarger and S. E. Vaala, "Screen Media and Language Development in Infants and Toddlers: An Ecological Perspective," *Developmental Review,* vol. 30, pp. 176–202, 2010.

[209] R. Barr, A. Lauricella, E. Zack and S. L. Calvert, "Infant and Early Childhood Exposure to Adult-Directed and Child-Directed Television Programming Relations with Cognitive Skills at Age Four," *Merrill-Palmer Quarterly,* vol. 56, pp. 21–48, 2010.

[210] T. A. Pempek, H. L. Kirkorian and D. R. Anderson, "The Effects of Background Television on the Quantity and Quality of Child-Directed Speech by Parents," *Journal of Child Media,* vol. 8, pp. 211–222, 2014.

[211] A. Sturn and J. Johnson, "Thinking Out Loud: An Exploration of Problem-Solving Language in Preschoolers With and Without Language Development," *International Journal of Communication Disorders ,* vol. 34, no. 1, pp. 1–15, 1999.

[212] M. Tanimura, K. Okuma and K. Kyoshima, "Television Viewing, Reduced Parental Utterance, and Delayed Speech Development in Infants and Young Children," *Archives of Pediatric and Adolescent Medicine,* vol. 161, pp. 618–619, 2007.

[213] D. Christakis, J. Gilkerson, J. A. Richards, F. J. Zimmerman, M. M. Garrison and D. Xu, "Audible Television and Decreased Adult Words, Infant Vocalizations, and Conversational Turns: A Population-Based Study," *Archives of Pediatric and Adolescent Medicine,* vol. 163, pp. 554–558, 2009.

[214] E. Wartella and M. Robb, "Young Children, New Media," *Journal of Child Media,* vol. 1, pp. 35–44, 2007.

[215] F. J. Zimmerman, J. Gilkerson, J. A. Richards, D. A. Christakis, D. Xu and S. Gray, "Teaching by Listening: The Importance of Adult-Child Conversations to Language Development," *Pediatrics,* vol. 124, pp. 342–349, 2009.

[216] Arterberry et al, "Early Attention and Literacy Experiences Predict Adaptive Communication," *First Language,* vol. 27, 2007.

[217] Demir-Lira et al, "Parents' Early Book Reading to Children: Relation to Children's Later Language and Literacy Outcomes Controlling For Other Parent Language Input," *Developmental Science,* 2008.

[218] Campbell et al, "Early Childhood Education: Young Adult Outcomes from the Abecedarian Project," *Applied Developmental Science,* vol. 6, 2002.

[219] Fletcher et al, "Joint Attention & Parent-Child Book Reading: Keys to Help Close Gaps